Peter Jones graduated in Classics from Cambridge University in 1964 and gained his PhD from London in 1971. He retired early as senior lecturer in Classics at Newcastle University in 1997. The author of numerous books on classical subjects, and a regular contributor to radio and a wide range of newspapers and magazines, he has been the *Spectator*'s 'Ancient & modern' columnist since 1996. He is involved in running the charity Friends of Classics, which he helped to found in 1991. He was appointed MBE in 1983 and lives in Newcastle.

D0924092

VOTE
⟫FOR⟪
CAESAR

Peter Jones

An Orion paperback

First published in Great Britain in 2008
by Orion
This paperback edition published in 2009
by Orion Books Ltd,
Orion House, 5 Upper St Martin's Lane,
London WC2H 9EA

An Hachette UK Company

3 5 7 9 10 8 6 4

A CIP catalogue record for this book
is available from the British Library.

ISBN 978-0-7528-8291-8

Typeset by Input Data Services Ltd, Bridgwater, Somerset

Printed in Great Britain by Clays Ltd, St Ives plc

The Orion Publishing Group's policy is to use papers that
are natural, renewable and recyclable products and
made from wood grown in sustainable forests. The logging
and manufacturing processes are expected to conform to
the environmental regulations of the country of origin.

Every effort has been made to fulfil requirements with regard to reproducing
copyright material. The author and publisher will be glad to rectify
any omissions at the earliest opportunity.

www.orionbooks.co.uk

Contents

Preface

For as long as I can remember, the ancient Greeks and Romans have done the job the BBC once did – informed, educated and entertained me on subjects as disparate as the purpose of the rich, educational selection, the advantages of leeks, People-power, astrology, prejudice, what children are for, religious experience, the proper function of prison, knowing oneself, the danger of law-makers, the ears of lampreys, the virtue of independence, the pointlessness of holidays, the source of evil, the benefits of elitism, responsibility, the unimportance of death and the vanity of metaphysics.

Here are the results, a few of which began life in my *Ancient & modern* column in the *Spectator*. Astonishingly, they reflect the interests, prejudices and ignorance of the author. The ancients, however, are not responsible for my selection from the vast variety of views they held on any number of the topics under discussion. I give due warning here that, for every view I attribute to an ancient, one could probably find a contrary one somewhere else; that there are occasionally some rather sweeping generalisations about 'ancient society' that a different sort of work would not have swept; and that statistics from and about the ancient world are the subject of much argument.

My son Tom shrewdly asked whether this book was history or manifesto. Even I am not so starry-eyed about the ancient world as to believe that the present should be wholly relocated in the past, at least not without the application of certain stern, mainly technological and medical, provisos. Nevertheless, Greeks and Romans were immensely fertile generators of ideas, as I hope readers of this book will discover, just now and again, here and there . . .

Finally, my very best thanks to Orion's Ian Marshall. No editor I have dealt with has ever given so much detailed and productive care and attention to a book.

Peter Jones
Newcastle on Tyne
January 2008

Readers who may feel temped to try – or re-try – their hand at Latin and Greek are recommended to look at Peter Jones' *Learn Latin* (Duckworth 1997) and *Learn Ancient Greek* (Duckworth 1998), originally written as jovial introductions to the languages in the *Daily Telegraph*.

[1]

Two capitals: Rome and London

Grinding you down

After any event that draws thousands into the city, or (even more catastrophic) a snow flurry, Londoners moan about the intolerability of the traffic. But then they moan about it anyway. Nothing is new. The Romans felt just the same about their city, and with considerably more justification. The Londoner, swept along by the heaving press of howling football supporters, or assaulted by the alien noises and smells of pop fans, or caught up in the mob reaction at another non-running train, feels like any Roman senator urging his slaves to get his litter through the marketplace, or any worker running an errand through Rome's choked and offensive streets. The satirist Juvenal (c. AD 120) gives an idea of what it was like:

> 'In the streets we pedestrians are blocked by crowds in front, harried by crowds behind. Elbows and poles poke in our ribs, someone brains me with a crossbeam, another with a barrel. There's mud all over my legs, feet kick me, here comes a soldier's hobnailed boot bang on my toes ... How much sleep can you get here? A good night's sleep is a rich man's privilege (most Romans die of insomnia). The wagons thunder through the narrowing, twisting alleys, carters swearing in the jams ...'

Nor are our crowds all upright, noble, honest, bold, true, right-thinking Englishmen. London is a centre of the world. Alien peoples and races gather here to live and work, from Scotland to Russia, from Australia to Syria, from Africa to France, from the USA to Poland and India. So it was in Rome where, incidentally, the most common everyday language was that of the whole Mediterranean: Greek. True to form, Juvenal is constantly moaning about all the bleedin' foreigners there, especially Greeks, but it is worth pointing out that Rome for the most part tended to ignore the differences between peoples, with the result that it was a fairly tolerant society. (It is only when you 'celebrate' your society as a 'multicultural' one and thus *emphasise* the differences that you get problems.)

Yet population problems would be much worse for all concerned were we living in Rome. Consider: London, we are told, has a population of c. 7.5 million inhabitants. But it doesn't. *Greater* London has that number. Those actually residing in the main city area make up a minute percentage of that figure. The rest labour in and out on what passes for the transport system (6.3 million trips a day are taken on London's increasingly bendy buses, 4 million on the tube).

Rome meanwhile had a population of a paltry million. But the crucial point is this: *Rome had no transport system.* Consequently, a good percentage of that million lived, worked, breathed and tried to move, all the time, in the 17.9 square kilometres that made up Rome itself (seven square miles – about the size of the first London congestion charge area).

So there was no such thing as a commuter in ancient Rome. Where Romans worked was where Romans lived – in the city itself – and if you had to travel, you did so by foot or, if rich, by litter (unless you were an aristocrat going walkabout, surrounded by your friends and supporters). The rich did not go to their suite of go-getting offices in some widely-acclaimed excrescence designed by an architect in dark glasses wearing boxing gloves. Surrounded by slaves, advisers and family, with their commercial agents (often slaves) waiting to do their bidding in town, country and province (aristos could not dirty their hands), they stayed where the action was: in their own homes, the hub of their world. There is a lot to be said for it, CEOs.

There is also a lot to be said for workers working from home too, as they did in Rome. Two hundred years ago there was an outcry when, as a result of industrialisation, workers had to leave home to work in 'manufactories'. But thanks to modern communications, there is in many cases no real need for that; indeed, there is evidence that businesses flourish where home working is encouraged. However, bosses still seem incapable of getting out of the 19th-century factory mentality.

None of this is to deny the problem London would have if it turned into Rome. Greater London is made up of thirty-two boroughs plus the City of London, which cover an area of 1,572 square kilometres (over 600 square miles). London's population density is therefore nearly 5,000 per square kilometre. Rome's may have been ten times that. Nevertheless, if only more people lived in the middle of London, it would set an excellent example for today's world: workers free from all the hassle and expense of travel, and no pollution from commuter traffic. Home working from the suburbs would produce the same results. All those roads could then be put out to grass and Green Belts, started in the 1930s, expanded, though admittedly in long thin strips. But then, what is a belt if not a long, thin strip?

So Rome was never free from crowds by day or noise and bustle by night. The sheer numbers of people clogging up the streets, especially by day, made any movement difficult, and traffic-access a nightmare. Trying to walk the streets in Rome must have been rather like trying to move down a carriage in the tube during rush hour. Rome's 'Ken Livingstone' moment came when they introduced not a congestion charge but a ban on any vehicles entering Rome by day, except for those involved in building.

Rome 'ground you down', as the epigrammatist Martial groans. Pliny the Younger puts it another way:

> 'At the time when you do these things, they seem important and necessary, but when you realise you have been doing them every day, these same things appear pointless.'

Every modern commuter knows precisely what Pliny is talking about, even though city centres increasingly experiment with keeping traffic out. Fascinatingly, the London Lorry Ban, set up in 1986, reversed Roman practice: it banished lorries at night to allow people a good night's sleep! (Juvenal would have approved.) More common still is blocking off roads and creating pedestrian precincts, standard practice in Pompeii and other Roman cities (see p. 14). In the modern world too, air pollution from traffic is now a factor, as is the threat to buildings from the vibration caused by massive containers. Traffic did not create these problems in Rome. It had not been overtaken by the demands of the motor car, the single cause of the most disastrous environmental change in our cities over the last hundred years.

Racism

It is commonly claimed that Greeks and Romans were 'racist'. A racist defines certain types of humans as inferior because of features of their make-up about which they can do nothing (e.g. because they are white or Jewish). The racist then concludes that they must therefore be deprived of the human rights accorded to their 'superiors'. In those terms, Greeks and Romans were not racist.

The main reason is that the ancients generally thought the sort of person you were was determined by your way of life, not your heredity. Since they thought way of life was determined by environment, all one had to do was change it to become 'one of us'. Further, since Greeks, naturally, thought their way of life superior to all others, everyone else must by definition be a *barbaros*, whatever their colour or origin. They had no interest in distinguishing 'barbarians' by genes or physiology.

So the Roman architect Vitruvius asserts that southerners, living in a hot climate, have quick intelligence but are cowardly, while northerners are mentally sluggish but brave to the point of foolishness. In so doing, he is telling us nothing about their colour, or how he thinks northerners and southerners should be treated, let alone that they cannot change. He is simply making a general observation

4

of the 'Italians have a snooze at lunchtime' variety.

For a Roman, anyone who grew up in a good, healthy Roman environment – whatever their heredity – would be fine. Romans were perfectly happy to make Spaniards and North Africans emperor. As long as they had been brought up like proper Romans, played the Roman game and climbed the ladder to the top, who cared?

If 'racism' means prejudice, xenophobia and stereo-typing, the ancient world was as prejudiced and xeno-phobic as everyone has been and will be for the whole of time. There is nothing illegal or immoral about that. But racism is an eighteenth-century invention. It arose from black chattel slavery, imperialism, and the huge tech-nological and cultural differences between whites and non-whites. The result was a mentality that put rich/white/master at one end of the spectrum and poor/black/slave at the other, and claimed this divide was 'nat-ural' and the gap could never be bridged. Greeks and Romans nurtured their prejudices as devotedly as we do. But racism so defined was not one of them.

Tower block terror

To accommodate the vast population, Romans did what we do: they built upwards. Their apartment blocks (*īnsulae*, lit. 'islands') reached up to six or seven storeys high despite efforts by people like the first emperor, Augustus, to do what we also do and impose a height limit (in this case, 70 feet). One ancient estimate puts the number of such blocks at 46,602, compared with private homes at a meagre 1,790. Plenty of graffiti survive on ancient walls adver-tising the delights awaiting a new tenant. Here from Pompeii:

'Available for let from 1 July: shops with upstairs (fine upper rooms), and a house in Arnius Pollio block. Landlord: Gnaeus Alleius Nigidius Maius. Anyone interested in being a tenant can apply to Primus, his slave'; 'Available to let for five years from 13 August, the Baths of Venus, equipped for persons of quality, shops, rooms above the shops, and upstairs apartments in the property owned by Julia Felix, daughter of Spurius.'

But rents seem to have been fairly high, and that would encourage overcrowding. Apparently Hong Kong high-rises built in the fifties to deal with overcrowding housed five people per 10' x 12' room.

People tend to think of these tenements as slums. It is true that minimal planning went into them and they collapsed with alarming frequency (*ruīna* was the term), usually from fire or flood (the Tiber was as much a threat to Rome as the Thames is to London, and they had no flood barriers in the ancient world). When a large building came down, the mortality rate could be fearful. In AD 27, for example, the gladiatorial amphitheatre at Fidenae collapsed. It had been shoddily built to produce instant profit and the result, the historian Tacitus tells us, was 50,000 dead. Juvenal again:

'Here we live in Shored-up City, with creaking stays and props. Landlords merely paper over the cracks to keep them up and tell the tenants they can sleep secure, when the whole building is balanced like a pack of cards. Give me somewhere to live where fire and midnight panics are not such everyday events. By the time the smoke reaches you fast asleep on the third floor, your neighbour down below is already well alight and roaring for water . . .'

But again, as in any big city, workers needed homes, and big money was at stake. These buildings were put up by the rich to house the urban population, the people who kept the whole show on the road. The politician, lawyer and philosopher Cicero records in a letter the *ruīna* of two buildings he owned, and cracks in the others ('even the mice have fled, along with the tenants'). But Cicero was not perturbed: his friend Vestorius had made a re-building proposal, he tells us, which would turn it all to profit.

Town planning – or the lack of it

Like London, Rome was not a 'planned' city – or only when a good fire (like the Great Fire of London in 1666) gave the chance to rethink its structure. Rome had an equivalent in AD 64, at which (we are told) Nero 'fiddled'. Not true. If he was there, he sang the whole of a popular opera 'The Fall of Troy', one source tells us (Nero fancied himself as a great opera star and aesthete). But the fact is that he was not there. He was on holiday in Antium 35 miles away when it started, and returned at once to organise the firefighting and provide for the dispossessed.

Roman firefighting

Government is always keen to reorganise (i.e. cut) services, of which the fire brigade is one. The Romans established the principles.

Fire prevention in Rome was originally in the hands of a committee of three, in charge of a body of public slaves who had been stationed around the gates and walls of the city. But they were in the wrong place and ineffective. The emperor Augustus got a grip on the problem in AD 6. With a 4 per cent tax on the sale of slaves to fund the operation, Augustus put a *praefectus* with his own headquarters and office staff in charge of seven cohorts of firefighters (*vigilēs*). Each cohort consisted of 500 men commanded by a tribune and divided up into seven 'centuries' (i.e. c. 70 per 'century'). Each cohort looked after two of the city's fourteen administrative *regiōnēs*, and was housed in barracks.

They patrolled extensively at night when the danger was greatest, since (in the absence of matches or other instant sources of fire) householders kept burning fires unsupervised. Owners of houses were required to keep a supply of water available and other *īnstrūmenta* for fighting fires – vinegar, mats, poles, ladders, sponges, buckets and brooms. In the absence of hoses, man- and bucket-power was

---

essential; the brigades brought pumps, hooks, mattocks, axes and *ballistae* to knock down nearby houses and create firebreaks. Four *medicī* were attached to each cohort.

On average there seem to have been about a hundred fires a day in the city, twenty large, two serious. There were probably no more than four large fires at any one time, and, given their size and careful distribution, the patrols could deal with them. The secret was to get in early (smell was very important).

So: the fire brigade must keep fully staffed night patrols. At the same time, there needs to be military-style organisation for the whole force: fire engines should be relocated at specific times to places where fires are most common, and property owners ordered to take preventative measures.

The fire burned for nearly ten days, at the end of which only four of the fourteen city *regiōnēs* remained untouched. When it was all over, Nero threw himself enthusiastically into the job of redesign and reconstruction. Narrow, winding streets were straightened and widened; building height was limited (again); party walls were forbidden; the use of wood was discouraged, and fireproof materials (e.g. concrete) encouraged; firefighting equipment was to be kept at hand; and the *īnsulae* were surrounded by supported walkways (*porticus*) to help firefighting or act as fire escapes. Further, anyone who lit a brazier in their home for the purpose of heating or cooking ran the risk of being clubbed or flogged on the orders of Rome's Firewatch Authority. If you wanted food cooked, you went to the local cookshop.

This looks like enlightened planning, but like the Corbusier tower blocks that have disfigured our landscape for so long, it does not seem to have made much difference. Later writers like Juvenal do not give the impression that post-Neronian Rome was a less dangerous place to live in, and the change to the road system seems to have made little difference to the traffic.

But Nero's measures did have one consequence, again evident in any big city. They lessened the amount of space available for building. As a result, the historian Tacitus tells us, the cost of renting accommodation and borrowing money was driven up. Then, as now, there were economic consequences of large-scale town reorganisation, not all of them benign. Today, in the middle of London, unbuilt penthouse flats overlooking Hyde Park attract queues of people wanting to buy at £84 million a throw. As Mark Twain said, 'Buy land: they don't make it any more'.

Street violence

Rome's problems were compounded by other features of ancient urban existence that continue to plague us today. Street lighting – or rather its complete absence in many areas of large towns at night – is a good example. Rome's *īnsulae* blocked out the light anyway, but at night there was no street lighting of any sort (let alone street names and addresses: messages were addressed to, for example, 'the shop on the corner opposite the water fountain by the temple of Jupiter'). Those who could afford it walked the streets at night accompanied by slaves holding firebrands to light their way, but in the absence of protection or if you did not know your way, it must have been terrifying to be out at that time.

Juvenal again talks of the dangers. Rubbish and waste tipped from upper-storey windows were the least of it. Materials loaded onto wagons could tumble off and crush pedestrians, or run away down the steep hills of the city. Mugging was an ever-present threat. Even

'when the house is shut, your shop secured with chains, every shutter fastened, and all is silent, there will be someone to rob you or settle your hash the quick way, with a knife'.

Indeed, Juvenal goes on, most of Rome's iron these days

'is used to forge prison fetters. Ploughs, hoes and mattocks will soon be unobtainable.'

The point is that high-density living brings with it high levels of violence, then as now. We have no statistics for Rome, but in London there were almost 700,000 crimes in 2006–07, including 34,000 robberies, 4,000 GBH, 2,500 gun crimes, 1,800 rapes and 125 murders – vehicle crime and residential burglary making up the rest. The historian and civil servant Suetonius tells us that the emperor Augustus thoroughly enjoyed watching punch-ups in the narrow streets, suggesting that there was little by way of official interest in controlling disorder. A typical graffito indicates that self-help was the usual order of the day:

> 'A copper pot has been stolen from this shop. Anyone returning it will receive a reward of 65 sesterces. Anyone who gives up the thief will be rewarded.'

Legal digests back up Juvenal's picture of the violence of back-street Rome (cf. pp. 148–9). In one incident a shopkeeper puts his lantern on the pavement. A passing thief grabs it and runs, the shopkeeper in hot pursuit. The thief lashes out at him with a whip, and in the ensuing fight the shopkeeper knocks out one of the thief's eyes. At the other end of the scale, a moving epitaph records a sad death:

> 'To the spirit of Jūlia Restitūta, unluckiest of people: in her tenth year she was killed for the sake of her jewellery. Jūlius Restitūtus and Statia Pudentilla, her parents [set this up].'

In another respect too, Rome mirrors the modern world and the legal dangers involved in trying to defend yourself. Juvenal describes himself 'trudging home by moonlight or with hand cupped round the guttering flame of a tiny candle' when he is confronted by a drunken bully itching for a fight:

> 'whether you try to answer back or creep away in silence, it's all the same: you're beaten up anyway, and then your furious "victim" takes *you* to court!'

We cannot tell how commonplace such incidents were; one suspects they were fairly frequent. But they feature on the pages of historians only when the violence reaches a level serious enough to have political repercussions. A famous example occurred at Pompeii. The gladiatorial amphitheatre there is the earliest we know of in Italy, built c. 70 BC, telling us something about the wealth and ambition of this provincial town. The arena could hold about 20,000 spectators and, to create ease of access for away fans, was built near two of the main gates leading into the city.

Much as soccer matches do these days, contests unleashed the emotions of the masses. Some were harmless enough: we find, for example, graffiti expressing the fans' feelings for celebrity gladiators (see p. 162). But, as the historian Tacitus reports, uglier emotions were unleashed after a gladiatorial contest there in AD 59 in a riot so notorious that it was recorded in a fresco.

It all started, Tacitus tells us, when the nearby town of Nuceria sent a gladiatorial team to take on Pompeii's best. 'An exchange of taunts, characteristic of these disorderly country towns', took place, which led to 'abuse, stone-throwing and drawn swords' – and a full-scale riot. The Nucerians came off worse, many being wounded or killed. News of the event reached Rome, and the Senate decided it was too serious to be allowed to pass off as just another provincial incident. The result of their deliberations was a ten-year ban on gladiatorial contests in Pompeii and exile for the contest's sponsor. Could one ever imagine our spineless footballing authorities taking such a line? After the Heysel stadium disaster in 1985 (39 dead), English clubs were banned from European soccer for five years, Liverpool for eight.

Sanitation

Conditions in such an overcrowded environment cannot have been exactly sanitary. We can guesstimate that a Roman would produce about 1.5 pounds of body waste a day. So a million inhabitants would produce nearly 700 tons of body waste per day, some of it deposited in those (few) tenements that had communal ground-floor latrines. One might conclude that a domestic sewage connection in every house would be desirable, but that was not necessarily the case. While great sewers like the *cloāca maxima* dealt with much of the waste, if the Tiber rose, the waste would back up into any connected houses. Further, since the Romans had not invented the u-bend, in-house lavatories would smell extremely unpleasant, and vermin would be able to get in through sewage connections (we read in one case of an octopus swimming up a house-drain each night from the sea to eat pickled fish stored in a house).

But there was a more practical reason for not having a lavatory in the house. Human excrement is a good fertiliser and made good money. Collected regularly by *stercorāriī*, 'cess-pit men', it was sold on to farmers on the outskirts of the city – an unpleasant but useful occupation. One is reminded of 'night soil men', still to be found in the UK in the 1960s, who collected the waste from outdoor privies located on the back lane; and the Victorian crossing sweepers who cleared away the horses' dung that covered the streets so that women would not begrime their skirts, and sold it on. Another option can be seen in a few houses in Pompeii, where waste was led directly onto the garden, though this must have smelled rather unpleasant. In our environmentally conscious age, there would be something to be said for exploiting human excrement productively rather than treating it as 'waste' to be got rid of.

Urine collection was also good business. This was used by the cleaning industry to mordant (i.e. fix, make permanent) dyes. It was usually collected in terracotta jars placed in streets, though these were known to crack and break open, with disagreeable consequences. The people of Ostia, the port of Rome, did things more efficiently: they brought urine directly from a urinal in the Baths of Mithras into the cleaning shop in the basement, via a lead pipe.

Indeed, so profitable was this business that urine was taxed by the emperor Vespasian. When his son Titus rounded on him for it, Vespasian held a coin from the first payment to his nose and asked him whether he was offended by the smell. 'No' said Titus. 'Yet it comes from urine,' replied the emperor. (This story is the source of the later saying *pecūnia nōn olet* 'money does not smell'.)

The authorities have not quite descended to this level yet in their search for taxes, but they are trying hard. Councils are now threatening us with a rubbish tax. All taxes are rubbish, of course, but this is to be a tax *on* rubbish. We keenly await a Rubbish Czar, fit promotion for some eager young trainee politician with the stench of high office in his nostrils, running squadrons of highly trained Rubbish Inspectors.

The Romans were keen on rubbish too. The first step on the ladder to high office in Rome was the post of aedile, whose responsibility to keep the streets of Rome clean of filth came under the general heading of *cūra urbis* 'care of the city'. Not that there was any official street cleaning of the sort regularly alleged to exist today. It was the responsibility of those with properties on the street-front to keep their own frontage of the street clean – something else we might usefully learn from the Romans instead of moaning on about 'the council'.

Apart from that, nature was left to play its part. Aqueducts fed water into public fountains which, since there was no way of controlling the flow, bubbled away day and night. That must have had some detergent effect as it poured down the streets. Dogs and carrion birds dealt with food, excrement and even corpses, which the poor or destitute would simply abandon in the street. Suetonius tells us that the emperor Vespasian was lunching one day when a street dog deposited a human hand under the dining table; perhaps it had been burrowing away in shallow graves or mass burial pits. In a poem about the hardships of a beggar's life, the poet Martial imagines the dying man listening to dogs howling in expectation of eating his corpse, while he flaps his rags at birds of prey to keep them off.

Among the unwanted would also have been infants, abandoned at birth. The names *Stercorōsus, Stercorius*, etc. ('found on dung heaps') are attested, presumably given to such infants who were rescued and sold onto the slave market; and dead gladiators who had been slaves may also have been thrown onto garbage tips. The island on the Tiber was reserved for slaves who had become too old or sick to be of further use. If all this sounds quite ghastly, a city like Cairo or Bombay can offer its equivalent in the third millennium AD.

Design centres?

All very grisly. But both Greeks and Romans (as most ancient societies) had a sense that problems could (to a limited extent) be 'designed out'. A Greek called Hippodamus invented the 'grid plan' design for towns, well illustrated in Pompeii. Here the earliest parts are all higgledy-piggledy; the later parts spacious, regular and ordered. Villa roofs in Pompeii are huge water-funnelling devices. Control of traffic through street-blocking and one-way systems was standard. Aqueduct systems of great sophis-tication transported water for miles into towns (see p. 32). Inev-itably, great care went into the design of all things military – from blow-deflecting armour, for example, to insta-build, overnight army camps.

We too know the importance of design. Car crime and credit-card fraud have dropped by about 50 per cent each as a result of better security measures and chip-and-pin. Light, spacious, airy tube stations are safer – and create less fear of crime – than dark, narrow alley-ridden ones. Some designs are universal. Modern football stadia imitate the design of Roman amphitheatres to give maximum ease of access and crowd flow. Riot police are equipped exactly like a Roman legionary. The Israeli wall is almost identical in strategic layout to Hadrian's Wall, especially in the control zones on the home side.

Power centre of the world

But what was Rome *for*? How did it work? Why on earth did a million people come to live in what seems like a hellhole? The reason behind the growth of Rome is the same as for any city – where there is power there is wealth, and wealth creates demand, and demand attracts people to meet it. Take London. The *City*'s business has always been to make money: cheques, notes, bills, bonds. It is now the major economic powerhouse of the nation: the 335,000 workers in the City produce 8.8 per cent of the UK's total GDP. The daily turnover in foreign exchange is over $1,100 billion (32 per cent of the global total); it has 40 per cent of the global foreign equity market and trades 70 per cent of all Eurobonds (see p. 22 on Roman 'banks').

London's main business has always been government: royalty, Parliament, the Courts, the Treasury, the Foreign Office, etc., and in their train, media and communications. These are the greatest engines of London's economy, and as such generate business and commerce to serve their particular needs. They also produce substantial numbers of London's 'elite', which in these meritocratic days means 'the rich', who themselves require 'elite' services. But since money is king, many of the services that the rich demand are also available to the moderately well off, non-elite middle classes. And the only way in which all these varying demands and needs can be met is by employing people who will meet them, who themselves bring their own needs and demands with them . . .

This must all be infuriating for the super-rich, who have to find more and more expensive ways of distinguishing themselves from the everyday rich. Apparently, Selfridges have on sale replicas of Lord Nelson's coffin to cater for their departure. Way to go. In the Republican period, the Roman super-rich paid for whole *armies* – to fight for them, of course.

For 500 years Rome was the greatest power centre of the ancient world. From here the Roman Senate during the late Republican period (c. 260–31 BC) and the emperor from then on until the collapse of the Roman Empire in the West in the 5th century AD issued orders that dispatched armies and controlled the lives of men and women from Britain to Iraq, from Germany to Libya and Egypt.

The result was a complex and highly developed economic, social, military and cultural infrastructure across the provinces that generated wealth for the provincial as well as Roman elites.

It was a system that could place fine pottery made in Tunisia on tables in Iona. If some provincials felt unhappy about the idea of Roman rule, others probably took the same attitudes as Iraqis today: as a shop owner there said, 'anti-American sentiment does not extend to commerce'.

A city of shopkeepers

But this raises a problem. In the absence of an industrial revolution and manufacturing of goods on the scale that we know it today, agriculture and minerals were the only source of wealth in the ancient world. And they are still critical today, as the battles over, for example, the ownership of the massive mineral wealth lying under the Arctic and Antarctic begin to be engaged – indeed, even more critical, since the minerals now include oil and gas, irrelevant to the ancients but at the heart of modern economies. The ability of the land to produce food was the critical one in the ancient world, since it both fed the population and enabled them to turn a profit (if there was a surplus) to be used to buy other goods and services. But where did a huge urbanised centre like Rome fit into this pattern?

The answer is that Rome 'added value' – in other words, it took in raw materials, and in the myriad *tabernae* (cf. English 'tavern') throughout the city 'retail shops' turned them into needed or desirable and therefore saleable items. Epitaphs record 160 different kinds of job, from cobbler, laundryman, cook, spinner, clerk, garment-mender and barber to baker, metalworker, gardener, hairdresser, litter-bearer, diver, bath-heater and dyer, providing services or working with every imaginable sort of material: wool, leather, metal, clay, straw, oil, wine and so on. Luxury items too were in demand – jewellery, fine clothing and perfume.

England was once dismissed by Napoleon as a 'nation of shop-keepers' – and we all know what the shopkeepers did to him. Rome was a *city* of shopkeepers. When the Roman general

Camillus, expecting a battle, entered Tusculum to see if the town itself was as peaceful as it seemed, he

'found doors wide open, shops doing business with all their contents out on display. Each artisan was intent on his work. He could hear the learning games of children, voice against voice. He saw the streets were full of people, women and children wandering at will to do whatever they needed.'

That, in a nutshell, was Rome – one huge shop. And as it grew wealthier from its conquests, so the standard of living and the quality and range of goods rose, attracting yet more people to try their luck. The result was a whole range of interlocking economic interests, from emperor to slave, from luxury goods for the elite, to sausages and cheap clothes for those serving them. It was a flexible market too. Many of the *plēbs* simply hired themselves out as 'general labourers' to do anything required. One graffito reads

'You've had any number of different job opportunities – barman, baker, farmer, at the mint, now you're selling pots. Lick cunt and you'll have done the lot.'

Labouring away

Whoever this bloke was, he was typical. The point is that the concept of the 'job' was different in Rome from what it is in our world. In our world, businesses employ people to do what they are told to do, in order to serve the needs of the business. The great majority of people find work like this. In the ancient world, almost the only type of person to whom that applied was the slave: (s)he was bought on the market, fed and watered, and told what to do by the owner. To that extent, we are all slaves. Romans, however, were freelance. Unless you worked in a family business, you found what work you could, wherever it was available – like the 'general labourer' above. So when the papers announced in shocked tones that more than half of new

British jobs between 1997 and 2006 went to 'foreigners', Romans would have wondered what on earth they were worrying about. Anyone who came to Rome had to find their own way, or die. No one else would find it for them.

But that did not mean people could not help each other. We hear of a workers' association – a sort of 'friendly society' – of forty-nine men (including slaves and ex-slaves) and four women co-operating to run the grain warehouses of the emperor Galba. It was dedicated to the emperor and the gods of Good Health. Solidarity among the poor has a long history.

Sex and the city

We can say nothing about sexuality from a woman's point of view in the ancient world because no evidence on the topic from a woman survives. The male experience, however, is very well documented; largely, that is, through the literature that males produced, mostly for the enlightenment of other males. And there are legal documents too. A marriage contract from Greek Egypt, for example, says 'it shall not be lawful for [the husband] Philiscus to bring home another wife in addition to Apollonia or to have a concubine or a boy lover'. The Greek moralist Dio argues that women these days are so easy to seduce that men will soon turn to boys instead. It is as if women and boys were merely passive objects designed to serve the male desire to penetrate. That is what ancient males were supposed to do, and to do anything else – especially to be penetrated – was shaming. So 'lick cunt' was an insult: an unmasculine activity. The important thing for men, it seems, was for the man to dominate.

On the other side, women were thought by males to need such penetration because that was what their bodies were *for*. This was why women had a reputation among men for sexual voracity. But women were perfectly capable of dominating too. The famous story was told of the blind

---

prophet Teiresias who had been both male and female. Asked by Hera, wife of Zeus, who got more pleasure out of intercourse, Teiresias replied that the woman did, by a ration of 10–1. Hera blinded him for his pains.

That is not to say that (according to males) males and females did not fall madly in love. Pompeii is full of graffiti on the subject: everything from romance ('Marcus loves Spendusa') to realism ('I came here, had a shag, went home') and sad irony ('Lovers, like bees, lead a honeyed life. I wish'). Epigrams and the poetry of, for example, Catullus make it quite clear that the flames of passion ran high between lovers. Mutual pleasure, too, is often the aim. This from Petronius:

> 'What a night that was, gods and goddesses,
> how soft the bed. We clung, hotly,
> and each to each transfused with our lips
> our wandering souls. Farewell, mortal cares ...'

This poem plays with the ancient idea that we will never be fulfilled until our souls enter the one we love, and their soul enters us. Further, to the mutual sensual ecstasy is added the sense that lovemaking of this intensity raises both participants from the mortal to the divine.

If one wants a sense of harmonious married relations, Homer (for example) provides it, especially in his *Odyssey*, where Odysseus talks of marriage in terms of 'like-mindedness', and when he and Penelope are re-united, Odysseus 'weeps to have his wife in his arms', while she 'rejoiced to look on her husband, and her arms around his neck would never let him go'. (And so to bed ...)

It is, incidentally, a rich irony that Greeks, often thought of as the great beacons of Western homoeroticism, thought pederasty inspiringly wonderful, a source of Light, Truth and Goodness, but homosexuality perfectly disgusting.

Express either of those views in public today and you would find yourself strung up pretty sharpish.

The famous 'old Roman' Cato gives some idea of the sheer range of Rome's business. Writing on agriculture, he recommends Rome for basic stuff like tunics, togas, blankets, patchwork, nails and bars. But the author of the *Book of Revelation*, envisaging the collapse of the city, indicates exactly what Rome meant to the traders in luxury goods:

'The merchants of the earth will weep and mourn . . . because no one any longer buys their cargoes, cargoes of gold and silver, jewels and pearls, cloths of purple and scarlet, silks and fine linens; all kinds of scented woods, ivories and every sort of thing made of costly woods, bronze, iron, or marble; cinnamon and spice, incense, perfumes and frankincense; wine, oil, flour and wheat, sheep and cattle, horses, chariots and slaves, and the lives of men.'

The Roman comic playwright Plautus (c. 200 BC) imagines what the rich man will have to put up with if he marries a spendthrift wife:

'The creditors stand at the door. There's the cloth-fuller, the embroiderer, the gold-smith, the wool-weaver, the fringe-designer, maker of underwear, inventor of veils, dyers in purple and saffron, sleeve-stitchers, linen-weavers, perfumiers, shoe-makers, slipper-makers, sandal-fitters, leather-stainers, repairers, corset-makers, girdle-experts. They're all waiting to be paid. And when you've got rid of that lot, in come another 300 waving their bills – needlewomen, cabinet-makers, bag-makers, then more dyers . . .'

Immigrants

So Rome was a magnet. Overcrowding, as we have seen (p. 3), was endemic, and Romans tried to deal with the problem. Free hand-outs (see p. 35) went only to those who had a fixed address in Rome, but fraud was as common then as now: Cicero complained that men working on his villa twelve miles away had left it to claim free grain in the city! The workless were forcibly sent to work in agriculture – good, honest Roman toil – in depopulated parts of Italy. Julius Caesar considered sending job-scroungers to the sea-port of Corinth, where there was much more chance of picking up easy money. Both New Labour and the Tories currently agree that benefit fraud and getting people back to work are two issues that need urgently to be dealt with and are busy working out policies.

But Romans did not stop foreigners coming, especially well heeled ones. When senators moaned at the emperor Claudius for being willing to let Gauls into the Senate, Claudius pointed out that this sort of move was one of Rome's strengths. Newcomers proved their worth by 'assimilating our customs and culture and marrying into our families'. Precisely. Assimilate and inter-marry away.

Athenians had no problem about immigrants either; they simply demanded that every immigrant had an Athenian sponsor (see box, p. 49). Interesting idea. The renowned orator Lysias, who made his money writing speeches for others (see the case on p. 110), was one such; his father Cephalus, a Syracusan by birth, made a huge fortune from arms manufacture in Athens, and Plato set his most famous dialogue *The Republic* in his house. Athens was a magnet as well.

So, London. Whatever its functional difficulties, from wretched transport systems to crime rates, it is nevertheless a desirable place to be. That is why its population is expected to grow to over 8.15 million by 2016. But the picture of Rome that our sources offer suggests that, however desirable it may have been for the wealthy elites, there wasn't much going for the rest. There was, after all, no welfare state in Rome.

Which brings us to, in Juvenal's famous (mistranslated) phrase, *pānem et circēnsēs*, 'bread and (not) circuses'. That phenomenon will be the subject of the next chapter, and the contrast with London's much-loved Millennium Dome and impending Olympic Games will be on the stark side.

Update: Banking on trouble

Romans did experience the occasional economic crisis but nothing on our current scale because it had no financial instruments (e.g. stock markets) to create credit. The Senate could spend only what it had – i.e. hard coin – though in times of crisis (e.g. the war against Hannibal) it took special action, e.g. special taxes on the rich. So no national debt either. Individuals, in the absence of banks, could only borrow from wealthy friends or money-changers, always for short-term projects, e.g. Caesar borrowed zillions from the billionaire Crassus to finance his early political career. There was not concept of 'furthering economic investment'.

Banks are massive wealth-generators, but they have forgotten poet Horace's *aurea mediocritās*, 'the golden middle way'. His point was that the real gold lay in *not* going to extremes. It should be the motto of every bank today, where going to extremes has landed us in fearful trouble (cf. p. 256).

>─┼─◆>─•─O─•─<◆─┼─<

Reading list

Peter Jones and Keith Sidwell (eds.), *The World of Rome* (Cambridge 1997).

Juvenal, *The Satires* (World's Classics 1991).

Plautus, *The Pot of Gold* (Penguin 1965).

Nicholas Purcell, in *Cambridge Ancient History* (second edition), IX and X (Cambridge 1994, 1996).

A. Scobie, in *Klio* (1986).

Frank M. Snowden, *Before Colour Prejudice* (Harvard 1983).

Suetonius, *Lives of the Caesars* (World's Classics 2000).

[2]

Bread and (not) circuses

Funding entertainment: London 2008

Keeping the population of London amused is not one of the most pressing problems that politicians face. Quite apart from the spectacle of London itself – its churches, shops, restaurants, parks and so on – there is an established tradition of professional performance – exhibitions, plays, sports, films, opera – for which people are happy to pay. Entertainment, then, is a business which responds to the demands, and forms the tastes, of the market (and an offshoot of the entertainment business, tourism, is London's second biggest money-spinner).

Admittedly, it is a business heavily subsidised by taxpayers (Alan Bennett's *The History Boys*, for example, got a cool £16.5 million) but that is the way with the Arts. The one redeeming feature of the subsidy is that at least it goes to people who should know what they are doing. When government in its universal wisdom tries to ape them, the results are catastrophic. The Millennium Dome must be unrivalled as a monument to the inability of government and its advisers to have the remotest idea of what people actually want. One has little confidence that the Olympic Games will be any more successful, especially given the expense. The cost of the Olympic stadium itself has doubled since the original estimate two years ago (to £500 million), and will be largely dismantled when the three-week Games are over, leaving a small 'legacy' stadium that would have cost £75 million. Nice 'legacy'. The Romans should have thought of this for the Colosseum. The overall cost of the Games is estimated at nearer £9 billion than the original £2.3 billion – and the games are still four years away. The latest forecast is that the cost 'may rise' to ten billion. Do I hear fifteen? (After all, the government paid £431 million for the Scottish parliament building. Eleven times over budget.)

But the Romans knew about this already. The emperor Augustus' confidante Maecenas lamented:

> 'Cities should not waste their resources on number and variety of games, in case they exhaust themselves in futile exertions and quarrel over unreasonable desire for glory. They should not ruin the public treasury and private estates thereby.'

The demands of the *plēbs*

When the Roman satirist Juvenal, however, turned to the topic of keeping the *plēbs* amused, he brought an entirely different assumption to bear. In his third satire, he talks about the expense of living in Rome in much the same terms as those struggling to buy property in London today, but adds a vital rider:

> 'You can buy a first-class house, freehold, in the country, for the price of a year's rent for some shoddy, badly-lit attic here in Rome – *if you can tear yourself away from the races.*'

In another place, he famously observes:

> 'Time was when the people elected generals, heads of state, commanders of legions. No longer. They've only got two priorities now – *bread and (not) circuses.*'

In both instances, he is talking about exactly the same thing – free entertainment, laid on by the state: the best a Roman could get.

As explained in the last chapter (p. 15), the Roman Empire existed to serve the needs of Rome, and the greatest need of all was to ensure that Roman citizens (*plēbs urbāna*, 'city people'), who kept the show on the road, were broadly content with their lot. These citizens were the original, or freeborn, or freed (i.e. ex-slave) inhabitants of Rome, not immigrant slaves or foreigners. But if they compared their own fortunes with those of the aristocratic elite, they might have been very discontented. Money, indeed, could be made – *salvē lucru(m)* ('Hello, Profit!'), announces a mosaic inscription in the doorway of a house in Pompeii – but it was at heart a dog-eat-dog world. If you survived, you were doing pretty well, and if you didn't, you died (to that brutal extent, poverty was not endemic). If you survived for a few generations, you might even do well enough to leave Rome altogether. But when discontent surfaced, things could turn very nasty.

One of the turning points in the demise of the Roman Republic was triggered by such discontent. As Rome conquered or made alliances with its neighbouring Italian towns, and slowly grew from a small city-state into (by about 260 BC) the master of the whole of Italy, it annexed Italian territory as *ager pūblicus*, 'state-owned land'. Here the Romans built new cities, or assigned, sold or rented the land to individuals who applied to work it. The purpose was to give a leg-up to honest peasant farmers, who had always formed the backbone of Rome's all-conquering citizen army. But – and this is crucial – unworked land, or a farm that was unworked because its owners were serving in the army, could be taken over by anyone who wanted to, in return for a rent. And anyone did want to – notably, the rich.

As a result, by the second century BC, wealthy aristocrats had come to monopolise the ownership of this land – and illegally too, because there was supposed to be a limit on how much of such land you could hold. Further, they farmed it not with free men, who might be called up for military service, but with slaves. Such vast expropriations also tended to make nearby small peasant farms unviable, with the result that these too were taken over. (Europe's Common Agricultural Policy, originally designed to prop up small French farms, has the same effect, rewarding the big producers in particular. Likewise, it is the large farms in Zimbabwe that Robert Mugabe has his eyes on to hand over to his cronies.)

So, in 133 BC a tribune of the *plēbs*, Tiberius Gracchus, proposed to revive the law that limited the amount of 'public' land anyone could own. The released land was to be divided up among poor citizens. The people were obviously in favour of this but the Senate, many of whose members had ignored the law and taken control of great swathes of it, was hostile. The historian Appian puts both sides:

'They [the aristocrats] had worked for a long time to improve the land with plantations and buildings; some of them had paid good prices to buy it – were they to lose their money along with their land? Some had family tombs there, had accepted it as their portion of the family estate, had spent their wives' dowries to buy it or given it as dowries for their own daughters. Money-lenders pointed to loans they had on the security of these lands.'

But the poor who had lost their land (often given to them as a 'pension' after fighting in the army) equally had a case, as Appian explains:

'They had been reduced from a decent livelihood to poverty and consequent childlessness, since they could not afford to raise a family. They listed the campaigns they had fought in to win this land, and expressed their anger at being deprived of their share in the country's wealth. They turned on the rich for employing slaves to work the land instead of free citizens who had fought in the army.'

Anyway, Gracchus invoked the right to by-pass the Senate and appealed directly to the people. Amid chaotic scenes, the bill was passed. That one incident was to trigger a decade of street violence, during which both Tiberius and his equally reforming brother Gaius were murdered by senators opposed to their re-distributive plans.

The culture of benefaction

The Roman *plēbs*, in other words, did not complacently acquiesce in whatever the Senate decided. They were free Romans, members of the greatest city in the world, and were prepared to let their rulers know it. The Roman authorities were well aware of this, and developed tactics to make them feel wanted. If religion was the opiate of the masses for Marx, for Romans it was state-sponsored largesse, providing the *plēbs* with what they thought of as pleasures available only to aristocrats.

Cicero for one did not approve. He remarked of Julius Caesar:

'He had wooed the ignorant masses by shows, buildings, hand-outs and banquets. He had bound his own followers to him by rewards and his adversaries by a demonstration of clemency. In brief, he had brought a free community to servitude.'

But at least Caesar paid for it with his own money. One hates to think what Cicero would have said about our welfare state – much the same, one imagines, as Arthur Laffer, an economic adviser to Ronald Reagan: 'If you pay people to be poor, you will never run out of poor people'.

But whatever one makes of Cicero, the fact is that the Roman state was able to generate a feeling among its people that not only were they living in the greatest city in the world, a showcase of power and privilege, but also (unlike, I suspect, those celebrities with their hair shampoo) that they were worth it. Despite the dangers of living in Rome – fire, flood, disease, debt, fierce competition for work – the Romans developed a culture of benefaction intended to make up for it all. Time, then, to look more closely at how the Romans set about making the masses feel that their life was an aristocratic one, and that living in Rome was worth all the hassle – and to wonder what our politicians have ever done to make the poor feel like aristocrats rather than (on the Ciceronian model) servile dependents.

It could be argued that, for example, the Docklands development and regeneration round the Dome and the Olympic stadium area are similar projects. My feeling is that such schemes are more like necessary infrastructure than projects designed to make one feel proud to be a Londoner.

Buildings

Transporting goods

Rome was a 'hanging city', built on its famous seven hills, which were originally far steeper than they are now. The river Tiber played a vital part in its development. The reason is that, before the invention of the steam engine, the transport of heavy materials was an extremely slow process. Only oxen could pull really weighty loads, and oxen nipped along at a whole 2 mph – quick, admittedly, by South West Trains' standards – consuming vast amounts of food as they did so. So up until the 19th century, the only way to transport heavy goods over long distances was by water – the further by water, the better. (This explains why, for example, a place like Venice became so wealthy. It was the furthest point into the Middle and Eastern European land masses that one could reach by sea from the Mediterranean.) For Rome, awkwardly located twenty miles inland, the Tiber at least made it relatively easy to bring in the necessary materials by barge.

The arch and concrete

The Alban hills (21 kilometres – 13 miles – south-east of Rome) were also crucial. Being volcanic, they provided lava (*silex*) for paving roads; and volcanic tufa is easily carved, worked and cut, making it perfect for construction. The (effectively) Roman invention of the arch and barrel vault was of great value for a city built on hills: it enabled builders to construct platforms, terraces, ramps and so on, and thus extend the hillsides.

Finally, and most importantly, the Romans invented concrete, which was to have the most dramatic constructional and architectural consequences, then and ever since. The original 'binding' substance was mortar, made by 'burning' chalk or limestone in a kiln and then adding water. When the water evaporated, the substance had adhesive qualities, and could be bulked out by adding sand or the like into a form of cement. This is very old technology indeed (found in Egypt in the 3rd millennium BC), and

Romans used it from the 4th century BC to bind the in-fill for walls, pouring it over a rubble interior, which was then faced with brick or stone.

But in the 1st century BC the Romans found that by mixing mortar with pozzolana, a volcanic sand found in regions like Naples (Vesuvius) and the Alban Hills, and adding broken rocks, they could create concrete – an extremely strong, comparatively light material, that could be poured into moulds and shaped and would set hard even under water. Arches, vaults and bridges were now comparatively easy to construct; and the speed with which one could knock up a defensive wall greatly increased. It also made possible the building of huge structures, like the Colosseum and aqueducts, which earlier technology – columns, cross-beams, solid stone and bricks (think Greek temple) – could never have done without gigantic expense. The aim was to turn Rome into a great contemporary Greek city, like Alexandria.

Roads and more

Extensive building work in Rome was one of the many ways in which the *plēbs* were made to feel proud to be there. By the 2nd century BC, Rome boasted streets, extensive shopping precincts and brick-built blocks of flats. In the 120s BC Gaius Gracchus, equally zealous reforming brother of Tiberius Gracchus (see p. 25), set about a massive building programme. The construction of roads was a particular concern:

'He took great pains to ensure that these should be graceful and beautiful as well as useful. His roads were planned so as to run right across the country in a straight line; part of the surface consisting of dressed stone and part of tamped-down gravel. Depressions were filled up, any watercourses or ravines which crossed the line of the road were bridged, and both sides of the road were levelled or embanked to the same height, so that the whole of the work presented a beautiful and symmetrical appearance. Besides this he had every road measured in miles, and stone pillars erected to mark the

distances. Other stones were set up at shorter intervals on both sides of the road so that horsemen should be able to mount from these without help.'
(Plutarch)

In 55 BC Pompey built Rome's first permanent (stone) theatre, to hold 10,000 people. In 33 BC, Augustus' side-kick, Agrippa, renewed the aqueducts, constructed new ones, made 700 cisterns, 500 fountain heads and 130 water towers in Rome – all in one year. This was at a time when Augustus (then Octavianus) was about to fight it out against Marc Antony and Cleopatra for leadership of the Roman world, which ended with Augustus' victory at Actium in 31 BC and (eventually) him becoming Rome's first emperor.

Roman roads

Roman roads were originally planned with the military in mind, and were therefore built to provide a firm footing for legionaries to march along under all conditions. They were constructed on firm bases and surfaced with paving blocks of flint or basalt, secured by kerbstones. The poet Statius leaves us our only account of Roman road construction in a poem praising the emperor Domitian for building a short cut along the *Via Appia* in AD 95, reducing travelling time from a whole day to two hours (beat that, Arriva): trench – secure grounding – foundation material – paving stone – kerbs, and all involving vast squadrons of workers. Designated public highways were constructed at state expense, sometimes with help from local landowners. Other roads were public–private partnerships, funded by a combination of state subsidy, imperial donation and local financing from townships and roadside inhabitants. This is not uncommon today; for example, Westfield is putting in £170 million to upgrade Shepherd's Bush tube station ahead of their new shopping centre complex.

But construction practices varied all over the empire,

---

and while some roads lasted for hundreds of years, others required continual upkeep. Inscriptions, often on milestones, describe how so-and-so, usually at his own expense, repaired a road that had collapsed, subsided, broken up, been long neglected or badly constructed in the first place (ouch!). The emperor Tiberius tried to persuade the people of Trebia to put into their roads money left to them to build a theatre (he failed). In the provinces, there was always a terrified scramble to repair the roads if the emperor was due to make a friendly visit (the reaction is similar when Her Majesty drops in). Upkeep of the roads for military use made heavy demands. In Macedonia, for example, we find Trajan (at war around the Danube) demanding that an important through road be repaired to military standard, and the rich from a neighbouring city rallying round to help the locals bear the vast expense.

All roads, of course, led to Rome: an expression of Rome's control over the empire's landscape – river, marsh, desert and mountain alike – and populace. Roads sped communication and cultural and economic exchange. But, like the railways, they did not come cheap.

Already Augustus knew what was required to win hearts and minds. When he became emperor, he ordered the renovation of many of Rome's temples that had fallen into disrepair and constructed others, as well as introducing a number of new religious rituals. Here was a man who, after the bloody havoc of the last years of the Republic, wanted to restore Rome's healthy relationship with the gods and therefore guarantee its long-term security under divine benediction.

Today's universal taxation means that we are in a much better position to put in place such schemes of public works. One crucial question is the extent to which they offer value for money. London's Crossrail, having been promised twice already in Labour manifestos, has recently been promised again and costed at £8 billion. No bookies, I guess, would be willing to quote odds on the reliability of that costing.

But there is another issue too: since it is all our money anyway, it is often hard to feel emotionally attached to the results unless, as well as being obviously value for money, they are also stunning with it. The ghastly discord in our streets between graceful 18th-century buildings and most modern constructions, designed (it would seem) not to catch the eye so much as to wrench it from its socket, tells its own story.

Water

Most of us take water for granted most of the time, except when the south-east of England has a hosepipe ban. Then there is a tremendous fuss and dire warnings about supplies running out, all oblivious of the fact that everyone else in the UK is swimming in the stuff (unless they are being towed through it by burly firemen). But 'everywhere else', of course, does not count if London goes short.

Aqueducts

The Romans were the first people to start supplying water to cities on a vast scale. Water engineers of staggering technical precision, they spread comfort far down the social ladder. The first aqueduct was commissioned in Rome in 312 BC; in time Rome alone came to be served by eleven aqueducts, totalling over 300 miles in length, delivering something in the order of 1.2 million cubic metres of water a day to its million or so inhabitants. The record length for an aqueduct is one serving Constantinople, 75 miles long as the crow flies, but in fact 155 miles with all the twists and turns.

Since the strength of the flow depended on gravity, gradient was all-important, and across the empire there were dazzling examples of engineering to control it. The water came into reservoirs with settling tanks, taps and sluices; and there being no serious storage facilities and no way to moderate the flow, the water poured out day and night, keeping the sewers flushed. Street fountains served the general populace; water could be fed into private houses through pipes of regulated size and at a price – a useful source of revenue.

Water cleanliness was a serious issue. The Roman architect Vitruvius (1st century BC) gave rules for checking it at source: are the inhabitants there strong, without physical distortions or inflamed eyes? Does the water leave traces when sprinkled over certain alloy vessels? When boiled in a copper pan, does it leave a sludge? Will it cook vegetables quickly? Is it clear, from an untainted source? Vitruvius knew that lead-working was an unhealthy occupation ('observe the lead workers' pallid complexion') and that lead piping (whose great virtue is that it does not corrode) was not as good for you as earthenware. Not that lead poisoning caused the fall of the Roman Empire: water flowing through the pipes laid calcium deposits that masked the lead. Interestingly, people have been aware of the effects of lead for thousands of years, long before Vitruvius; only with the advent of chemistry have the dangers been quantified and public policy put in place to do something about it (including lead in paint and petrol).

Baths

In many towns where aqueducts were built, the water itself was not vital for existence. Springs, rivers and rainwater must have been sufficient, or the town would never have existed in the first place. No: the water's primary destination – the main reason for the whole vast network – was the public baths: every Roman's relaxation centre of choice, and demanded by the legions wherever they were stationed across the empire. Emperor, toffs, struggling workers and slaves alike, all naked, took advantage of them, women included (mixed and separate bathing was available, depending on local tastes).

The entry fee was minimal. Romans came there to be olive-oiled up, work out – physical fitness was an important 'lifestyle' priority (see pp. 206, 236) – and then bathe it all off: first in the sweating room, then the hot bath, the medium and the cold (Marcus Aurelius comments that bathing is all 'oil, sweat, filth and greasy water'). Baths were the equivalent of today's (abominably expensive) work-out gyms and pubs rolled into one. They offered everyone a taste of what was felt to be the way toffs lived.

But although all classes used the baths, there was never any question of social levelling or integration: people knew their place and mingled with their own kind. The wealthy, for example, would come surrounded by slaves, be oiled with the finest unguents, be dried with thick woollen towels, drink wine from superb goblets, sport expensive jewellery, bring a range of clothes to choose from and depart well perfumed. Doubtless they would be deferred to in the general hubbub. The sharp Roman satirical poet Martial admits that however much he bathed with his wealthy patrons, they did not like him any more for it.

In this respect the baths were exactly like our comprehensive schools. Unlike the Roman baths, comps were specifically designed with an apparently vital educational purpose in mind: to mix the classes. No one has ever explained how, precisely, mixing the classes would have the slightest advantageous educational effect but, in fact, it does not mix the classes at all. Comprehensives just put them side by side, where they continue to gaze at each other in fascinated horror.

Gossip, news, business, laughs (and the rest): all Rome was there in microcosm. As the famous elegiac inscription says:

> *balnea, vīna, Venus corrumpunt corpora nostra;*
> *set vītam faciunt balnea, vīna, Venus.*
> 'Baths, drink [and] sex destroy our bodies;
> but they make our life, [do] baths, drink [and] sex'.

No wonder at the start of his treatise *dē aquaeductū* the super-intendent of Roman aqueducts Frontinus (AD 97) exclaimed:

> 'I ask you! Just compare the vast monuments of this vital aqueduct network with those useless Pyramids, or the good-for-nothing tourist attractions of the Greeks!'

Not that one could say anything so complimentary about *our* water supply. It remains a constant mystery why, when Romans could convey water huge distances into towns, our supine companies are unable to keep the south-east supplied from the aquatic superabundance of the rest of the country.

'Bread and (not) circuses'

The Roman satirist Juvenal made his famously acid comment that people were now interested only in *pānem et circēnsēs*, 'bread and (not) circuses', around AD 100. By this time, emperors had been installed for over a hundred years. The assemblies where the people had indeed been able to appoint their leaders (see p. 75) had been dissolved by the emperor Tiberius in AD 14. He handed the duty to the Senate.

Bread

By 'bread', Juvenal meant hand-outs of grain offered by the state to nominated groups of Roman citizens. The practice was begun in 123 BC by the great reformer Caius Gracchus (see above, p. 29). Gracchus' hand-outs were not, however, free. Instead, grain was charged at something less than market price to those who qualified for it. The aim was to ensure that the price of grain was not subject to seasonal fluctuation or the exploitation of the grain merchants. The grain's dietetic value was also high, calculated at about the equivalent of 3,000–4,000 calories a day (about 3000 a day is reckoned to be needed by an adult male).

This was not a welfare scheme. It did not provide especially for the poor or for large families. But it did attract large numbers of people to move to Rome and even increased the manumission (liberation) of slaves. This came about because, on manumission, the household could retain a limited hold on the freed slaves' services, but now without having to find the total cost of feeding them.

As a result, grain became a political hot potato, and politicians leapt on various grain-wagons to win popularity by extending the range of recipients or cutting the cost – one thinks of medical prescriptions, TV licences, changes to inheritance and income tax today – until in 58 BC Clodius made the distribution free, which it remained from then on. This increased further the drift of people into Rome.

Hand-outs and bureaucracy

The real problem, as ever, was registering those qualified for the hand-out. In 46 BC Julius Caesar, then effective dictator of Rome, drew up a new granary roll across Rome, district by district, worked out with the help of the tenement overseers. In so doing he struck out illegitimate claimants, halving the number of recipients from c. 320,000 to 150,000 (the problems of today's social services are not new).

From then on the emperors made consistent efforts to keep numbers within the 150,000–200,000 range. No one was debarred for bad behaviour. As the Roman political adviser and essayist Seneca said:

> 'Everyone whose name appears on the register, thief no less than perjurer or adulterer, receives the state hand-out. Whatever else he may be, he gets it, not because he is good or bad, but because he is a citizen.'

Some principles are very ancient.

Over time a huge bureaucracy was put in place to organise it all. The grain was harvested, stored and loaded onto grain ships in Africa and Egypt; received in Rome at its port of Ostia; stored there; then loaded into barges and towed upstream for storage in the capital itself, every step under the closest state supervision. About 200,000 tonnes (up to 4,000 barge-loads) of grain a year would be required to feed Rome.

Then, in the 3rd century AD, the grain hand-out was replaced by a bread hand-out. The 260 or so baking establishments in Rome immediately came under strict state control. Bakers' estates and goods were frozen by the state; bakers could not change jobs; their sons had to become bakers. We even hear of people being lured into bars and brothels to be kidnapped and swell the bakers' numbers (probably not the way to deal with today's critical short-age of physics teachers, though it might be an effective way of closing down brothels). Bread was baked and distributed daily (it would not keep) under the official gaze; each recipient had a token, marked with the amount due to him, and where he was to collect it. Meanwhile, later emperors added further dispensations: Septimius Severus added an olive oil hand-out, and Aurelian dis-tributions of pork and wine.

But, again, certain things never change. Though Romans were a very practical people, bureaucracies are not renowned for their smooth workings. We find orders being endlessly repeated – they clearly had not been carried out – granaries misused, and so on. The greater the number of laws we find published to control the system, the more we can be sure it did not work efficiently.

Nevertheless, here was another aspect of the 'aristocratic' life for the people of Rome: high-quality bread from grain grown in North Africa and Egypt (none of your nasty local-grown stuff), shipped at enormous expense to the capital, all free, for them and them alone; and olive oil, meat and wine too. What it was to be a citizen of the greatest capital in the world!

(Not) circuses

As for circuses, it is important to point out that these had nothing to do with what we call a circus. The word meant 'circuit', and referred to the chariot races. Juvenal was using that single example to stand for all the public entertainments that were laid on for the pleasure and aristocratisation of the *plēbs* – the main one of which was, indeed, the races.

Legend had it that chariot races were invented by Romulus and were the spectacle that led to the famous '(Not) rape of the Sabine women' (see box). Horses, the equivalent of Ferraris in the ancient world, were the privilege of the very rich, and chariot racing (two- or four-horse) phenomenally expensive (like today), not least because the best stud farms were in Spain and Africa.

The (not) rape of the Sabine women

The Latin word translated as 'rape' in this context actually means 'seizure'. The story was told by the Roman historian Livy. Early Rome (traditionally founded in 753 BC) needed to boost its population. So Romulus started by turning Rome's Capitoline hill into a place of sanctuary where the dross of the world could find refuge and start life afresh. It was just like Australia. This was very successful, but still left Rome with a shortage of women. So Romulus sent envoys round the local tribes, asking for volunteers. The envoys were decisively rejected. Romulus therefore advertised that he was planning to lay on a sensational set of chariot races. People from outlying areas flooded in both to watch and to find out what this new town of Rome was like, and the Sabines sent their wives and children too. In mid-race, the young girls among them were abducted. Romulus explained that the Romans' only desire was to make honest women of them, but all the tribes which had attended dismissed this excuse and attacked. They were easily beaten off, except for the Sabines. But the abducted women had by now become persuaded by the Romans' 'desire and love, which are always the most effective appeals to a woman's heart' and intervened themselves 'among the flying missiles', begging both sides to make peace. Which they duly did. That is Livy's story, anyway.

Here, then, was true aristocratic entertainment for the masses. The Circus Maximus was the major venue, able to hold 150,000 spectators in its heyday. These races generated the same passions as horse racing and Formula 1 do today. Carrier pigeons, we hear, instantly spread the news of winners to outlying towns. One man became so excited that he covered his head when the team he backed was running, fainted when it won and had to be revived with a sponge.

Theatre and banquets

In 366 BC Rome was subjected to a 'fearful plague'. In an effort to placate the gods, Romans started laying on free theatrical shows – the first time (Livy says) the Romans had ever done anything so novel. These were slowly 'romanised' into knockabout entertainment called 'mime'. They were noted for their obscenity and licence (especially female nudity) and involved a range of features, from song and dance, acrobatics and conjuring to melodramatic tales of kidnapping, shipwrecks and adultery. They were hugely popular. We tend to think of classical drama as enormously serious, but that is merely a reflection of what survives. Low knockabout and sentimental schmaltz were the staple diet of the *plēbs*. Just like the telly, in fact.

Further, the state-funded *lūdī* ('games', 'entertainments') also came to include mass banqueting, 'aristocratic' feasting for all the people. As Seneca put it, 'on feast days, the right of luxury is given to the people at large'. This sentiment is, in fact, a good summary of what the public religious festivals were all about: a taste of the 'good life', usually associated only with the very rich of Rome – felt to be shocking when enjoyed only by the toffs, but entirely justified when spread among the whole people.

Spin-offs

But there were further beneficial consequences that sprang from such entertainments. Old facilities needed to be renovated and new buildings to be put up, especially for the dramatic performances. Open-plan porticos were ideal for public feasting. All this gave work to building contractors and labourers and developed a city of which the *plēbs* could feel a part. As for feasts, the *tabernae* came into their own: no one could eat unless provisions were available, and on a huge scale. In other words, these festivals provided important economic opportunities for Roman workers: a community of interests linked rich and poor, elite and masses alike.

As Rome became larger, and life there more precarious, it became more and more essential to give the vast masses of the *plēbs* a reason for staying. 'Bread and (not) circuses', which made the general populace feel a sense of pride in having such extraordinary largesse freely available to them, was a key part of the strategy. But there was nothing patronising about it. The grain distribution was not a charitable hand-out to keep citizens alive (though doubtless it was for some); the *lūdī* were not a gratuitous sop. They were a bonus, an indication of Roman citizens' unique status and importance in the Mediterranean world. It was what living in Rome did for you. The result was that most of the Roman citizenry for much of the time felt somehow incorporated into the wealth of the city and had a sense of proud solidarity with what it stood for. SPQR, *Senātus Populusque Romānus*, Rome's 'signature', meant what it said: 'the Senate and the Roman People'. What sort of a hollow laugh would it raise today if someone were to announce that 'Parliament and the English People' was the signature/motto of England?

The contrast between SPQR and the resentment generated by the modern welfare state, which does far more for citizens and spends infinitely more public money than Rome ever did, could not be more pointed. One reason, I suspect, is that, for all its rhetoric, modern government at heart regards 'the people' not as an asset but as a liability, requiring to be fed, watered, pregnancy-tested, slimmed, educated, medicated, bussed, given 'rights' and lectured at not to smoke, drink wine with meals, throw snowballs, play conkers, take toothpaste on aeroplanes or publicly reprimand recalcitrant youths. Where governments cannot do this themselves, they run nearly 900 unaccountable quangos, costing us nearly £170 *billion* a year (more than five times the defence budget of £32 billion a year), to do it for them. Secretly, they would really prefer us to go away. The feeling is often reciprocated.

Votes for fun

Perhaps it is something of a relief that government does not also try to entertain us with our money. We have already mentioned the Millennium Dome fiasco. One could throw in the BBC too – or throw it out, as government should have done long ago, whatever its bleatings about 'public service'. Since government does not need to make a profit and is not therefore constrained by the market, it is far more satisfactory to leave entertainment to private initiatives, which will soon find out whether they have got it right or not. Government could start by letting listeners and viewers vote on the amount of BBC money to be given to the various programmes – and presenters.

Of course, if government could use our money to make money in a way that gave people pleasure, it would be different. Gambling (the National Lottery, Premium Bonds) and National Savings seem to be their only big ideas on this front. The latest idea, to hold a TV vote-in to decide which of four projects will win £50 million from the Big Lottery Fund, is right on the button (see Aristotle, p. 217). It tells you much about the modern world that the contestants – projects relating to the Eden Project in Cornwall, Sherwood Forest, the Black Country and more bikeways – all *loathe* the idea that the public might have a say.

But if government were to turn prostitution into a state-controlled service, as is often advocated, they could make a bob or two. Three of the most heavyweight ancients would have approved – the Greek poet and political reformer Solon (early 6th century BC), Cato the Elder (234–149 BC), Roman statesman, moralist and prose stylist, and St Augustine (AD 354–430).

Cato once saw a young aristocrat coming out of a brothel and applauded, on the grounds that the more easily sexual desires were satisfied, the better the chance that the young would spend more of their time on the important things in life. St Augustine regretfully admitted that if prostitutes were banned, society 'would be reduced to chaos through unsatisfied lust'.

But it was Solon who took the sentiment to its logical

conclusion by instituting a legalised brothel in Athens. He did this, we are told, because of the crisis developing in the lives of Athenian youth. They were, he felt, under the compulsion of nature, but were going astray in directions that were not appropriate. So Solon:

'purchased and stationed women in various quarters, equipped and ready for all alike. They stand there naked, so that you will not be deceived ... No prudishness, no bullshit, no pulling away – you just get on with it. You leave, that's it. Tell her to jump in a lake if you want – she is nothing to you.'

An ancient brothel?

All sorts of shenanigans went on in Roman baths. Many of them housed brothels, and in the so-called 'Suburban Baths' at Pompeii there is a changing room decorated with a series of illustrations of sexual positions, numbered I to XVI. Were these a *table d'hôte* of what was on offer? ('And what would you like to day, sir? Number VIII is fresh in and, I am told, very good', 'Can I have it with a portion of XII, drizzled with IV?', 'You can have it any way you like, sir.') Or were they a graphic reminder of where you had left your clothes? ('Now: where did I put it? Yes, Caelius, *very* funny, but I was talking about my toga.') It did not last. It had been painted over long before Vesuvius exploded in AD 79.

Charming, but not quite the whole story. Solon did more than just set up the brothels – he diverted the profits from them to building a temple to *Aphrodītē Pandēmos* ('of all the people'). Solon saw that, for a public institution that was essentially somewhat shady, popularity was not enough. Such a venture needed a higher purpose to justify its existence. Temple construction fitted the bill perfectly. I am sure our government could think of some equally worthy cause that would tempt us all to do our bit (as it were) for the nation. Something to do with harmful emissions, perhaps? Carbon is, after all, something 'bad' (like brothels) being taxed for public 'good'.

But Roman elites knew what the people liked and found advantage in providing it. By the time of Julius Caesar, there were 59 festival days during the year; with Augustus this went up to 77. Which raises some acute questions: given that Rome did not tax its citizens, who actually *paid* for such extraordinary largesse, not to mention the building work that it all entailed? Does that hold any lessons for us? And why has there been no mention of gladiators?

>─┤─◆>─○─<◆─┤─<

Reading list

Appian, *The Civil Wars* (Penguin 1996).

Richard Beacham, *Spectacle Entertainments of Early Imperial Rome* (Yale 1999).

G.G. Fagan, *Bathing in Public in the Roman World* (Michigan 1999).

A.T. Hodge, *Roman Aqueducts and Water Supply* (Duckworth 1992).

E. Köhne and C. Ewigleben (eds.), *Gladiators and Caesars* (British Museum 2000).

Juvenal, *The Satires* (World's Classics 1991).

Livy, *The Early History of Rome* (Penguin 1960).

I.D. Margary, *Roman Roads* (London 1967).

Plutarch, *Makers of Rome* (Penguin 1965).

Nicholas Purcell, in *Cambridge Ancient History* (second edition) IX and X (Cambridge 1994, 1996).

Geoffrey Rickman, *The Corn Supply of Ancient Rome* (Clarendon 1980).

[3]

The Roman way of tax

Tax? No tax!

'HM Revenue & Customs collects tax to pay for public services. Each year the Chancellor's Budget sets out how much it'll cost to provide these services and how much tax is needed to pay for them. Key taxes that individuals may have to pay include: Income Tax, Capital Gains Tax, Inheritance Tax, Stamp Duty, Value Added Tax and certain other duties.'

So says a government website: and don't we just know it. Of the £457 billion raised in taxes in 2005–06, approximately £331.3 billion (75 per cent) came from our pockets, and the remaining 25 per cent (£125.7 billion) from business. And the whole point about it is that the Chancellor is extracting on his terms and then spending, on his terms, without reference to us, *our money*. Further, he expects to be applauded for it. The contrast with the Romans could not be starker. With certain relatively minor exceptions, they never spent their own people's money because they did not have it to spend. They spent other people's money.

Rulers of states in the ancient world had two functions – first, to be able to wage war successfully and second, to stay in power (because power bestowed status and wealth). For both of these functions they needed wealth. In the absence of a manufacturing industry, there were only two sources of wealth available – agricultural and mineral, agriculture being by far the more important – and the more a state could get of both, the better.

The crucial point is this: since neither Greeks nor Romans ran police states (in fact they both put a high value on the concept of citizen liberty), there was no question of bleeding their own citizens dry. Besides, that was not the way to stay in power. The aim, therefore, was to bleed *other people* dry – by conquest and empire building. Fighting, in other words, was good business – as long as you won. As a result, the Mediterranean world was in a fairly constant state of conflict either for self-protection or in order to extract the wealth (usually by taxes) of others. Nowadays, fighting in the Western world for precisely the same reason usually takes place between companies trying to take each other over.

Economics of knowledge?

All this raises a nice question: to what extent was Rome a 'knowledge' economy (i.e. did it use knowledge to produce economic benefits)? These days, it is reckoned that in the last thirty years the ratio of the UK economy based on 80 per cent tangible assets and 20 per cent knowledge has been reversed. Apart from the fact that the Senate did not control 'the economy' as government does today – trade was in the hands of the very few, very rich, acting in their own interests – the ancient world was generally a technologically conservative place, with occasional breakthroughs changing things for ever (e.g. concrete, key-stone arches); and farming the main source of livelihood. To that extent, it was almost all tangible asset. The necessary, traditional skills to make the most of the asset were passed down from generation to generation, with very little prospect of any alternative 'career' – if anyone ever thought in such terms – unless you lived in the city, where anything went.

Yet the main driver of the Roman economy was the army, the means by which the Roman Empire was won and kept. This was an all too tangible asset if you were unlucky enough to come into contact with it, but it needed a superb general like Pompey or Julius Caesar and experienced legionaries to get the best out of it, and their contribution was 100 per cent knowledge. Knowledge, likewise, refined over the centuries into experience, was the key ingredient for the successful running of the provinces. It is not surprising that technical books on soldiering, farming and history were hugely popular in the Roman world – rather like computers today and books about cooking (the celebrity chef Nigella Lawson was outsold in hardback last year only by Harry Potter).

Lucky strikes and liturgies

Occasionally a state *might* hit pay dirt in its own territory. The foundation of 5th-century BC Athens' wealth and power, for example, was the discovery in 483 BC of a phenomenally rich vein of silver in its working lead mines at Laurium. This was used to construct a powerful fleet of 200 ships, which enabled the Athenians to build up and control a maritime empire. On the back of these imperial revenues, it built the Parthenon and turned Athens into the 'education for Greece', as Pericles put it. But such strikes were, indeed, rare. (By the way, at an early stage the Athenians became so fed up with the cost of the Parthenon that they decided to fund it no longer. Pericles retorted that he would fund it personally, calling it the Pericleion. The Assembly swiftly discovered its reverse gear.)

Athenians did not tax themselves except in serious emergencies, when a war tax could be levied on the property of the rich. They did, however, hypothecate: that is, they expected certain predetermined services to be paid for by the richest men in Athens (usually someone with property worth about 70 times a skilled workman's annual wage). The services included:

- The state drama festivals in January and April in honour of Dionysus, god of transformation. At these times tragedies, satyr plays and comedies were staged in competition, the context in which some of the world's greatest masterpieces were performed, e.g. Sophocles' *Oedipus the King* and *Antigone*, Aeschylus' *Oresteia*, Euripides' *Medea* and Aristophanes' famous sex-strike comedy *Lysistrata*.
- The equipping and manning of a warship (the trireme), the basis of Athens' wealth and power.

But what if A, who was selected for a *leitourgiā* ('public duty', source of our 'liturgy'), thought old B down the road was in fact richer? He could challenge B in the courts to an exchange of property! If B agreed, they would exchange property and A would do it; if B did not agree, B would do it. Ingenious.

These *leitourgiai* were not necessarily resented by the wealthy. They gave them a wonderful opportunity to show off, in public, what they really could do. So they competed keenly among themselves to put on the best theatrical shows (and, most of all, they fervently hoped, *win*) and equip the most lavish and well appointed triremes.

If government gave the same sort of public duties to big businesses in lieu of tax and told them to get on with financing and overseeing a stretch of new motorway on condition that their names were plastered all over it, one might well see fairly dramatic improvements in our road system. Signs saying 'Built under New Labour with *your* money' might be equally productive. But governments are unconditionally opposed to hypothecation of any sort because it is felt to interfere with their right to spend taxes on anything they want. But this is to miss a big trick – the opportunity to win public sympathy for taxes. Imagine what credit they would be given were they to impose on every packet of cigarettes (say) a 2p tax, hypothecated to treat lung cancer. The point is that smoking, like drinking, creates problems which put burdens on the public purse. Let those who smoke and drink, therefore, pay specifically to relieve that burden. It has frequently been argued that fuel duty and road tax should be spent on roads and nothing else. National insurance, now a tax in all but name, was originally designed in 1911 largely to fund contributions to state retirement pension and unemployment benefit. It now yields nearly 20 per cent of the total tax-take.

Greek citizenship

These days we nurture a concept of human rights applied, by definition, to everyone, without distinction. The trouble is that we allow this worthy concept of universal applicability to drift into areas where it has no right to go. One such area is citizenship. We feel it is a sort of 'human right' to be a citizen, and therefore all must be citizens. We therefore find the idea of an *ex*clusive citizenship hard to handle, especially since we live in a multi-ethnic, 'global' world where 'inclusivity' is an endlessly repeated mantra.

For Greeks and Romans, 'rights' tended to mean 'what the law said' (see p. 90), and they found no problem with *ex*clusive citizenship at all. Indeed, for Greeks the whole *purpose* of citizenship was to privilege those who, by parentage (which, virtually always, meant location as well), had a natural stake in, and therefore commitment to, the society of which they were a part. By giving their own people citizenship, and denying it to others, the state reinforced that sense of their citizens' peculiar and precious privilege. It also gave them a focus, a sense of belonging, a feeling that today's multiculturalism, globalisation and demands for an 'emotional attachment to a European identity' threaten. Has the British 'brand' ever been weaker?

For classical Athenians, citizenship after 451 BC depended on having an Athenian father and mother, the baby's status being ratified soon after birth in various neighbourhood ceremonies. Citizenship meant one did not pay tax; males over eighteen could discuss and vote on all issues raised by the Assembly and serve in executive positions (see p. 91ff.); one could partake in state and local religious ceremonies (see p. 184); one could own property; and one could go to law in one's own right.

And Athenians reciprocated by competing among themselves to pay back the privileges through service to the state. To show in this way that you were indeed a good citizen – what you could do for the state – was a way to earn high honour and respect in the community: and every Greek loved to be honoured and respected (see 'euergetism', p. 54). No wonder Aristotle said 'anyone who is not an active citizen in the community is either an animal or a god'.

None of these privileges (bar some legal ones) was allowable to aliens, who were permitted to work in Athens only if they had an Athenian citizen sponsor who would act as guarantor. But if you were an alien who had given outstanding service to the state, you could be granted citizenship by the Assembly. It was a very rare honour indeed.

To that extent neither Greeks nor Romans would have had the slightest problem about ID cards, as long as they did nothing other than certify you as a citizen. But the government plans an ID system that creates for each citizen a single database collating all official and non-official personal records, from passports and medical and criminal records to social service usage, car journeys, foreign travel and even visits to pubs, that can be shared at will among officials. No free Greek or Roman would have put up with that.

War and fleece

In 500 BC, Rome was a small but growing city state. Over the next 230 years, by a process of conquest and alliance, it was master of most of Italy. It then took on and defeated the might of Carthage in the two Punic wars (264–241 and 218–201 BC) for mastery of the Western Mediterranean. In the process, Sicily (the location of the former war) and Sardinia became Rome's first provinces, to be followed later by North Africa with its rich grain and olive fields and Spain with its phenomenal wealth in precious metals (Carthage had major bases there). Greece, one of whose kings had supported Hannibal, followed; so did Asia Minor (actually *bequeathed* to Rome by its king) and in the 60s BC Pompey brought in states further east; in the 50s BC Julius Caesar made Gaul a province.

Further, Rome's military success was not down to any preternatural bellicosity. Every ancient state aspired to become a Rome if it could. It was just that Rome had a much larger, better trained and extremely loyal citizen population to draw on for its army; and it was also the master of diplomacy, knowing how to turn conquered enemies into reliable allies. That was why its empire in the West lasted some 700 years.

As a result of this expanding empire, Roman revenues (it has been calculated) quadrupled between 200 BC and 70 BC. Pompey's campaigns in the East in the 60s BC immediately doubled or even trebled that amount. His sensational triumph in 61 BC lasted two days instead of the usual one and even so, the historian Plutarch tells us, he had enough undisplayed material for another triumph besides. In the course of it, his men dragged through the streets coins to the value of over 70 million *dēnāriī* (280 million *sēstertiī*), far more than Rome's annual revenues and enough to feed the whole of Rome for two years.

This explains why Romans endured only indirect taxation, for example 5 per cent on legacies, duties on goods and (the most resented) a half per cent sales tax hypothecated for the retirement of soldiers. The result was that roads, building programmes, bread and (not) circuses and pay for the army (which kept the show going) did not come out of citizens' pockets: it came out of revenue raised elsewhere. So when Cicero said that taxes 'are the sinews of the state', he did not mean taxes on just its own citizens.

There is surely a lesson for our government here. In no moral or ethical system known to man is 'taxation' a virtue. Instead of spending all its time wondering how to screw more money out of us, government could more profitably concentrate on wondering how to screw it out of someone else. That's the way to stay in power, too.

The Tory party has finally come to see the sense in this, and has recently suggested that all non-domicileds (i.e. foreigners who have chosen to live here but not become citizens, nearly always for tax purposes) should pay an annual levy of £25,000 (a policy Labour immediately snaffled). This, apparently, will raise £3 billion. This is paltry set against the £457 billion total tax take of 2005–06, but is at least a start. All that money lurking in offshore bank accounts might well come next – about £11.5 trillion, it has been calculated, a tax loss of £225 billion a year. Think how much of that could be stuffed down the throats of the obese to slim them down!

By the same token, cutting taxes is enormously popular. So it was in the Roman world, that is, among those who actually did pay taxes (i.e. provincials). The emperor was always happy to relieve towns or provinces of taxes when they did him especially good service. The principle is currently being applied to civil servants who have been working in Iraq. Why not to the troops too? Why not adopt the strategy more widely, for example, to lure people into jobs that the government decrees are 'essential to Britain's future' (e.g. physics and maths teachers)? Also, to remove the tax from state pensions would be a terrific vote winner.

Caesar's show time

But in the ancient world, government spending was only half the story. The other half was the incredible sums of their own money that wealthy individuals, lusting for power, poured into benefactions to win the favour of the Roman people. The history of the development of gladiatorial shows offers a prime example of how this worked.

The last chapter ended with the observation that gladiators had not featured in the account of the games laid on by the state for the Roman people. That is because gladiatorial shows were, originally, no part of them. They had their origins in funeral games for dead male relatives, and were always laid on privately by very wealthy individuals. But a lavish, novel and thrilling spectacle like gladiatorial combat had potential for mass appeal, of the sort that would do no harm to a wealthy family with political ambitions. The Roman forum, therefore, became the obvious place to stage them, and anyone could roll up.

Once that idea had taken root, aristocrats started to compete with each other to raise the funerary stakes. We hear of elite funerals in 216 BC featuring twenty-two pairs of gladiators, in

200 BC featuring twenty-five pairs, in 183 BC sixty pairs and in 174 BC seventy-four pairs. When Julius Caesar was appointed aedile (see pp. 13, 53–4, cf. p.27) in 65 BC, he promised to finance a gladiatorial show featuring 320 pairs! His enemies in the Senate promptly placed legal restrictions on the amount of money an aedile could allowably spend on such events.

But Caesar finally did the business in 46 BC, after he had defeated Pompey's men in the civil war and made himself effectively dictator for life. He celebrated his various campaign victories by laying on a stunning sequence of shows, one day for each victory, superficially in commemoration of the death of his daughter Julia. To give some idea of this sensational monstrosity, I quote from the historian Suetonius' description:

'Caesar climbed the Capitol by torchlight, with forty elephants bearing lamps to the right and to the left. In the show celebrating his triumph over Pontus, one of the carts in the processions had on the front of it a placard with the words "I came, I saw, I conquered", emphasizing the speed with which it was completed rather than giving details of the campaign (as was the case with the others).

'To every foot soldier of his veteran legionaries he gave as booty ... twenty-four thousand sesterces [*sēstertius* = c. £5]. He also gave them plots of land ... To every male citizen he gave, besides two *modiī* of wheat and two pounds of olive oil, the three hundred sesterces he had once promised, along with an extra hundred to make up for the delay. He also remitted a year's rent to those in Rome who paid up to two thousand sesterces and in Italy up to five hundred. He added a banquet and a distribution of meat and, after the celebration for his Spanish victory, two dinners. For when he decided that the first had been rather mean and not served with his usual lavishness, he provided another extremely lavish one five days later.

'He sponsored spectacles of various kinds: a gladiatorial contest, plays in all regions of the city (performed by actors in every language), as well as circus performances, athletic contests, and a sea-battle ... Five days of animal fights were provided. For the final one, two battle lines were drawn up, with five hundred foot soldiers, twenty elephants, and three hundred knights assigned to each side. To make more space for the encounter, the central barriers were removed and in their place two camps were set up, one facing the other. In a temporary stadium constructed in an area of the Campus Martius, athletes competed for three days. In the sea-battle, which took place on a specially excavated lake, ships with two, three, and four banks of oars from the Tyrian and Egyptian fleets engaged, manned by a huge number of fighters.

'Drawn by all these spectacles, so vast a number of people flooded into Rome from every region that many had to lodge in tents put up in the streets or along the roads. And on a number of occasions the crowds were so great that many people, even including two senators, were crushed to death.'

(Adapted from Catherine Edwards, *Suetonius: Lives of the Caesars* [World's Classics 2000])

The point to emphasise is that this spectacular was Caesar's *personal* benefaction to the people of Rome: it was not officially financed by the state. And this practice was absolutely typical throughout the ancient Graeco-Roman world. In other words, it was not just the state that saw advantage in offering the *plēbs pānem et circēnsēs*; very wealthy individuals on the make, whether politically or socially, did so too.

Buying power

Clearly, men holding office who wanted to climb the political ladder found it advantageous to act in this way. Those appointed to the post of aedile (the first rung on the ladder), for example, were responsible for putting on state-run festivals, and they would frequently subsidise them out of their own pockets to ensure the people enjoyed the best actors and charioteers that money could buy. Sometimes they would even find reasons to repeat the festival, for example, on the grounds that there had been some ritual failure.

To give another sensational example, in 58 BC the aedile Scaurus, who had been the first Roman governor of Syria (63–2 BC), decided to show the people he had not been sitting on his hands in the East, only on his money. So he put on a show featuring 150 leopardesses, the first hippopotamus ever displayed in Rome, five crocodiles and a skeleton from Jaffa / Yafo (now in Israel), said to be that of the monster, eventually killed by Perseus, for whom Andromeda was chained up as an offering. For this spectacular he had constructed in Rome a temporary theatre three storeys high, the first storey veneered with marble, apparently decorated with 3,000 statues and able to hold 80,000 spectators (information, naturally, courtesy of Pliny the Elder). Eat your heart out, Sir Cameron Mackintosh – and, of course, the Olympics Committee. Wealthy Romans of the Republican period would have loved to have sponsored the whole thing.

Euergetism – you what?

But rich citizens without any specifically political agenda would also pour money into projects. The wealthy aristocrat Pliny the Younger, for example, endowed his home town of Como with a school and a library, and in his will bequeathed it a public bath and a capital sum to give everyone a free annual dinner. His letters span eleven years, and in that time alone he spent some 2 million sesterces (say £10 million) on the town in benefactions. The *quid prō quō* for Pliny and all like him was public acclaim and therefore public status. Pliny was feted, celebrated and remembered in his home town, like all those whose generosity extended to the people in this way. The technical term for benefactions of this sort was 'euergetism': Greek for 'doing good', both for others and oneself. The problem to which euergetism was a partial solution in the ancient world was the massive disparity between the rich and the poor, and the destructive envy that it could generate. And I do mean massive. For example, in the 70s BC Rome's annual revenue was 200 million sesterces. Crassus alone was worth 192 million. Contrast poor old Bill Gates, vying with an Indian and Mexican tycoon to be the richest man in the world, who racks up a pathetic $62 billion against an American GDP of $12.3 trillion – 220 times poorer!

One way the Roman rich created jobs was to hire tens of thousands of Romans as soldiers in their private armies. Caesar recruited about 80,000 men for the civil war with Pompey (the Roman army was finally professionalised under Augustus). Another was to disburse their wealth among the people in hand-outs, shows, building work and other public benefactions. Crassus, for example, once paid for three months' corn supply for the Roman people out of his own pocket. Public use of the money mitigated the public consequences of personal abundance: as Cicero pointed out in a speech, Romans hated private luxury but loved public display.

The moral is: since you can't have it all ('where would you put it?' as someone pointed out), you might as well use it for good, all the more creditable if it is for others' good too. It was as if, in today's world, one's status as a wealthy man was judged by the taxes one paid, not the money one earned and the taxes one did *not* pay (in 2006 Britain's 54 billionaires paid income tax totalling just £14.7m on their £126 billion combined fortunes, and only a handful paid any Capital Gains Tax).

The pay that the seriously wealthy pull down is grotesque, but it is the same the world over. The richest 1 per cent of Americans earns $1.3 trillion a year, we are told – more than the national income of France. More than half of America's total wealth, it is claimed, has been created in the last ten years, on the back of new technology, deregulation and free markets. The same is probably true of Russia, where the gap between rich and poor is even huger, as it is in India (but cf. on banks, p. 22).

Rich justification

One would like to believe that euergetism would rise parallel with the astonishing growth of this wealth – or do the rich still spend all their time competing over the size of their helipads, submarines and football clubs as wealthy Romans in the 1st century BC did over the size of their fishponds? These were briefly all the rage, as Pliny the Elder tells us, like tulip-mania in 17th century Holland and dot.com mania in the 21st century. One woman so admired one of her lampreys that she fitted it with earrings. Lampreys do not have ears, but such trivial considerations never influenced a fashion-crazed Roman.

The point is that in a dynamic, capitalist world, grotesque pay and therefore grotesque inequality of earnings are essential, and inevitable. The question is how one makes a virtue out of this necessity. The answer would be a truly Roman one.

First, conscript all the rich into the front line of the army. After all, they can afford the smartest and latest weapons, armour and gear, and they have the most to lose. This is what happened during most of the Roman Republic, because only the rich could afford the armour, not to mention the horses (and they had everything to fight for). Less wealthy men occupied less prestigious (and less well armed) places within the ranks. Below a certain wealth level, a man could not be conscripted. But I am not sure this is practical these days.

Better, present these salaries as an aspiration, a fantastic prize to be grasped, the route to fame and glory, but only if one understands that one thereby has a duty to personal 'public service'. Let today's plutocrats take that route and nurture, by their example, a tradition of plutocrats endowed equally with money and a sense of duty to society. The Gettys and Gates of this world set an example in this respect, as do Americans giving vast sums to their universities. Is there as much of this sense of public service about now as there was, say, in the 19th century?

Perhaps the most striking example of businessmen using their fortunes for public pleasure – though not without an eye on private profit, but so what? – is the purchase of football clubs. Sir John Hall at Newcastle United talked enthusiastically about the 'Geordie nation' and genuinely believed that a thriving team would do enormous good for the region. As a result he is a much-admired figure in the north-east. It is not clear that Roman Abramovich at Chelsea has quite the same vision, though he has bought (rather than brought) plenty of joy for his supporters, not to mention his team. Randy Lerner, the American who is pouring a fortune into Aston Villa, has shown that he also appreciates the good things of life: he has just given £5 million to the National Portrait Gallery.

Second, aristocratic Romans maintained a polite distance between themselves and the slightly sordid business of making money (see p. 2). They found glory in other terms. But these days businesses creates jobs, and therefore wealth and therefore taxes and therefore schools'n'hospitals. This, surely, is where glory should lie. Barclays, for example, pays billions in corporation tax and employs c. 50,000 in the UK. But then again, how much does it (legally) avoid? If it could spend it on, for example, Barclay's schools, it would be keener on paying because it would get the credit instead of the money disappearing into the Chancellor's bottomless pit for him to spend how he likes (and then boast about it). It should become businesses' greatest ambition to pay all their taxes, and in full, and reap the rewards thereof.

Finally, an observation. Our politicians and government employees eat up billions in salaries, expenses and pension rights, as we know all too well. How much did Roman bureaucracy cost in salaries? The answer is – nothing. Zilch. Zero. O. Because the holders of office were paid nothing. *In other words, the Roman state was run for free.*

Of course the state had expenses to meet (e.g. fighting wars; see below, and p. 50 for the cost of Augustus' standing army). But the rich who ran for political office took no salary for it. Their reward was simply power, and the *prospect* of all the perks that might go with it, such as a juicy province when you had served your term as consul – if, that is, you became consul. Tony Blair knows all about the prospect of perks. The (big) buck(s) stopped there.

Romans would have been appalled at the idea that we pay our MPs salaries and expenses. So the argument that those who want to boss us around should pay for the privilege might be worth considering. One could put the idea to Shaun Woodward, Secretary of State for Northern Ireland. He is married to a multimillionaire Sainsbury's heiress, and they also own houses in France, New York and the West Indies. He still claimed from the taxpayers £130,000 of MP's allowances, to include expenses on his second home. Where is his sense of public duty? Romans would have burned it down by now.

Further, the idea that we should also pay for the survival of the parties themselves because they cannot generate the money to survive on their own, as New Labour is now considering doing, would have struck Romans as outrageous. What duty do we have to keep *parties* going that cannot keep themselves going? No political party has a right to exist. But if government does decide to use our money to pay for the parties, I suspect Romans would have demanded the parties pay us to vote for them. Fair's fair, after all.

Taxing issues

So how did Rome function on this system? One answer is: because they preferred to use private individuals to deliver their services. So, from early on, wars were fought, roads built and mines worked on the back of service contracts offered out to hopeful private contractors. With a piece of spinning quite the equal of anything New Labour has attempted, these contractors called themselves *pūblicānī*, 'public servants', the hated 'publicans' (and sinners) of the New Testament. The right to gather dues from harbours and toll stations was also sold off, and in 123 BC came another great leap forward when Gaius Gracchus proposed that the right to collect the taxes in the new Roman province of Asia should be sold off every five years.

The sums involved were gigantic, and *pūblicānī* formed themselves into consortia (*societātēs*) to bid for the rights. They further developed the business by diversifying into money-lending and mail delivery, sometimes even forming cartels. The great advantage to Rome was that they got their money up front from selling off the rights, without any of the costs, time and effort of a huge state-run collection service. Admittedly, the total take might have been less than was theoretically possible, since the *pūblicānī* had to be allowed their cut, but Rome wisely preferred its bird in the hand.

Naturally, there was a degree of corruption and extortion, for the most part only when the *pūblicānī* worked hand-in-hand with corrupt provincial governors. But precisely the same occurs in the UK with HM Revenue and Customs, once separate bodies but now, united, even more able to impose their arbitrary reigns of terror at whim. No government has ever dared to rein them in. Why not scrap them entirely? We could then improve on the Roman model by encouraging any number of bodies to bid for the rights to raise a percentage of total tax-take. They would provide government with its money up front and would then have to compete among themselves for our custom. We might finally get intelligible tax returns and a little fairness. Admittedly, the government would have to control abuses, as Augustus tried to do. Augustus in fact failed, with the happy result that in Nero's reign it was suggested that the only way to end the abuses was to end tax-gathering . . . Nice try.

The obvious place to start such a scheme is Northern Ireland, where it would be greeted with shrieks of joy by the publicans and Shinners, who have long experience of this sort of dealing.

Corrupt practices

This raises the question of corruption generally. We are much stricter than the Greeks and Romans on this, probably to our disadvantage; the concept of corruption in the ancient word was necessarily a fluid one. First, there was no such thing as 'Big Business' in Roman times. Individuals dealt with individuals. For example, a newly discovered document from Egypt is a copy of a document dated 33 BC and authorised by Cleopatra herself. In it, she permits Canidius Crassus to export wheat from Egypt (Egypt was the bread basket of Rome), import wine into Egypt and live there, entirely tax-free. Canidius Crassus was a lieutenant of Cleopatra's lover Marc Antony.

The deal with Canidius was a perfectly legitimate exercise in keeping powerful friends faithful to her and Antony's cause, and thereby serving what she considered Egypt's interests at a critical time. Canidius profited from it, of course. But ancients expected their great men to do deals with the wealthy in other countries, as long as it was in everyone's interests. After all, no one complains today when government does tax deals with Big Business to profit from it, save jobs and win elections (unless they are private equity businesses, of course).

Second, gift exchange in the ancient world was the oil which kept the wheels of all relationships, social, political and business, smoothly running. The whole point of money was to use it for one's own – and that included one's friends'– advantage, and what was corrupt in one light could be seen simply as dispensing and receiving legitimate and justifiable benefits in another (rather like paying for private medical care today and thereby saving the NHS money, regarded by some as utterly corrupt). The only condition was that, at the end of the day, the deals 'advanced, and did not hinder, the interests of the people' (as a Greek orator put it).

Third, no one thought another country's ethical codes were anything but that country's concern. Pliny the Elder boasted about the way Rome 'civilised' barbarians (see p. 145) and Alexander the Great caused himself much trouble by intervening in one tribe's burial practices (p. 172), but no one would dream of refusing to deal with a people on those grounds alone. So the inclination of countries today to lecture other countries about 'their human rights record' (oppression of women, torture and so on) would have bewildered the ancients. What had that got to do with them? 'Custom is king', as the Greek historian Herodotus said as he observed the totally contradictory practices in which different countries engaged.

So when BAE Systems made what were alleged to be shady

deals with the Saudis in 1985 to sell them billion of pounds worth of Tornado jets and other military equipment, Romans would have cheered them on. The idea that this was a chargeable offence would have struck them as barking. By the same token, they would (unlike most media) have applauded King Abdullah's visit to the UK in 2007: Saudi oil, trade and help against terrorism are all in our vital interests. They would have been baffled by the logic of refusing to take the King's money in exchange for British goods because Saudi women were treated differently from British.

Greeks and Romans would be fascinated to discover what the origin of all this moral posturing about other countries' practices actually was, and might uncover a paradox. It probably starts with the assumption that we must not be 'judgemental', and all values are as valid as any other, and the UK, being Western and therefore a natural-born oppressor of human rights, has no right to tell others what to do, etc. etc. (sage nodding from transfixed studio audience). But the moment one actually does a deal with someone whose values are different, one can self-righteously denounce it because one's own values *are* superior after all.

This combination of cultural cringe (at which the English seems especially adept, unlike, for example, the French) and out-raged self-assertion is a particularly delicious hypocrisy. Guilt-laden breast-beating about 'values' was not a notable feature of ancient life. Greeks and Romans were proud of their past and took the view that they were models for others (cf. Pericles on Athens, p. 179). That did not mean that they could not be severely critical of aspects of their own cultures. Neither Thucydides nor Plato, for example, had any time for democracy, and Tacitus not much for the imperial system.

The emperor strikes back

Dynasts like Caesar, Crassus and Pompey were able to compete in using their wealth to appeal to the people only for as long as the Republic lasted. When it collapsed, and Caesar's adopted heir Octavian emerged as the first emperor Augustus, an important change came about. The emperor became the universal euergetist and patron of the people. Not that the rich stopped their benefactions: but they could no longer put them so openly to political use as they had before. No one could be seen to challenge the emperor.

Not, of course, that anyone acknowledged the change as such. It just happened, and life went on as normal. The contrast with our politicians is striking. They spend most of their time boasting about the need for 'change' as if it were a good thing (Gordon Brown used the word thirty times in his prime ministerial acceptance speech). But change is needed only if things have gone wrong. It is a sign of *failure*.

One of the things Romans liked to boast about was the permanence of their system, and that change was the last thing anyone needed. When the Republic collapsed and Augustus became emperor, he did not announce with shining face that 'he was the change' and the bright new era of an imperial system had dawned. Far from it. He emphasised that nothing had changed, the Senate still ruled, and so on. It was all nonsense, but it was what the Romans wanted to hear: as the great epic poet Ennius said, 'Rome stands firm on the foundations of its men and its age-old traditions'. Come to think of it, the only system that ministers tell us never changes these days is the EU ... now I wonder why that can be?

One could gain no clearer picture of what the change in euergetistic practice actually meant to the Roman people, not to mention the emperor himself, than the account of his benefactions that Augustus ordered to be displayed all over the empire on his death, a practice now regularly followed by every tin-pot dictator in the world (one longs to see Mugabe's).

Augustus (emperor 31 BC–AD 14) had in fact intended to memorialise his legacy by writing a thirteen-book autobiography. Its purpose seems to have been to answer his critics, who were accusing him of being a merciless, criminal, cowardly, jumped-up nobody (which in terms of family background was spot-on). But in 23 BC he discontinued it. Instead, he concentrated on refining a document known as the *Rēs Gestae* ('My Achievements', lit. 'things achieved'), which was inscribed on two bronze plaques and placed outside his mausoleum in Rome, and copied elsewhere across the empire.

This c. 350-line document is, at one level, simply a stupendously boring list of honours, titles and achievements ('I restored these buildings, built these temples, put on these shows, conquered these lands, took these offices', etc.), interspersed with the occasional comment emphasising his conservatism (e.g. 'I did not accept office contrary to our ancestors' customs'). But it is the sub-text that is crucial: as he says, most of this was done out of 'the private expenses which I devoted to the state and the people'.

These 'expenses' run to billions. Assume the *sēstertius* (*s*, pl. *ss*) to be, as already suggested, a fiver (it is impossible to come up with a truly meaningful exchange rate). Augustus lists hand-outs to every single Roman of three hundred *ss* in 44 BC (under Julius Caesar's will) and four hundred *ss* in 29, 24 and 11 BC. He bought land for troops in Italy and the provinces to a sum of 860 million *ss*; and gave another 400 million *ss* in 'rewards' to soldiers later on. He transferred private funds of 320 million *ss* to the treasury; he paid for grain distribution among the people when treasury funds ran short and laid on games. In all, he gave (we are told) 600 million *dēnariī* to the treasury, people and soldiers (= 2,400 million *ss* = £12,000 million, or £12 billion, at a time when a soldier's pay was £4,500 a year, if a *s* = £5). Public buildings, banquets, free bread, extravagant games, cheap baths (etc.) – all were treated as if they were his own personal benefactions. That is what it meant to be universal patron/euergetist of the whole Roman people.

Quids prō quō

But where did these gigantic sums come from? It is tempting to say that it must have been the state's money all along, and Augustus was indulging in a little creative accountancy (it is not unknown in our day and age). But this was not the case. War booty belonged to the general, and in 44 BC Augustus inherited Julius Caesar's vast bank balance (much of it down to his famous wars in Gaul). In 30–27 BC Cleopatra's fabulously wealthy Egypt fell to him.

Again, while he was in power, Romans shovelled huge legacies his way. Agrippa, for example, left him the whole of the Gallipoli peninsula. In the last twenty years of his life he was left 1,400 million *ss* in wills alone. Not that the donors left their own families destitute, but a serious legacy to the emperor was a long-term family insurance policy. All this money was salted away in his *fiscus*, the term for the private imperial account (the state treasury was the *aerārium*). One is reminded of the fantastic wealth from the oil revenues that do actually belong to the Sheikhs. The result is that some oil states pay no tax at all; it is the Sheikhs who pour their own money back into their country.

Coinage and transport

There is a big question about how money was transported. On one model of the Roman Empire, a total weight of 775,000 kilograms of coinage (760 tons) – 10 per cent of annual revenue from the provinces – would be dragged round the empire every year. To do that all in one go would have required 1,610 wagons and 6,440 oxen. Rome did have a credit note system, but at the end of the day people needed to be paid in coin: it had to be got to places somehow or other, but there is no shred of evidence for how this happened. One imagines it would have been a brigands' paradise.

To that extent it was foolish of our Parliament not to think a little more clearly about the Queen's decision a few years ago to start paying Income Tax. Tax, as we know, simply disappears down the cavernous maw of the Treasury, never to be seen again. If the Parliament had considered the matter, it would have realised how much to its advantage it would have been to have invited Her Majesty to spend that money, backed up by government support, in providing benefits for the British people on the Roman imperial model. She is, after all, a woman who does command high respect among the people, and it would have done New Labour a power of good to be associated with her and her benefactions, rather than (as usual) just grabbing her money and running. Further, as Her Majesty's reign draws to a close, there might be a case for proposing a royal *Rēs Gestae*, suitably explicit on all these benefactions, to be posted all over the Commonwealth. It would surely make compelling, and probably quite cheering, reading.

Can we then argue that, in our system where virtually everyone pays taxes, the state has taken the place of the beneficent euergetist? We can, but it will get us nowhere. It certainly sets itself up as the universal provider, but with our money and without reference to us. The crucial point about ancient euergetism is that it was personal and reciprocal: the giver was spending his money (however he had got it), and that act served the interests of the giver – everything from patriotic display to political self-advancement – as well as that of the recipient. There was, in other words, a *quid prō quō* about ancient benefaction, entirely absent from our state spending.

So when Gordon Brown poured nearly £150 million into revamping the Treasury for himself and his pals, the British public did not exactly feel like standing and applauding. It is not merely the self-serving nature of this boasting about spending other people's money that is so infuriating: it is also the fact that governments all bang on endlessly about inputs (we have spent vast sums on X, Y and Z) and very rarely about outputs, i.e. the results of it all. When they do discuss both, they are never put side by side – 'Admire the billions we have spent on education and look! A quarter of the population cannot read or write, half of schools do not reach a "good" standard,' and so on. When that is pointed out, the response is 'That just proves we must spend even more to ensure our children of the future . . .', etc. etc. All it proves is that government has got it wrong.

When Augustus came to spend money, he was very careful to give the appearance that it was not to feather his own nest but to benefit the people. He did not build magnificent gardens and villas for himself on the outskirts of Rome, as the rich tended to do, but emphasised the fact that he lived in modest comfort. When he did build, it tended to be public squares, courts and colonnades for everyone's use. He affected a quiet private life, disapproving of luxury and cruelty. The story is told of his visit to the Naples villa of Vedius Pollio. When a slave broke a goblet and Pollio (another member of the 'fishpond set') ordered him to be thrown to the moray eels, Augustus intervened.

He asked to see Pollio's complete collection of goblets, and promptly smashed the lot. Pollio got the message. When Pollio died, Augustus had his villa destroyed and a public walkway built there. Like Julius Caesar before him, Augustus' idea was to turn private land over to public use. Incidentally, the resort of Posilippo on the bay of Naples takes its name from the name of Pollio's villa – Greek *Pausilūpōn*, 'Free from cares' ('*Sans souci*').

All this was a lesson Nero singularly failed to learn.

Nero's golden end

We have already heard of Nero's heroic efforts to rebuild and restore Rome after the great fire of AD 64 (see p. 7). As it turned out, however, his heart was really set on using this opportunity to build himself a proper palace. Seizing 200 acres of prime property in the middle of Rome, much of it belonging to the senatorial classes, he started to have built not a monument that everyone could enjoy but one dedicated to his own private pleasure, his 'Golden House'.

It was, admittedly, an astonishing architectural and structural feat. Using all the latest building techniques made possible by concrete, it revolutionised the idea of what an emperor's palace should be – soaring vaulted ceilings, vast domes, mechanical rotating rooms and ceilings, endless sequences of complex interlinked corridors, dining rooms and chambers (the one side that survives has 150 rooms), the whole decorated with fabulous frescoes and works of art. It was an architectural masterpiece.

The luxury of the interior – gold and jewellery in abundance, flowers and perfumes showering over diners from the ceilings – was to be expected. What was new was the architectural and artistic breakthrough in the stunning use of interior curved, vaulted, domed, concave space – no more boring straight lines for progressive, modernist Nero – and the integration of this huge palace into a series of woods, lakes, fields and long open vistas. It was the countryside reconstructed in the city centre. At the front of it, he had set up a *colossus*: a huge statue, 120 feet tall, of himself. 'Now at last I can live like a human!' Nero exclaimed.

But the cost of it all was immense. The finances of Rome began to creak. Nero devalued the coinage by more than 10 per cent. Complaints at the seizure of private property came in from the senatorial classes serving in the provinces in Gaul, Africa, Egypt, Spain, Judaea and Britain.

Nero's paranoia increased with the general chaos and it all ended, eventually, in open revolt against him, starting in the provinces – Gaul, Spain and Africa. Nero's personal Praetorian Guard abandoned him and instructed the Senate to declare Galba, governor of Spain, as emperor. Nero fled and committed suicide. 'Dead – and what an artist!' were his last words, for reasons that will become clear later (see p. 163).

Imperial duties

Later emperors were not about to make the same mistake. They buried the Golden House under buildings designed for public use. Nero's successor Vespasian filled in Nero's lake and started the gladiatorial building we know as the Colosseum – named after Nero's *colossus* – and Trajan (emperor AD 98–117) built 25 acres of public baths over it.

These were the proper duties of the emperor of the Roman people, as Trajan well knew. He was, indeed, responsible for probably the single most spectacular example of imperial benefaction. When he finally ended the trouble on the northern borders of Romania (Dacia) in AD 106, he had lost a lot of men. But the result was that Dacia became a province, and Trajan returned to Rome with five million lbs of gold and ten million of silver – about thirty times Rome's total annual revenue.

Coins were struck throughout the empire to celebrate the occasion. Foreign embassies from as far as India came to greet him, keen to avoid a similar fate. And in celebration he gave every Roman citizen 2,000 sesterces, and over a two-year period laid on nearly 150 days of games, at which 11,500 gladiators fought, 11,000 animals were killed and mock sea-battles were fought – an unprecedented extravaganza.

>·+·◆·•·O·•·◆·+·<

Reading list

Julian Bennett, *Trajan* (Routledge 1997).
P. M. Brunt and J.M. Moore, *Res Gestae Divi Augusti* (Oxford 1967).
Edward Champlin, *Nero* (Harvard 2003).
Pliny, *The Letters of the Younger Pliny* (Penguin 1963).
Thomas Weidemann, *Emperors and Gladiators* (Routledge 1992).

[4]

Control Greeks – and Romans

Keeping in with the crowd

In the last chapter we saw how, during the Roman Republican period, the rich and powerful – Pompey, Crassus, Caesar – used their wealth for the benefit of the public and themselves, and the results it had; and how and why, in the imperial period, the emperor took upon himself alone the duties of universal bene-factor, dispensing *pānem et circēnsēs* (now including gladiatorial combat) for the people.

A fascinating letter from Cornelius Fronto (c. AD 95–166), looking back to the emperor Marcus Aurelius, reveals the reason why the emperors were such dutiful benefactors. It emerges that the emperor's position *as emperor* was actually at stake. Fronto writes that Trajan paid especially close attention to the stage, the races and the gladiatorial arena because (in his view) these won the people's favour.

Further, Fronto goes on, Trajan drew a distinction between giving out bread and laying on public shows. Bread, he says, was less effective because it placated only those who qualified for it; but the whole people, rich and poor alike, adored shows and could therefore be won over by them. In other words, general popularity was *politically* as important as 'policy'; the emperor's position did in fact depend as much on entertainment as on the serious busi-ness of running the state.

Consider the implications of the following three anecdotes, the first about the young Octavian, soon to become the first emperor Augustus. He had defeated Marc Antony and Cleopatra at the battle of Actium (31 BC) and was entering Rome as its (effective) sole ruler, being greeted by crowds of well-wishers. Among them was a man holding a crow that croaked 'Hail, Caesar, victorious commander (*imperātor*)'. Octavian was so impressed he gave the man the incredible sum of 20,000 sesterces for it. It then emerged that the man had a collaborator who also had a crow, which said 'Hail, victorious commander Antony'! Win-win, therefore, for the imaginative duo (who presumably split the proceeds).

The second anecdote involves the emperor Hadrian on one of his (incessant) tours of the provinces. Hurrying off to give judgement at a local assizes one morning, he was stopped by a woman with a request. He shook her off, telling her he was too busy to listen. 'Then don't be emperor,' she replied. He stopped. He listened.

Thirdly, Julius Caesar laid on some games for the people, which he had to attend. Having little interest in them himself, he used the time to do some work. The crowd noticed and started booing. He put down his work and paid attention.

These stories may or may not faithfully record an actual incident. But that does not matter for our purposes, any more that it matters whether or not the ex-MP David Mellor wore a Chelsea shirt when he went to bed with the actress Antonia de Sanchez. They are history to the extent that they represent how people of the time found it plausible to imagine those in power. What emerges from all three is this: emperors and *plēbs* alike understood that there was something that bound them inescapably together, however immensely powerful the one and immeasurably insignificant the other. This was the sense that the powerful could not divorce themselves from their obligations to the ordinary people, however much they may have wanted to – and both sides knew it.

Even the humblest citizen could approach the mighty emperor with a request and expect a 'personal' reply. One among hundreds of examples is a letter sent by a sick worker to the emperor, complaining at his father's treatment of him. The emperor (Antoninus Pius) replied: 'If you approach the relevant authorities, they will give orders that you should receive upkeep from your father, provided that, since you say you are a workman, you are in such ill-health that you cannot sustain your work.'

In replies to petitions from women, the emperor allows that the many children of one Flavia Tertulla, who had been married off in ignorance to her uncle, should be regarded as legitimate; that Sebastiana should be allowed to bring a case (against, presumably, her husband) for bigamy; that another woman should be allowed to act if it was found that she had been defrauded by her son-in-law; and so on. Here is the mighty emperor of the greatest empire in the known world listening and responding to the pleas of individual subjects on the most trivial of matters – trivial at least to him, but not to them. And they got a reply. How many of us can say that we have written to one of our Cabinet ministers with a problem which (s)he has immediately fixed?

Life for the emperor, in other words, was not one long series of orgies, however much the Roman people liked to believe it (what would you do, after all, if *you* were emperor?). In the early years in particular, when the imperial bureaucracy was incredibly small, life was one long series of tiresome problems to solve with, presumably, the occasional orgy thrown in to relieve the tedium. As one emperor said 'If the people knew how laborious was the mere writing and reading of so many letters, they would not pick up a crown which had been thrown away'.

Occasionally the strain showed. We have much of the correspondence between the younger Pliny, governor of Bithynia (northern Turkey), with the emperor Trajan. Many of Pliny's questions seem footling but Trajan always replies with great courtesy until, replying to a particularly tiresome enquiry about gift-giving on social occasions, he finally snaps (roughly paraphrased): 'Look, Pliny old boy, I appointed you to exercise your own judgement. Bleedin' get on with it.'

One can imagine Gordon Brown, controller of a gigantic bureaucracy which he does not trust an inch, equally snapping 'Look, Darling, I appointed you to exercise *my* judgement. Bleedin' get on with it.'

Voter rotas

It is one of the most important features of Roman and, as we shall see, Greek political life that 'freedom' was a constant watchword of these societies. Indeed, they are the place where Western conceptions of 'freedom' were born. 'Freedom for whom?' the cynic will ask. If that means freedom to be involved in making political decisions, the answer for the ancient world was quite a lot for citizens, but none for the rest. Such political power (though in some ways more limited) has been available in much of the West only in the past hundred years or so. What marks Greeks and Romans out is the idea that their leaders were there, in a very basic way, to provide for the needs and interest of their citizens. That, perhaps, is to tinge those hard and unforgiving worlds with an excessively and undeservedly roseate hue, but it is, at bottom, importantly true.

Take, for example, the citizens of Pompeii. Nearly 3,000 municipal election 'posters' bedeck the walls and houses of that provincial town. These supported candidates for office, who then went on to join the local council of 80–100 citizens. This body, like the Senate in Rome, was responsible for general policy and the conduct of the officials. Hand-painted in red, the 'posters' cluster along main roads, busy junctions and candidates' homes, and analysis suggests they were not posted at whim, but organised by the candidates themselves.

Roman citizenship

Romans, whose empire stretched from one end of the known world virtually to the other, took a more pragmatic attitude to citizenship than Athenians did. Citizenship was still a great privilege. But among the disparate millions living at the far ends of the empire, its grant could generate a unifying and therefore stabilising sense of loyalty to Roman rule. It was therefore politic to hold it out as an achievable object of desire. So Romans established intermediate grades of citizenship. These they granted, in stages, to those provinces that earned it, the culmination being full citizenship. Become a full citizen and you could:

- make legal contracts
- hold property
- have citizen children
- stand for office
- have full rights before the law (e.g. to a trial, to appeal a decision, not to be tortured or scourged, cf. St Paul p. 146).

It was one of Rome's most original and successful ideas, and in AD 212, the emperor Caracalla granted full citizenship to all Roman provinces, irrespective.

To barbarians outside the empire who wanted to settle inside it – and Rome needed them to keep up their military strength – Rome adopted different tactics. A mere handful were granted citizenship; but all seem to have been allowed to deal with Rome under the terms of Roman civil law (*iūs cīvīle*), for example, to own property in the Roman world. This allowed barbarians to act like citizens in all but name, without compromising any nationalistic, ethnic and religious feelings they may have had; and many made a good career for themselves in the army especially, learning the Roman way and thus climbing the Roman ladder.

Romans, in fact, were masters at integrating cultural practices. When they took over a province, they had no worries about provincials practising their own religions or settling disputes with their own jurisdictional methods. The Romans' only demand was that the provincial governor should have the final say about which legal cases must be settled under Roman law. To that extent they would have wondered what all the fuss was about with the Archbishop of Canterbury's suggestion that aspects of sharia law should be integrated into the English legal system. Integrate if you want to, would have been their response, but why bother? Let Muslims do what they want to do – as long as they do not threaten the bases of the English legal system, and the English courts have the final say.

Couched in terms of personal attachment ('a good man', 'young man of integrity', 'blameless', 'worthy' and so on), the posters highlight the strength of the bond between candidate and support. Individuals make their feelings known ('I ask you to support A', 'B urges you to support C for office') and so do workers' co-operatives: we have exhortations from fruit-sellers, mule-drivers, goldsmiths, carpenters, cloth-dyers, innkeepers, bakers, porters and removers, chicken-sellers, mat-makers and grape-pickers to vote for this or that person. Even a teacher and his class feature ('Teacher Sema and his boys recommend . . .').

By the same token, some posters mock a candidate: one Vatia is supported for the post of aedile by 'All those asleep, and Macerius', 'The little thieves' and 'The late drinkers'! Fifty-one posters survive in which a woman announces her choice ('Fortunata desires Marcellus', if that is a poster and not a come-on). But when two local prostitutes, Cuculla and Zmyrina, announced their choice, an outraged citizen demanded it be erased. It is, however, striking how uninformative the pleas on the posters are. None is attached to a manifesto or policy. One begins to wonder if anything that we would call 'policies' existed.

It is also interesting that candidates do not support themselves. After all, only supporters can truly support. It is a tactic that seems to have escaped the attention of today's self-inflating parties. But there is something to be said for our system, i.e. that the candidates have to suck up to us once in a while. In Pompeii, where the patronage system was hard at work, we would have had to suck up to the candidates. Still, euergetism (p. 54) was also alive and well, and those keen for power could win popularity (and votes) by offering free bread and baths and putting up a building or two – and all out of their own pockets. How agreeable it would be if our politicians stood for election in order to spend their own money on us, rather than our money on them (well, on their expenses and pensions and, coming shortly, if Gordon Brown has his way, their party machines too).

Nevertheless, there is another side to this coin. The Romans, said the late historian Procopius, were 'the most city-proud people on earth'. Wherever they went, they planted cities and introduced the barbarians to Roman urban, and urbane, values. The city was the place to be. But there was a cost. The exploitation of the countryside was intense, and if famine threatened, it was the rural population that lost out. The Greek doctor Galen describes the consequences for the peasants of famine. Their wheat, barley, beans and lentils were commandeered, leaving them a few pulses and leguminous fruits. When those gave out, it was a diet of twigs, tree-shoots, bulbs and roots. In fact, country dwellers were in the majority, and the driving force behind the whole agricultural economy. But the cities exploited them ruthlessly. The problem does not go away in the modern world: the rural population is constantly telling politicians that they favour the city and 'do not understand' the country.

Plēbs and toffs

It is a nice question: 'How democratic or free was the Roman Republican system?' The historian Livy's account of early Rome and the development of the Republic is full of incidents in which the people take on the ruling patricians, the wealthy aristocrats defined by their noble family status, who alone had the right to hold high office and then served for life in the Senate, Rome's main advisory/legislative body. Livy tells how, bit by bit, the people won the right to the same offices, to their own People's Assembly, whose agreement had to be won for the purpose of passing laws and appointing top officers of state (consul, praetor, etc.) and to officials called 'tribunes of the *plēbs*', who were specially appointed to serve in the Senate with the people's interests at heart and with the right to veto any business in the Senate that they did not like (see Tiberius Gracchus, p. 25).

This is in principle far more democratic than our system, in which the ruling party in Parliament makes all the decisions and passes all the laws without reference to us. No tribunes of the *plēbs* for us (well, OK, there is Dennis Skinner, but he is toothless if his party is not in power – though given his views, he is if it *is* in power). Greeks and Romans alike would have been even more outraged by the idea that Parliament should accede to the demands of 'Europe', a body which by definition does not act in *our* interests, but is adored by politicians because it gives them seats at the top tables of a power gradually becoming much greater than their own.

Nevertheless, it remained the general rule that, in the Republic, wealthy aristocrats from usually ancient families continued to dominate the political scene: money, connections and experience all told. It is also true that actual debate about the laws put before the people to vote on was virtually non-existent, and that the voting procedures, by colleges, gave excessive weight to the votes of the upper classes. But politicians who made it to the top of the greasy pole did so largely because they could take the people along with them.

Productive liaisons

The ancients used marriage to forge dynastic relationships when it suited them, at home and abroad. Alexander the Great married the princess Roxane from Bactria (roughly the Hindu Kush), as Antony did Cleopatra. They used sex too. The emperor Augustus, we are told, committed adultery to find out his opponents' plans from their wives – well, that was his excuse. Julius Caesar, as a young man on duty in Bithynia (northern Turkey), had an affair with its king Nicomedes; on his death Nicomedes bequeathed his kingdom to Rome.

That example makes one wonder why our politicians

---

cannot do the same. Who knows what benefits might not now be flowing our way had Robin Cook and John Prescott turned their melting gazes not on their secretaries but on, say, the lovely Mrs Putin or one of the heart-stopping Mrs Bin Ladens? That President Amhadinejad looks a bit of a goer, too. George Galloway should be sent to exert his considerable charms over him, a sacrifice that would surely win him redemption in all eyes.

But whatever the answer to the Roman question, there is no question about the Athenians. In 508 BC, they invented the first, and last, democracy worthy of the name – where the people (*dēmos*) really did have the power (*kratos*), however Great and Good and Wealthy the Great and Good and Wealthy were.

Power play

Picture, for a moment, a Parliamentary Question Time in which the Defence Minister is being accused of incompetence. Hard to imagine, I realise, but it has been known to happen. A member of the opposition leaps up and says a mate of his who lives next door could do better on the back of an envelope. The minister immediately suggests his mate takes over. The chamber vociferously agrees. The minister hands over his red box, and we have a new Defence supremo.

Unlikely, on the whole. Let us now take ourselves back to the Athens of 425 BC. The Peloponnesian War between Athens and Sparta is in its sixth year. The Athenians have trapped a large contingent of Spartans on the island of Sphacteria and desperately want to take them hostage. That would be the coup of coups. With all those elite troops in their hands, Sparta would settle on almost any terms to get them back. But the Athenians are unable to winkle them out. Winter is fast approaching. That means they will soon have to sail back to Athens and lose their prize. So the situation is getting desperate.

The subject, therefore, is being discussed in the Assembly (*ekklēsiā*) of the Athenians. This is the sovereign governing body of Athens. It consisted not of elected politicians, but of *all male citizens over the age of eighteen*. That is, if you are male and over eighteen and a citizen, you. Yes, you. No one, but no one, can override *any* decision that you aged-over-eighteen male citizens, gathered in the Assembly, agree to take.

One of the participants in this particular Assembly is a controversial figure. His name is Cleon. He had already persuaded the Assembly, on an earlier occasion, not to make peace with the Spartans on the grounds that, if they actually managed to capture the Spartans, they would be in a much stronger negotiating position. But now things were going badly wrong: the Spartans were slipping out of their grasp. So Cleon got up and said, if the reports were true, that the elected generals should get their act together. The historian Thucydides, a contemporary of these events, narrates what happened next:

'Then Cleon pointed his finger at Nicias who was a general [an elected military official], a personal enemy of his, and said scornfully that if the generals were real men, they could easily set out with an armada and capture the enemy soldiers. If he were in command, he continued, that was what he would do.

'The Athenians then excitedly encouraged Cleon to sail immediately, if he thought it would be so easy; and Nicias reacted to Cleon's rebuke by telling him that, as far as the generals were concerned, he could take whatever force he wanted and give it a try. At first Cleon thought that Nicias was just *saying* that he would relinquish command; so Cleon declared that he was ready to go. But when he realised that Nicias really *was* handing over power, he backed off in alarm and said that not he, but Nicias, should lead the campaign. He had never thought that Nicias would go so far as to yield the command to him.

'But Nicias repeated his demand. Nicias then resigned his command, and called on the Athenians to witness his act.

They behaved as crowds will, and the more Cleon tried to back out of what he had said and avoid sailing, the more they urged Nicias to hand over his command, and called on Cleon to sail. Cleon had no way to free himself from his own words, and reluctantly took on the expedition. He said he was not afraid of the Spartans ... he said he would either bring the Spartans back alive in twenty days or kill them right there.

'The man's boasting struck the Athenians as funny, but the most thoughtful people were quite pleased with it. They figured that this was a no-lose situation. They would either be rid of Cleon – which is what they expected to happen – or, if they were mistaken in their opinion, he would defeat the Spartans for them.'

In the 'democratic' UK, all decisions about the running of the state are made by the majority party in the House of Commons, i.e. usually about four hundred mostly white males, under orders from a Cabinet of about twenty members, under orders from a Prime Minister. In democratic Athens, every decision was made by male citizens over eighteen meeting in Assembly, by majority vote, under no one's orders. That is real democracy – People-power in action – as the next chapter will explain.

By the way, Cleon did lead the expedition and did take the Spartans alive – and, as he had boasted, in twenty days.

⪢─┼◆─○─◆┼─⪡

Reading list

Alex Butterworth and Ray Laurence, *Pompeii* (Weidenfeld and Nicolson 2005).
R.W. Mathisen, in *The American Historical Review* vol. III, no. 4 (2006).
Fergus Millar, *The Emperor in the Roman World* (Duckworth 1997).
Thucydides, *History of the Peloponnesian War* (Penguin 1972).

[5]

Power to the people! Athens 508–323 BC

Bragging wrongs

Gordon Brown has informed us that he 'wants to involve the public more in policy' – though not, presumably, that of appointing Prime Ministers – and have a 'national conversation'. I am waiting for his call. By the time this book is published, we shall know how true this is, along with other traditional promises 'to slash red tape' (for 'slash' read 'rearrange'), 'restore public trust in politics' (note: not 'in politicians'), 'offer progressive common-sense solutions' (a contradiction in terms), 'make Parliament more accountable' (but to whom?), while 'engaging in full and frank discussions' (yes, yes), 'forging a new progressive consensus' (as opposed to an old progressive consensus) and 'providing firm foundations going forward'. But if only firm foundations had been provided going backwards, we might not continually need them going forward, but that's politics for you.

Had Brown said this before the Athenian people, they would not have understood what he was talking about – because the public, not elected politicians, made all the decisions. So Athenian Gordon Browns would have argued that it was the politicians that you needed to involve more in policy.

As we saw at the end of the last chapter, the Athenian Assembly, Athens' sovereign body consisting of citizen males over eighteen, happily accepted the resignation of an elected top military official and replaced him with one of the crowd, with instructions to lead a military expedition of the very highest significance. The Assembly was sovereign. It could do what it liked, unless persuaded otherwise.

Not, I imagine, what Brown exactly has in mind since, like

most politicians, he has no time for popular interference with his decisions. He prefers the mindset of the East German Writers' Union which, after the 1953 anti-communist riots, commented: 'the people have forfeited the confidence of their government'. So he has forbidden a referendum on the new European Constitution – sorry, 'Reform Treaty' – because he knows the British people do not want it and he would lose it. That tells you how 'democratic' a country we inhabit. It is well known how democratic Brussels is.

So we do not live in anything remotely resembling a democracy, and never have. Indeed, it is some indication of how devalued – indeed, almost meaningless – a concept democracy has become that virtually every country in the world claims to be one – from Zimbabwe to Iran, from Russia to Venezuela.

The rhetoric in which we proudly enrobe our 'Constitution' says as much. 'If there is a single trait in our character that has historically set us apart from other nations, it is our determination to limit the authority of those who rule over us', proclaims a pop singer Billy Bragg, bidding fair with Bonio and Bob Geldof to stand up and be counted as one of the most incisive political, social and historical commentators of the day. Not half as determined as the ancient Greeks, dearie: they ensured no one ruled over them in the first place. They ruled themselves.

War, women and slaves

It is important to start by getting two quite ahistorical, and mindlessly repeated, objections to Athenian democracy out of the way – first, that the Athenians did not give slaves or women the vote; and second, that Athenians were militaristic and nationalistic.

There is no ancient society that was not a slave-owning one. Ancients held human life cheaply, and saw certain categories of humans (e.g. war captives) as useful tools. The idea that such people, humans kept in subjection to serve your needs, should be given the right to make judgements about the way your world was run would have struck ancients as absurd: obviously, the first things slaves would vote for would be the end of slavery.

Clearly, if Athenians were *unique* in owning slaves, the observation would have a point. But they were not. Slavery was endemic down the millennia, and remained so until the 19th century in the West, though no one condemns Cromwell/Shakespeare/Paine/Burke (continue almost *ad inf.*) because of it, or claims that their work would have been impossible without it. By the same token, there is no good reason to believe that Athenians could not have invented democracy without owning slaves. No doubt slaves helped to create free time for them to visit the Assembly once every eight days, or serve on the various democratic bodies, but I can think of no argument which would demonstrate that their presence was the one necessary condition for the invention of democracy.

As for votes for women, they were first given the vote at a national level in New Zealand in 1893 (cf. France 1944, Belgium 1948, Switzerland 1971; the state of Wyoming got there in 1869). In the UK it was not until 1918 that *all* males over twenty-one got the vote, and (for the first time) females as well (at age thirty; age twenty-one from 1928). So it has taken us a long time to reach even that position. The Athenians got there in *principle* 2,500 years earlier. Again, had other societies been dishing out votes like confetti to women, the point might be worth making. But since they never dished out votes to *anyone*, it is not.

Finally, Athens did indeed fight people to extend its empire, hold on to it and defend itself. It is hard not to drop into ironics at this point. Fighting! What an outrage. No society has ever done that in the whole recorded history of the world, and certainly not in the 5th century BC. Fighting? Greeks? Absurd. Further, Athens was surrounded by peace-loving states like Sparta, to whom the very idea of fighting was absolute and unconditional anathema. It was only under the greatest provocation that Sparta forced its unwilling Spartiates into battle, but then they only had 300 of them, didn't they? Like the film said? True, they had been trained to fight since the age of seven – indeed, it was the only occupation they had ever known – but that was because they were so peace-loving. Obviously.

To drop the ironics, in terms of women, slaves and fighting, Athens was acting like any other state in recorded history until very recent times. But what they *did* do was unique: their own citizens had the power to control all decisions about their own political future. I would have thought that was a 'value' worth 'celebrating'. It has hardly happened anywhere since.

One wonders what it is about classical Athens that attracts such self-righteous finger-wagging. I rather suspect it is to do with liberalism, an 18th-century invention associated with the age of Enlightenment. The reason is that academics, being liberal, are convinced democracies have a *duty* to be liberal too, and are shocked if they are not. They therefore get an attack of the Polly Toynbees when they examine Athens' record because Athenians made no effort to disguise their blind and unforgivably stubborn-headed inability to have the foresight to acknowledge everything liberals hold dear. The ancient refusal to fund a generous system of pension rights for the old is equally culpable. Oddly, academics do not get heated about that.

Hand up to be counted

At the heart of real democracy lies the art of persuasion – persuasion of the people who make up the democracy to take *this* decision rather than *that* one. It is the complete absence of public persuasion on any matter that invalidates virtually all Western so-called democracies. No wonder the public are so apathetic about politics and join admirable organisations like the National Trust and RSPB (with far more members than all parties combined) because they serve their interests and get things done.

I say 'virtually' all democracies because of Switzerland. Here, uniquely, it is still the case that something approaching direct democracy plays a part. For example, citizens have a right to demand that *any* Parliamentary measure be put to popular vote. For a vote to be triggered, 50,000 signatures are needed; recent years have witnessed votes on nuclear power, the abolition of the army, and reforming health insurance and unemployment benefit. Citizens also have a right to propose an amendment or addition to the constitution (100,000 signatures needed to put it to a popular vote); while all constitutional amendments proposed by Parliament *must* be put to a popular vote.

At the level of the 26 Swiss cantons, 24 use the ballot box to decide which laws to pass. In the other two cantons, direct democracy in the form of public citizen-debate takes place. Here citizens gather in the square once a year, argue for and against proposed laws (e.g. to raise local taxes) and vote on them by a show of hands (as ancient Greeks did, p. 97).

Switzerland does not seem to be suffering as a result. Even its incomprehensible refusal to join the EU has, bafflingly, had no effect on its extraordinarily high standard of living or its ability to cooperate with its neighbours on issues like policing and drug control, despite the obvious fact that EU bureaucrats will know far better than they what is good for them, and would save them all that dreary voting too. Amazingly, the level of participation in politics is very high. Let us hope the UN can be persuaded to move in a task force and sort things out soon, before anyone else gets the idea.

Demockery

The contrast with our own palsied 'democracy' could hardly be more acute. In England, two-thirds of the population rarely bother to vote; public referenda are fiercely resisted by politicians and virtually unknown at any level, for all politicians' talk of 'involving the people'; and the majority party in Parliament ensures that no one else's proposals but its own can become law. MPs that do not nod as they are told are democratically hauled over the coals by the whips and politically ostracised. One cannot help but wonder whether things would improve if MPs were ordered to vote in secret in Parliament (as happened occasionally in Rome). Then they really might be tempted to put country before party.

There is a serious consequence to all this. In Athens, the people met to solve problems among themselves as best they could. In our system, government decides how it thinks problems should be solved in relation to its own political positioning and the vote-winning potential of it proposals. In other words, the purpose of solving problems is to create political capital. The idea that the solutions might be best for the country never enters its collective head. The New Labour politician Charles Clarke made the point with exquisite precision when he said 'There is only one question for Labour – how do we win the next election?'

The recent debacle over Inheritance Tax demonstrates the point with dreadful clarity. Labour has been relentlessly hostile to increasing the amount that escapes the government's maw from this source. The Tories propose to more than treble that amount. Labour attacks it ferociously. But it turns out to be a hugely popular move. A week later Labour doubles the amount.

This is sometimes censoriously referred to by pompous commentators in the *Guardian* as 'the tyranny of prevailing opinion', which they accompany with dark hints about 'the fatal path to plebiscitary democracy'. There is something just faintly ironic about commentators talking disparagingly of 'opinion'; and one does wonder why the 'opinion' of a small Cabinet cabal with its own agenda in mind should be preferable. And 'fatal' – to let people exercise responsibility (cf. Aristotle, pp. 217–8)? But the *Guardian* was never wild about that.

Ostracism

Ostrakismos, lit. 'potting' – though not in a gardening or snookering sense – was invented by the Athenians. It was a means of getting rid of a politician whose loyalty was in some way suspect: the loser of the vote was sent into exile for ten years. The word derives from the Greek *ostrakon*, 'piece of pottery', on which the names of candidates for *ostrakismos* were scratched. Many *ostraka* (plural) survive;

one particular batch has the same name on each piece, clearly written by the same hand! Is this an example of vote-fixing? Or does it suggest that some Athenians were illiterate and needed to have someone write out the name of the candidate they wanted ostracised?

It is important to point out that there is nothing necessarily wrong with the English model of Parliament, best described as 'elective oligarchy' (Greek *oligarchiā*, 'rule of the few'). Aristotle would have argued that, if MPs were the experts, then (on the brain-surgeon model) the experts should make the decisions. But he would also argue that the system bears no relation at all to anything remotely resembling democracy. Yet, almost everywhere it is practised, elective oligarchy is all that 'democracy' adds up to. Why not just call it what it is, instead of pretending it is something it is not? It would save a lot of problems.

We might console ourselves that at least we get a chance to vote the brutes in or out of office every five years. But no ancient Greek would have regarded that as having anything to do with *dēmokratiā*. The reason is that we have no say in the decisions that Parliament then proceeds to take. We have no say in how those decisions are put into effect, let alone who puts them into effect. Where is the 'People-power' in that? Even Aristotle, no democrat, agreed that 'ruling and being ruled in turn' made the basis for an ideal community. Contrast our system with that Assembly debating what to do about the Spartans trapped on Sphacteria. The citizens in Assembly accept the resignation of an elected general, and put in place a loud-mouthed citizen to do the job. Why? Because that is what they had decided to do.

In other words, in Athens the *dēmos* did actually have the *kratos*. In England, the *kratos* is in the hands of a small clique in the ruling party in Parliament. We, the *dēmos*, have no option but to do its bidding, which it imposes by law.

Talking the talk

In Athens, therefore, it is no coincidence that there began to appear many of the first known books about the rules of persuasion by public speaking (known as 'rhetoric', from Greek *rhētōr*, 'speaker'). The reason was that persuasion of the people in Assembly was the only means to political power, if by that you meant getting the Assembly to do what you wanted. As today, some people were naturally talented in that area. But if you were not, the means were available to anyone to *learn* how to become an effective speaker, even if not a brilliantly gifted one. Indeed, it was one of the main aims of both Greek and Roman education. In other words, meaningful engagement in *dēmokratiā* was for everyone. Even a John Prescott – remember him? – could have learned how to articulate his thoughts clearly and intelligibly to a listening secretary.

The ability to persuade, however, was not a neutral skill. Today people say, admiringly, 'X is a great communicator'. But so was Hitler. They do not tend to ask 'What is she communicating *about*?' So in the ancient world there was considerable debate about the moral value of what a speaker was trying to persuade you to believe. In other words, learning how to be persuasive was one thing; but what was its point if you were persuading people to be corrupt? That made understanding techniques of persuasion even more important because it helped listeners to decide whether the speaker had something to say or just had to say something – being (in our dismissive use of the word) 'rhetorical'.

Rhetoric

These days we are bombarded with 'rhetoric' in the sense of visual, auditory and verbal media designed to create needs in us so that we will buy products and services. It has never been more important to understand these exploitative means of persuasion so that we are able to see them for what they are. Plato put it at its clearest when he said (in a political context) of the *rhētōr*:

'He has no idea which of the beliefs and desires of the people is honourable or base, good or bad, just or unjust, but he employs all these terms in accordance with that great brute's (= the people's) beliefs, calling the things that please it "good" and the things that annoy it "bad".'

Thank heavens that, in this morally enlightened day and age, nothing could be further from the minds of politicians seeking our vote and advertisers and newspaper editors persuading us to buy their products.

So if anyone was to direct public policy in democratic Athens, it was the man who was able to persuade the Assembly to act in his way, rather than anyone else's. That is why, for example, the great Athenian political figure Pericles was able to exert such influence. Some indication of his popularity can be gauged from his appointment to the post of military general (*stratēgos*) fifteen times in succession; an unprecedented run. But that by itself gave him no authority whatsoever to *compel* the Assembly how to vote on any issue. He shaped Athenian policy over that time simply because he was able to persuade the Assembly that his way of doing things was preferable to anyone else's. The Assembly was the sovereign body. It could at any time reject his proposals. It rarely did, though it once prosecuted him for financial malpractice.

The workings of direct *dēmokratiā*

It had better be clear from the outset that, when one talks loosely of 'Greeks', one usually means 'Athenians' because it was from classical Athens that so much derived which continues to mean so much to us today. The distinction is important. The reason is that classical Greece (Greece of the 5th–4th century BC) was not a political unity. It consisted of hundreds of independent, autonomous 'city-states' (*polis*, pl. *poleis* cf. 'political'), each with its own customs, coinage, dialect, political system and so on, united only by the fact that they all spoke Greek and worshipped many of the same gods. Athens, Sparta, Corinth, Thebes and Argos are examples of *poleis*. Most of them fought each other, on and off, like rats in a sack. And it is worth pointing out that, of the city-states we know about on the classical Greek mainland, about half were democracies and the other half monarchies and oligarchies. Democracy was not universal.

Greek-speakers lived in *poleis* all round the Mediterranean. This is why you find Greek temples (stating proudly 'Greek civilisation has arrived') everywhere. The parallel with McDonald's does not bear thinking about. A recent calculation put the total number of *poleis* at 1,035. They are usually called 'city-states' because many of them – not all – consisted of an area of territory (like Attica) controlled by one major city (Athens); 'citizen states' might be a better description of those that were democracies and therefore run by their citizens. Athens, with a total population of c. 300,000 across its territory known as Attica, was by far the largest *polis*. Plato thought the ideal number was 5,040 citizens (i.e. about 20,000 in all).

The function of the state

Since we live in a tax-raising, capitalist world which funds a vast welfare state, one of the main functions of politics is to control the country's most vital activity: money-making. One of the ways it does this is by providing 'jobs' for people from whom it can then take enough money in taxes to pay for welfare, including redistributing the money to those it favours. It has developed a gigantic bureaucracy to help (or hinder) this cause, and since there is only one long-term aim of a bureaucracy, i.e. to gain yet more power and therefore jobs for itself, it is unlikely ever to shrink.

States in the ancient world did not make it part of their

'policy' to 'create jobs', though they did when public works were required, for which skilled slaves (among others) would be hired. Ancient Greeks were peasant farmers, and the main activity of the ancient economy was agriculture. The aim was self-sufficiency. Usually living in small city-states (Athens was the exception), the peasants had one priority – survival – and that meant security (claiming and defending territory so that they could live in peace) and farming their land so that they could survive.

So the job of the state, in as far as it had one, was not to raise taxes but to fight successfully (the Romans later changed that, raising taxes and fighting superbly too). The state therefore needed brave citizens. Here language comes into the equation. The Greek for 'brave' is *agathos*. It has its root in the ideal of 'manliness' – it is a male virtue. In time it comes to mean efficient, excellent, good *at* something, and good in the sense of 'virtuous'. Ancient political thought, in other words, was all about the production, not of money for the state to spend, but of 'good citizens' who would serve the state well.

The result is that ancient political thinkers tended to conduct their discussions of the role of the state at an extremely rarefied level. Issues of goodness, justice, right and wrong predominate, as if politics were simply one long moral philosophy tutorial, with practical applications – the duties and responsibilities of public service, benefaction, ambition, friendship, patriotism and so on.

So ancients would not have welcomed our insistence that the individual is all-important. He was all-important only in as far as he fulfilled the duties and obligations he owed to the state. To that extent, Greeks do not seem to have had a concept of 'rights': they had the laws, and the only question was whether you had acted within them or not. So when the failed bus-bomber Ibrahim Muktar Said came out in his underpants with his arms up, surrounded by armed police and heroically shouting – it makes one howl with derision – 'I have my rights', they might have asked him 'On what grounds?' Had he replied 'Because I am human,' they would have replied 'What on earth has that got to do with it?'

The ancient world was not a place where Polly Toynbee would have felt at home.

Benn novice

When Tony Benn made a TV programme about democracy, he agreed rather reluctantly that the Greeks invented it, but described it as nothing much more than a few people getting together for a little chat. This tells you everything you need to know about Benn's interest in and grasp of history. Ignorant, complacent, self-satisfied codswallop springs to mind.

The world's first and last democracy was invented by the Athenian Cleisthenes in 508 BC. It evolved over time, and the following description gives the main outline of the democracy in its fully developed form. In order to keep it simple, a number of technical complexities have been omitted, but not (I hope) such as to distort seriously the overall picture.

Assembly (*ekklēsiā*)

The sovereign body that made all the decisions was the Assembly (*ekklēsiā*, 'those called out', the word used much later for 'church', root of our 'ecclesiastical', etc.). The only conditions of attendance and voting were being male, over eighteen and with an Athenian mother and father. There were probably about 30,000–40,000 adult male citizens in Athens (most city-states were much smaller and had only about 500–2,000 adult male citizens). The Assembly met routinely about every eight days. How many citizens attended we do not know, but some meetings required a quorum of 6,000. One assumes those living in or near Athens rather than the out-skirts of Attica made up the regular clientele (it was a thirty-mile journey to Athens from Cape Sounion, the village furthest from the city).

Council (*boulē*)

As anyone who has run a committee knows, a meeting needs an agenda; and that needs a smaller committee of people who will prepare it. The agenda for the Assembly was prepared by the Council (*boulē*, 'plan', 'scheme', 'advisory body'). This consisted of 500 citizens over thirty, appointed for one year, who could serve twice in all, but not in succession. The result was that about half of the Athenian citizen body would have served at least once on the Council!

Councillors were appointed from the 139 'demes' across Attica (*dēmos*, pl. *dēmoi*: 'parish/neighbourhood'). Each deme appointed a number of members proportionate to its size. The deme appointed them by the only truly democratic means available to any society – by lot. Elections are, as Aristotle saw, not democratic but meritocratic. Nothing wrong with meritocracy. It just isn't democracy. Compare, for example, our National Lottery. There is nothing meritocratic about that institution. It is democratic in its purest sense – as long as you have a quid to spare, guv'nor.

The demands on the Council's time were high. It effectively oversaw the affairs of state. It met virtually every day, preparing and coordinating all Assembly business, and ensuring that the Assembly's decisions were put into effect. So Councillors were paid.

Standing Council ('Prytanes', Greek *Prutaneis*)

The political year was split up into ten 36-day 'sessions', and a Standing Council of fifty members of the Council (a different fifty for each of the ten sessions) was lodged at public expense in the Prytanes' Lodgings. For those 36 days, that fifty was on call 24 hours a day to receive political business and decide whether the Council needed to be alerted. (A good idea, that: when MPs are on duty in Parliament, it would surely be cheaper to lodge them all in some inexpensive MPs' hall of residence rather than giving them gigantic subsidies to buy houses for themselves in the area.) Further, for each of those days one of the fifty was (by lot) 'chairman' for the day, with power to veto any business – head of state for 24 hours! Socrates was chairman during one very fraught incident. That story will be told later.

From citizen to Assembly

Anyone with Assembly business – citizen, messenger, foreign embassy – went first to the Prytanes' Lodgings. There the matter would be received, discussed and (if deemed suitable) passed on to the Council. The Council in turn would discuss the matter and, if necessary, turn it into a motion for discussion by the Assembly. The Assembly could then accept it, reject it or send it back to the Council to be reworded.

Decrees into action

That's your lot

All Assembly decrees went back to the Council to be put into effect, and the Council detailed them off to the appropriate officials (citizens in good standing over thirty). It was these officials' jobs to see that the policy was carried out successfully and within budget.

It is at this point that modern jaws begin to drop. The most important feature of office was that, in nearly all cases, officials were appointed for one year and one year only; and that they were appointed, if you can believe it, *by lot*. In other words (to exaggerate rather), if you wanted to be minister for health, you put your name forward and if it came out of the hat, you were. Clearly, this was a seriously dysfunctional system. On Greek principles one could land up, for example, with someone like Roy Hattersley or Kenneth Baker in a position of real power and responsibility. Imagine the catastrophic consequences that would have!

But the Greeks were not stupid. They left that style of government to elective oligarchies. After all, elective oligarchies like our Parliament have only a minute fraction of a percent of the population to choose from to run the show because they have to make do with whatever dross they are lumbered with after the elections. The Labour Party, for example, has c. 350 MPs. From that lot, over a hundred are now needed to fill all the posts that they have decided Parliament requires, from top-of-the-range cabinet ministers to ministers of state, Parliamentary secretaries, under-secretaries and barrel-scraping whips. Ancient Greeks had, in theory, the whole citizen body to choose from.

Official power

The top ten, most influential officials were the *stratēgoi* (s. *stratēgos*, cf. 'strategy'). These were in charge of all military operations. In the 5th century BC they could also have considerable political influence over the Assembly (e.g. Pericles), though this political influence waned in the 4th century. These were *elected* and could (almost uniquely in the Athenian system) stand for office every year. This explains Pericles' dominance between 443 and 429 BC.

Most other officials – and Aristotle lists some 700 of them – were appointed to serve for one year only. Statute setters, auditors, state contractors, property assessors and corn guardians, legal arbitrators, temple repairers, dockyard overseers, and revenue collectors (and many more), all were citizens of Athens prepared to put themselves forward for official posts by a process of election at deme level and final selection by lot for the ultimate 'prize'. But what prevented any old Timotheos, Dikaiopolis or Harpagos from volunteering to do the job?

Keeping a check

'Examiners' are the answer. The point is this. Regular checks were carried out on the performance of officials. At any stage any citizen could accuse them of malpractice. Further, at the end of their year a full Examiners' audit was carried out, looking in detail at their performance and their financial accounts. If at any stage they were shown to have acted irregularly, the Assembly or the courts (also manned by citizens over thirty, and therefore effectively the same body, see pp. 107–8) could bring charges against them. Punishments ranged from fines, through exile, to execution.

Comparison with our system of Parliamentary Ombudsmen is telling. Their purpose is to examine complaints against Parliament. In March 2006 the Ombudsman found the government guilty of maladministration for telling various members of subsequently bust company pension schemes that their pensions were perfectly secure. The Secretary of State rejected the report, arguing that 'he, and not the Ombudsman, is the final arbiter of whether his own actions and those of his Department give rise to injustice in consequence of maladministration.' More recently, the Commons have laughed out of court the suggestions that there might be an offence of 'lying to Parliament' (as there is, *mutatis mutandis*, in the USA and elsewhere).

Brilliant! Any old Timotheos, Dikaiopolis and Harpagos would have been racing flat out for prestigious executive jobs in Athens offering *that* guarantee! Fantastic! As it was, however, knowing there would be Examiners waiting for them at the end of their term, they would have thought twice before putting their names forward, especially since the Assembly could be a very hard taskmaster indeed, with little time for excuses. Contrast the case of the recently disgraced MP Derek Conway, spending public money to featherbed his own family. Athenians would have found him out very quickly indeed in the annual public audit of his accounts – two and a half thousand years ago. But our Speaker's reaction was to set his face firmly against any external audit of MPs' expenses on the grounds that the oligarchy was 'sovereign'. Nice work if you can get it.

Further, Athenians were a litigious, highly competitive and very status-conscious lot, the more so the higher up the social scale one went. 'Help out those on your side and screw your personal enemies rigid' was a cliché of ancient Greek thought. Athenians were always looking for ways to bring rivals down, and bringing charges against rivals for being incompetent in the service of the people was a common way of setting about it. So taking on an official appointment was not to be lightly entered into. The price of failure, incompetence, or just bad luck, could be very high.

At which point one may pause and reflect on our system of dealing with failed politicians. They get directorships and are sent to the House of Lords. Perhaps it would make them think a bit harder about what they were doing if, at the end of their term of office, we could scrutinise their performance and if it did not come up to scratch, recommend a suitable penalty. In Athens, on average, two out of the ten *stratēgoi* were condemned to death every year ...

The People can do no wrong

Some flavour of the potentially very fraught world of the Athenian Assembly can be gleaned from the aftermath of a sea-battle fought between Athenians and Spartans in 406 BC. It also involves a bit part for Socrates. The account is based on that of the contemporary soldier-historian Xenophon.

The two fleets met off Arginousai (a small group of islands between Lesbos and the west coast of modern Turkey). The Athenians won, but a storm blew up. The eight military commanders (*stratēgoi*) in charge detailed off forty-seven ships to recover their dead, but the storm proved too strong for them. When the fleet returned home, it was without two of the *stratēgoi* who, presumably, foresaw what the consequences of their failure would be.

The other six *stratēgoi* were immediately imprisoned by the Council, and invited to address the Assembly. There the *stratēgoi* said they were not to blame, but also refused to implicate those they had sent to pick up the bodies: the storm was just too fierce. The *stratēgoi* seemed to be winning the argument, and many in the Assembly proposed they should be let out on bail. But since night was coming on 'and they could not have seen the hands' (see box), the decision was put off until the next Assembly, when it was agreed that the Council would make a proposal about how the men should be tried.

Voting in the Assembly

How was the vote in the Assembly actually taken? Xenophon tells us here it was by a show of hands. This is exactly how it works in those Swiss cantons referred to above where discussions and then votes are held (p. 84). In the cantons, the attendance is in thousands, and there are eight official assessors. When hands are raised, each assessor makes a judgement of the result and reports it to the chairman. It takes about a minute. If six or more agree, the chairman announces the result; if fewer than six, there is a re-vote and reassessment. If agreement is still not reached, an exact count is made, the crowd filing from the meeting place through 'yes' and 'no' exits. Witnesses of the proceedings say how easy it is to assess the majority, even in a close vote. In the Athenian Assembly, nine *proedroi* were chosen by lot from the *Prutaneis* to serve just for that day, to officiate at the Assembly. One of their jobs was 'to determine the result of the voting' (Aristotle).

That Assembly turned into a bear pit. When one Callixeinus tried to persuade the Assembly that the men should be tried *en bloc*, and if found guilty, executed, Euryptolemus said he should be summonsed for making an illegal proposal (because it was Athenian law that men could be tried only individually):

> 'Some applauded this, but the majority shouted out that it was outrageous for anyone not to allow the *dēmos* to do whatever it wanted'.

The summons was withdrawn, but some *Prutaneis* made the same objection. The crowd roared its disapproval, and the 'offending' *Prutaneis* yielded. But not Socrates. He was one of the *Prutaneis* at the time. This is his account of the proceedings, as reported by Plato when Socrates was on trial for his life:

'I have never held any office in our city, gentlemen, but I did serve on the Council. It so happened that I was serving on the *Prutaneis* at the time when you decided that the commanders who had not rescued the men lost in the naval battle should be tried *en bloc*; which was illegal, as you all later agreed. On this occasion I alone of the *Prutaneis* opposed your acting in any way contrary to the law, and voted against the proposal. The public speakers were quite ready to denounce and arrest me, and you were shouting and urging them on. But I thought that it was my duty to face it out on the side of law and justice rather than support you in your wrong decision simply because I feared prison or death.'

Socrates got away with it. Euryptolemus now spoke passionately and at length against the proposal, urging the Assembly to have the *stratēgoi* tried individually, so that only the guilty would be punished. A vote was taken, and Euryptolemus' proposal accepted. But then an objection was lodged under oath (see box: presumably the objection was that the nine *proedroi* had got the count wrong), the vote was retaken and the result reversed:

'After this they condemned all eight *stratēgoi* who had taken part in the battle; and the six who were there were executed. Not long afterwards, however, the Athenians regretted their decision, and voted to lodge complaints against those who had deceived the Assembly.'

But circumstances prevented them ever coming to trial.

So much for Tony Benn's little chat. This was a life-and-death matter, fought out in the highly charged atmosphere of an emotional Assembly, with the result on a knife edge until the last. Note in particular the sentiment that 'it was outrageous for anyone not to allow the *dēmos* to do whatever it wants'. The Assembly was sovereign. If it chose to break its own laws, it could, and in this case did. But note also the reaction after the event. The people realised they had made a mistake. But the Assembly was untouchable. So it summonsed those individuals who had led them into error. It was no good those individuals pleading 'But you agreed to the proposals at the time'. The Assembly could do no wrong.

Mob rule?

It would be easy to characterise this episode as an example of disgraceful mob rule and use it to condemn People-power as a serious option in a law-abiding society. There is, indeed, an element of the ghastly football crowd in full, brainless riot about it. Three points need to be made:

- The vote was clearly a very close-run thing indeed; not everyone had lost all judgement.
- The number of times the Assembly acted like this was very small.
- The Assembly repented of their decision after the event and attempted to see justice finally done. How many of our elected oligarchs do that? Or football crowds?

The fact is that the Assembly generally acted very responsibly. Had it so chosen, it could have decided to vote itself bags of gold to be deposited daily outside every doorstep. It never did.

For example, after the bonanza of the find of silver at Laurium in 483 BC (see p. 46), there was a debate in the Assembly about what to do with the money. One proposal was that the people divide it up among themselves (and, presumably, charge straight down to the travel agents and car showrooms and spend the lot). The long-term counter-proposal from Themistocles was that they use the money to build an all-powerful fleet which would give them the whip hand across the Aegean for generations to come. The far-sighted Assembly chose the latter. So when the Persian revenge assault for their 490 BC defeat at Marathon arrived, the Athenians were ready, and wiped out their fleet at Salamis in 479 BC.

Weapons of mass destruction

The ancients exploited the raw products of the natural world for all sorts of purposes, but they knew nothing of biology or chemistry, let alone nuclear technology. So they could not synthesise natural products. Without that, you cannot engage in biological or chemical warfare. Anthrax, for example, occurs naturally; but only in the modern world can you turn it into a powder and pop it in the post.

Further, nothing the ancients exploited in the natural world could be said to result in weapons of mass destruction, capable of killing thousands, indiscriminately, all in one go. Fire was the only practical ancient WMD. Water supplies were poisoned on only a few occasions. One might, of course, call on the gods to engineer something dramatic (e.g. Moses' Red Sea trick against the pursuing Egyptians) but gods could not be relied on.

There were plenty of interesting one-offs, however. Hannibal's elephants were a nice try, but elephants in battle were notoriously uncontrollable and found it lamentably difficult to distinguish friend from foe. Hannibal lobbed snakes into enemy ships on one occasion; Romans are said to have catapulted bee and hornet nests into enemy camps; and in AD 627 the Byzantines – inhabitants of the Roman Empire in the East – used naphtha (like napalm, distilled from wood, coal and tar) against the Arabs. It is very sticky, burns to a very high temperature, floats on water, and mixed with sulphur and quicklime is extremely nasty. But it did not cause *mass* destruction in any intelligible sense.

The dull fact is that ancient warfare was about humans ramming or boarding each other at sea, or fighting hand-to-hand on the land, with occasional help from arrows and horses. Improvements in military technology, tactics and training – like the inventions of the Greek trireme and Roman legion – were the best they could do.

This is not to deny that Athens acted on many occasions in ways that would have resulted in a UN sanction (which, being democrats, the people would undoubtedly have ignored). But it is important to understand that Athens was not unique in this respect. Far from it. Such non-UN behaviour was absolutely commonplace across the Greek world – as indeed it has been across the whole world, in every age and every society. It did not happen because Athens was a *dēmokratiā*. It happened because that is the way societies act.

The world's only democracy lasted 180 years. It ended in 323 BC, when Athens was subjugated by her all-conquering neighbours to the North, Macedon, which under their king Philip II and his son, Alexander the Great (both by then dead), had decided to bring the Greeks under their power.

>-+-<>-•-O-•-<>-+-<

Reading list

Aristotle, *The Athenian Constitution* (Penguin 1984).
Peter Jones, *An Intelligent Person's Guide to Classics* (Duckworth 1999).
Plato, *The Last Days of Socrates* (Penguin 1993).
Christopher Rowe and Malcolm Schofield (eds.), *Greek and Roman Political Thought* (Cambridge 2000).
Thucydides, *History of the Peloponnesian War* (Penguin 1972).
Xenophon, *A History of My Times* (Penguin 1966).

[6]

People's law and people's justice

Democratic Law

In 2004 the Law Lords – the highest legal authority in the land, whose judgements can be overturned only by the European Court of Justice – ruled that the indefinite detention of foreign terrorism suspects was incompatible with the Human Rights Act and the European Convention on Human Rights. Rachel Denber of Human Rights Watch said this was a profoundly significant decision: 'The Law Lords have reminded us of a self-evident truth – that no threat, however real, can justify abandoning basic principles of liberty and justice.'

Ancient Greeks would have been shocked by both the Law Lords' statement and Ms Denber's approval. Committed to People-power – the right of citizens in Assembly to run the state any way they wanted – Athenians would not have taken kindly to being told what to do by lawyers who had not been appointed or consulted by the Assembly; especially by lawyers appointed for life; and even more especially by lawyers acting on behalf of something called 'Europe'. What about the Athenian people, they would have asked? Do we not have a right of self-determination?

As for Ms Denber's views, Athenians would have wondered whether the principle of 'liberty' did not conflict with the idea that the decisions of a democratically elected Parliament could be over-ridden by anyone, even Law Lords. On the other hand, when they found out that a 'democratically elected Parliament' was actually an elective oligarchy (see p. 86), they might well have agreed that there needed to be supreme powers to restrain *them*. One obviously needed protection from oligarchs.

But, they might have asked, did one need protection from government that really *was* (in Lincoln's terms) of the people, by the people and for the people? That was a logical absurdity: what protection did people need from rulings the people themselves had made? In a genuine democracy, the people were the source of the law and could therefore repeal and enact at will. None of Engels' 'false consciousness' for them, i.e. the belief that people cannot be trusted to see where their true interests lie.

But that simply points up what a fraud, though a glorious one, Lincoln's magnificent sentiment is. There never has been government of the people, by the people and for the people except for that brief period of Athenian democracy 2,500 years ago.

Obeying the law

This is not to say that Greeks did not place a high value on the law. They saw it (together with language and reason) as the most important feature that distinguished men from animals because it enabled men to live together in communities in peace. True, they also saw that the way humans ordered their lives created possibilities for crime not open to animals (e.g. accusing a police horse of being gay), but that just made the law all the more important. But the value that Athenians placed on the law was tied up with the fact that *they* were the ones who made it, not a collection of oligarchs or lords, let alone Europeans. Of course the people had to obey laws they themselves had made.

Animal 'rights'

The ancients were fascinated by the question of the relationship between men and animals. For those who, like Pythagoras, believed that souls transmigrated from man to animal, killing animals was wrong, and that was the end of it. Others tried to analyse the differences. The sixth-century BC Greek thinker Alcmaeon argued that man alone had understanding, while animals had only perception,

---

divorced from understanding. Fifth-century BC Anaxagoras thought it was man's experience, memory, expertise and technical know-how that distinguished him.

Aristotle vigorously denied that animals possessed reason, thought, intellect or belief in any form. Their perceptions, he argued, allowed them to make propositions ('I perceive that what is in front of me is edible'), but that did not involve the reasoning faculty; animals, he thought, were certainly incapable of considering what action was demanded of them by moral virtue (controlled by philosophical understanding) in any situation. But the debate raged on. Later thinkers like Plutarch and Porphyry happily ascribed discrimination, memory and judgement to animals – otherwise, why would they run from enemies? Stoics argued (well before Chomsky) that it was syntax, or speech, that was the big difference. But do not animals respond to human speech, said Porphyry?

All this still leaves the question of animal justice. Followers of the philosopher Epicurus (p. 224) argued that justice existed only between those who could make legal contracts. Mutuality, in other words, was the key to justice. So no ancient thought animals had 'rights'. People like Plutarch and Porphyry, however, were ahead of their time in holding that animals should be respected as feeling and suffering creatures.

Socrates puts the argument at its sharpest. When he was awaiting execution in prison, his friend Crito suggested that he should nick out and go into exile instead. Socrates rejected the offer, imagining what the laws of Athens would say were he so to act. First, he says, the laws would point out that, by wriggling out of their decision, Socrates would be bringing the laws themselves into disrepute, undermining and destroying them.

Second, he argues, there is an agreement between the laws and every Athenian, rather like that between a son and his parents, requiring obedience to their rulings, irrespective of the danger and inconvenience it may bring. But since Athens

'is something far more precious, more venerable, more sacred, and held in greater honour among gods and all reasonable men than even your mother and father and the rest of your ancestors',

Socrates points out how much more important it is to obey country than it is even parents, for

'violence against mother or father is a unholy act. How much greater is a crime committed against one's own country'.

Socrates ends by pointing out that one can always go and live somewhere else: one does not have to agree to the 'covenants and undertakings' which a country makes with its citizens via the laws. But if one agrees to them and then breaks them, one has no right to complain, as if one did not understand the nature of the agreement into which one was entering.

Being imprisoned, and especially executed, for the principle that the law is supreme even when its verdict is (at least in our eyes) unjust is not common in the West. We would normally associate such behaviour with religious martyrs (Greek *martus*, 'witness'), but they were rejoicing not in the supremacy of the law but in their desire to defy it in order to reap a greater reward in heaven. Roman governors were used to this from Christians and tried to resist it. When Christians approached the governor of Asia in AD 185 demanding martyrdom, he said they could use ropes and cliffs themselves. But that, of course, would be suicide, not defiance of the state in the name of religious belief.

In the light of Socrates' passionate idealisation of people-made law, it is interesting that, when it came to Athenian legal proceedings, there is a distinct air of 'Forget about the law: how do I get off?' about them. On the other hand, that can hardly be surprising. Anyone nowadays who has been brought to court feels exactly the same, as does the barrister detailed to get them off. So while the technical business of the workings of the law is very different in Athens from what it is in England, when it comes to persuasion of the jury, we are in very familiar territory.

Good cop, bad cop, not much cop

One feature that will strike today's reader as bizarre is the role of the cops in ancient society. Naturally one assumes they will turn up (eventually), sirens blaring, dogs barking, breathalysers at the ready, tasers charged, cordoning off the streets with red plastic tape, arresting innocent bystanders, clipboards poised to take incriminating statements from anyone they can find as they put up crush barriers and carry out fingertip searches across waste ground in the increasingly desperate hunt for clues to find the obese youth seen playing conkers in the playground.

But they were nowhere in the ancient world. They had not been invented. Nor was there anything like our Crown Prosecution Service, making the decision about whom to bring to trial. All cases in the Greek (as in the Roman) world, from murder to treason, from impiety to theft, were brought by private individuals, to be settled by arbitration or court proceedings (as the box below explains, every effort was made to settle things privately before the matter came to court; it is salutary to note that most prosecutions in England were similarly private until the late 18th century). The incentive to do so was that in Athens the state made sure it was worth your while, i.e. in a number of cases, the successful prosecutor would gain financially. The only time when the state would step in, with the military or an equivalent, would be when trouble threatened its security or on special public occasions. So in Rome, when games took place, the emperor Augustus stationed watchmen round the city so that thieves would not have empty homes at their mercy.

'Increasing police presence' is a common practice today, but financial incentives for bringing and winning cases is not (though there are rewards in certain cases for 'information leading to arrests', cf. p. 149). Why not add a financial incentive for bringing a case – as long as its corollary too is introduced (as it was in

Athens) – that such prosecutors would be fined if they lost? The government is very keen on increasing our sense of what it means to be a 'good citizen'. If Poo Dogge-Fowler knew she might be more than just watched as she let Rover have his way all over the pavements, it could increase her incentive to act like a good citizen herself.

But the point is broader than that. The fact is that, without the help of the public, the police are virtually helpless. The culture which encourages people to say 'The police are paid to do this; let them get on with it' is self-defeating. Meanwhile, a father was recently murdered by a gang of juveniles with whom he was remonstrating, and another while playing cricket with his son. One cannot expect the police to be everywhere, but one does rather wonder to what extent crowds of fifteen-year-olds went round terrorising the adult population in the Greek and Roman world and killing citizens. One does not like to think what would have happened to them. Or perhaps one does. There are recorded instances of Roman heads of the family inflicting the death penalty on their sons, as they had the legal right to do. The *paterfamiliās* was felt to have not a private but a *public* duty to the integrity and soundness of his own family, in the interests of society at large.

Trials by jurors

Greek trials were lean, mean occasions:

- It is worth repeating: forget about police, solicitors or Crown Prosecution Service. If you thought you had been hard done by, or (for certain cases) seen someone else do wrong, you went to the authorities and launched an action yourself.
- Trials were held in front of juries consisting of usually 500 paid citizens aged over thirty, chosen by lot for that trial from an annually empanelled group of 6,000.
- Plaintiff (prosecution) and defendant made one timed speech each, usually in person.
- Witness statements were read out (no questioning, however).

- The jury listened, discussed *nothing* and voted.
- No judges controlled the legal side of the proceedings, telling you what you could or could not say; or making clear what the law was; or summing up the case; or imposing a sentence (sentence was usually automatic, depending on the offence committed); no barrister spoke on your behalf or made objections ('Objection overruled!').
- The only officials present were there to run proceedings and keep order.

That was it. It makes one wonder about the extent to which the law could be simplified today. Already the more thoughtful lawyers are pointing out how many of the law's often very expensive services (e.g. will-making) can, or might, be done by special agencies or do-it-yourself. The procedure for handling 'small claims' sets a useful precedent. You can already buy your own 'kits for winning' at £14.99 (wig extra). Online legal sources, call centres and outsourcing might all have a useful role to play.

The problem, however, is actually *getting* your money if you do win (ancient Greeks simply barged into a home and grabbed it, in kind if necessary). If simplified 'Dogge-Fowler Good Citizen' courts were ever established, at least you could be certain of the state paying up the reward (or extracting the fine if the prosecution failed). As long, that is, as the computer systems were working.

Arbitration

Then as now, strenuous efforts were made to prevent a case coming to court in the first place. The aggrieved party first gathered witnesses and confronted his opponent with his claim. That might settle the matter on the spot. If not, the parties could then go to *private* arbitration. They agreed on the arbitrators and their terms of reference, and contracted to stand by the decision, which had judicial force.

If they could not agree to this, a summons was served orally. The two parties were then told to appear with witnesses on the stated day before the *arkhōn* (a public legal official). The *arkhōn*'s job was to decide whether the case was actionable, this time by *public* arbitration. If it was, the complaint was formally lodged in writing while the accused could also lodge an official objection. Both sides put down a cash sum against costs (the loser of the case paid up), and the complaint was displayed in public.

On the day of the hearing, both sides swore an oath that they were telling the truth and presented their evidence before the public arbitrator (not an official, but an Athenian citizen beyond military age, selected by lot). If a decision was reached, the matter ended there. If not, it went to the full court. The evidence, which could not now be added to, was sealed up in a well defended box (*ekhīnos*, literally 'hedgehog' or 'sea urchin') to be read out in court when the time came. At any time, the parties could agree to revert to private arbitration.

Pleading to win

Under the conditions of the Greek courts, an action was pretty much no holds barred. Rather like one of those TV shows in which the young, bafflingly, compete to be humiliated by and then win a job with the unappealing Sir Alan Sugar, you had one speech in which to persuade a few hundred males over the age of thirty that right was on your side. The legal aspect of the case would obviously play a part, but blackening your opponent and presenting yourself as a picture of injured innocence were just as important. The only aim was to *win*: everything would be directed towards that end. Justice came a poor second.

Here, then, is the jury: 500, very average, citizen males over the age of thirty. What can I say to them, the litigant will ask himself, which will convince them that, even if I am guilty as hell, I am a good bloke, one of them, who deserve their sympathy and support? Nothing, for sure, that will make them rear up like startled horses; everything that will appeal to their own sensibilities and understanding of the world.

The same sort of judgement is made every day by, for example, editors who need to sell newspapers and barristers who, lacking any other means of defending their clients, fall back on, e.g. arguments from sympathy ('What a warm and loving person Mr Masse-Merdrer has proved to be in the community') or probability ('Is it likely that someone with the education and background of Miss Coak-Pedlar would deal in drugs?'). Greeks knew all about those sorts of argument. Indeed, Aristotle wrote a most informative handbook about them, *The Art of Rhetoric*, describing in detail what means of persuasion were most appropriate for what situations. It is all a modern barrister or politician needs.

A fool for love: X vs. Simon

Time, then, to look at an actual case; and a very pleasant surprise it will make too. Legal cases pleaded in ancient Greek courts make cracking reads. Not only can they tell us a great deal about Greek values but also about 'everyday life', and in a most vivid fashion.

The speaker, whose name is not known, is defending himself against a charge of 'wounding with intent', brought by one Simon. The speaker begins by buttering up the jurors – in this instance, a specially convened Council that heard such cases – and then describes what had happened between him and Simon, and why. Here the speaker admits he has made a fool of himself. This was not because he was having an affair with a boy. No Greek would have been surprised at that. Nor was it because he agreed he was a bit old for that sort of thing (males over forty were considered to be past it). No – the reason was that he had allowed himself to be drawn into humiliating, public street brawls over the matter:

'Even though I may seem to have acted rather foolishly for a man of my age in my relationship with the young boy, I ask you not to think the worse of me. Falling in love is natural. It happens to everyone. The best and most sensible man is the one who, when such feelings overtake him, tries to behave in the most controlled and responsible way. But this Simon has done all he can to frustrate me in this respect, as I shall show.'

Naturally, it was all Simon's fault. The case is an excellent example of the way in which a speaker attempts to shovel off responsibility for what happened by putting the blame on, while blackening the reputation of, his opponent. To read the whole speech, it looks as if Simon in fact owned the boy (who was not Athenian) as a slave and rented him out to the speaker, who had tried to lure him away without paying for him. Hence the clashes between them. The speaker now tells the story:

Simon drunkenly broke into my house

'I fell in love with Theodotus, a young boy from Plataea. I thought I would win his affection by treating him well. This Simon, however, thought abuse and maltreatment was the way to get Theodotus to accede to his every wish. It would take a long time to describe everything the lad had to put up with at his hands; but I think now is the occasion for you to hear the numerous wrongs Simon has done me.

'When he heard the boy was with me, he arrived at my house, by night, drunk, smashed down the doors and entered the women's quarters. My sister and nieces were there, women living so respectable a life that they feel embarrassed even for their own relatives to see them. But this man's humiliating behaviour knew no bounds. Here he was, in the presence of young orphan girls, refusing to budge an inch. He eventually left only when neighbours who appeared on the spot, and those who had accompanied him, threw him out, thinking his intrusion quite outrageous.

Simon found me and attacked me

'But did this make him regret how disgracefully he had behaved? Far from it. He found out where the boy and I were having dinner together, and proceeded to put on a most extraordinary, indeed incredible, performance – incredible, that is, to anyone who did not already know what a lunatic he is. He called me out and, as soon as I appeared, tried to hit me. I defended myself, and he backed off and starting throwing stones at me. He missed me, but one stone hit one of the people who had accompanied him to my house, Aristocritus, and split his forehead open!

'[I was so embarrassed by this incident that I decided to leave Athens.]

Simon was waiting for me to return

'So I took the young man with me – you must know the whole truth – and departed. When I judged enough time had passed for Simon to have forgotten about him and to have had regrets about his wrong-headed actions, I returned. I was on my way to Piraeus, but Simon found out that Theodotus had already arrived back and was staying with Lysimachus (Lysimachus was living near the house that Simon was renting). Simon called some of his friends to join him, began eating and drinking, and put watchers on the roof so that they could snatch the boy when he left the house.

When I returned, Simon's gang attacked me again

'It was at this time that I arrived from Piraeus. Since I was passing, I turned into Lysimachus' house, we spent some time there, and then left. They, drunk by now, leapt out on us. Some of them refused to have any part in this criminal act, but Simon here, Theophilus, Protarchus and Autocles began dragging the boy away. He threw off his cloak and ran for it. I, expecting he would get safely away and that these men, if they met anyone, would immediately feel ashamed and desist – well, thinking like this – I took off along another street. I was very careful indeed to steer clear of them; I was well aware that my every encounter with them had turned into a complete disaster. So, on the very spot where Simon alleges that a fight took place, not one of them or us had his head cut open or received any other injury. I shall provide witnesses from those who were there.'

[WITNESSES]

Simon grabbed the lad

'You have heard from those who were there at the time, Council, that this man was the wrongdoer, and that he had laid this plot against us, and not I against him. After this, the young man managed to take refuge in a cleaner's shop. But they charged in and took him off by force, while he shouted and screamed and called on people to witness what was happening. Many men came running up, protesting strongly at what was going on and saying it was outrageous. But they paid no attention to any of this, and beat up Molon the cleaner and some others who were trying to protect the lad.

I tried to fight back

'They had got as far as Lampon's house with him when I met up with them. I was quite alone. I thought it was a terrible, shameful thing to stand by doing nothing while this young man was being so lawlessly and violently abused, and tried to pull him away. I asked them why they were behaving so lawlessly, but they refused to answer. They simply let go of the boy and began hitting me. A fight now broke out, Council. The young man pelted them with stones and defended himself; they pelted us; then in their drunkenness they started hitting him, and I defended myself. The passers-by joined in on our side since we were the ones being wronged, and the result of the brawl was split heads all round.

Simon's gang apologised – but not he

'After the event, as soon as the others who had joined in Simon's drunken excesses saw me, they begged my forgiveness, like men who had done wrong rather than suffered it;

and though four years have passed since it all happened, no one has ever brought any charges against me. This Simon, who was the cause of all the trouble, took no action for a long time, afraid for himself. But when he became aware that I had failed in a private lawsuit, he saw me as an easy target and brazenly brought this serious action against me. I shall provide those who were present at the time as witnesses to the truth of my account.'

[WITNESSES]

Having sketched the story, the speaker then goes on to anticipate the arguments that he suspects Simon will deploy, and tries to demolish them. He ends with a swingeing attack on Simon's character and a statement of his own value to the city.

Character witness

It is the character touches that give the speech its charm. Simon, it appears, is always drunk and on the lookout for a fight; he has no sense of shame or propriety; even his friends desert him from time to time; and on one occasion Simon accidentally scores a hit on a chum Aristocritus with an ill-directed stone (loud chuckles around the court: is the speaker trying to create the impression that the whole situation is too farcical to be taken seriously?).

Likewise, the speaker is winningly self-aware. He admits he has made a fool of himself, though that is Simon's fault, he claims, not his own; he has tried to lead an orderly existence as a decent citizen and has never wanted to become involved in this sort of case, even though (he hints) the wrongs done to him would justify it. He feels a sense of shame at how things have worked out for him; but (he is quick to point out) when fights do break out, the bystanders always take *his* side – they know where right and wrong lie, even if Simon does not. Unfortunately, we do not know the outcome. Only the one speech survives.

When law was personal

It is possible to see what enormous strides Greek society had made by comparing what passed for law in Homer's day and the practices around 400 BC that we are considering. In Homer's *Iliad* (c. 700 BC), the warrior Ajax describes how murder was dealt with:

'Even in cases of murder, a man accepts a blood price for the death of a brother or a son. If the killer compensates the next of kin, he does not even have to leave his country, since that compensation holds the family's anger and injured feelings in check.'

This was the traditional way of doing things, law as 'custom and practice, agreed between the parties involved', the way ancients had always done it. And very effective it was too – it did indeed satisfy both parties. Nevertheless, the differences between this approach and that of a law-driven society are very great. In Homer's world:

- There was no sense of blame or culpability, of a crime committed by a criminal.
- There was no sense of punishment in an official sense, imposed by a statutory authority to deal with a moral failure in society.
- Punishment lay solely in the hands of the victim – which presumes he was powerful enough to be able to impose it. There was no legal sanction to help him.

So whatever we may think of the rather hit-and-miss process of the Greek law courts in the 5th century BC, it was much closer to what we would understand by 'due legal process' than anything in Homer's day.

Defensive tactics

When Aristotle drew up his 'rules' for rhetoric, he made a point of emphasising how important it was not just to get the technical arguments right but also to:

1 present oneself as an appealing person (arguments from *ēthos*, 'character'), and

2 understand what would move an audience (*pathos*, 'emotion').

In other words, like the omniscient servant Jeeves in PG Wodehouse's Wooster stories, Greeks were well aware of the importance of exploiting an understanding of the 'psychology of the individual' to help them win a jury over. Here, then, is another use for the rhetorical skills discussed above (p. 87), not this time in the political but in the legal and psychological arena.

The tactic is especially common in English courts, where being seen as a relaxed, friendly, winning personality goes down very well (think *Big Brother*). Of course, the top dogs in any world today – political, business, journalistic, educational, legal – fear defeat as powerfully as any athlete on the track or boxer in the ring, and fight among themselves ferociously to emerge, and stay, on top. But in a court of law it is only winning that counts, and if one has to swallow one's pride (a very difficult thing for a Greek to do), so be it.

Law frauds?

Greek and English legal practice, then, are similar in this respect: the body of written ('statute') law is one thing, but trials are all about winning, by whatever means. However, in the UK we have judges to control proceedings and ensure that the law is properly interpreted, rules of evidence adhered to, and so on. Barristers, in other words, whatever tricks they get up to in order to win a case, cannot ultimately bend the rules: the law of the land rules supreme. Indeed, while Parliament passes the laws, judges alone determine whether they can stand. To that extent, the judiciary, not Parliament, is the highest authority in the land. This 'separation of powers' lies at the heart of our political system.

It did not lie at the heart of the Greek system. In their radical democracy, the *dēmos* really did have the *kratos* to make whatever decision it liked, whatever the law said – as we saw in the debate about the generals at Arginusae (p. 96ff). There was no 'separation of powers' between those who made the law (the Assembly) and the courts because they were *exactly the same people*: those who filled the Assembly also filled the courts (as we have seen, 6,000 male citizens over thirty were annually selected at random to form panels from which jurors were, again, randomly drawn for each trial). And, as we have seen, there were no, for example, judges to instruct the courts about what the law was.

The result is that the Greek 'rule of law' often seems to add up to little more than 'the rule of men'. The law, of course, always requires interpretation, but it is worrying that the government increasingly puts on the statute book laws about subjects such as, for example, religious hatred, whose vagueness makes it almost impossible to know whether you have broken them or not. This is not the 'objectivity' to which the law should aspire, and does nothing to encourage confidence in it.

Roman law

Greek laws have had no historical influence (though its legal theory has). It is the Romans whose law has had the most profound effect on European and Scottish law, and to a lesser extent on English (because English law is based, for historical reasons, on a different set of assumptions). The reason for Roman influence is that the Romans were precise legal thinkers; they regarded the law as a system that should apply its *own*, internally consistent, rules to all situations (in other words, it was 'above' the world: it did not bend with every whim of fashion); the body of their law was written up, modified and developed down the centuries; and they produced a magnificent codification of it all which turned out to stand the test of time.

There are four sources of Roman law, developing over hundreds of years:

1 Every year the praetor, effectively the minister of justice, published his 'edicts', which informed the public of the grounds on which he would be prepared to grant a legal action (e.g. fraud, theft).

2 These edicts were accompanied by 'formulas', that is, details of the tests that would have to be applied to determine the outcome of the case. For example, in the case of theft that (i) if the property belonged to A, and (ii) it had not been restored to A, then (iii) B should restore its value to A; but if not (i) or (ii), B must be acquitted.

3 Laws passed by the people's assemblies were written up and put in the public domain, e.g. the original XII tables.

4 Jurists, individuals who were experts in law, were consulted on knotty points and their verdicts written up. Under the empire, jurists became professionals employed by the emperor for this purpose.

In AD 533 a *Digest* (or summary) of Roman private law, ordered by the emperor Justinian, was published, in fifty volumes, condensed by sixteen legal experts, in three years, from 2,000 volumes written between the 1st century BC and 3rd century AD; together with a four-volume version, the *Institutes*, a beginners' guide to the *Digest*. These two mighty works, complete with legal argumentation about cause, responsibility, precedent and so on, lie at the heart of the tradition of Western law.

Free-market law?

If that, then, was the way the courts worked, those were the terms on which the litigants played the game. So, for example, while the written laws could have a part to play in the proceedings, it was not necessarily a major one. If the laws helped a litigant to make his case, fine. If they did not, ignore them, misquote them or talk about something that would.

In a famous case in which a man caught seducing the defendant's wife was killed on the spot, the speaker argued that he had the right to do so because that was the law. In fact, the law offered a number of alternative responses, of which only one was instant execution: but the execution clause was the section of the law read out to the jury by the defendant. Presumably the prosecution speech, which does not survive, corrected the imbalance. But there was no one in the court whose job it was to point out that only part of the appropriate law had been quoted.

So, in practice, cases that came to an Athenian court boiled down to every man for himself in a legal free market. The result is that, time and again, both sides seem to be seeking not objective *justice* but rather plausible *justification* for their actions – legal or not – because that was the way to win. Naturally, barristers today regularly try to do the same in our system. But there are judges to prevent them succeeding.

Sentence structures

Nevertheless, there is a flexible element to our system too. While the law stands, for the most part, objective and remote in its majesty, sentencing remains (within certain limits) at the discretion of the judge; and it is usually here that problems arise. Even if a case has been *won*, protesters still prop each other up, scatter teddy bears and football shirts and cry 'Justice for tragic toddler Cyril!' if the judge (who is always 'out of touch') is not considered to have imposed a severe enough punishment.

The reverse can also be the case. Last year an American heiress called Paris Hilton was sentenced to 45 days in prison for repeatedly violating probation on alcohol-related, reckless driving charges. No one was complaining about the court's 'guilty' verdict. But some argued that far too heavy a sentence was imposed on her simply because she was a 'celebrity' and the judge wanted to make an example of her.

But at least the problem of the 'out of touch judge' was not one that affected ancient Greek courts. There were no judges; and in most cases the punishment for wrongdoing carried with it a fixed penalty.

Athenians, then, would have been baffled by our theory of law, that it should be prepared, in principle at least, to stand above the hurly-burly of everyday life and transcend all political, religious, social and other considerations. A democracy serves the people, they would argue: nothing transcends the people's wishes.

To that extent there is much to be said for responsible TV programmes like *Rough Justice* where injustices have been uncovered and corrected. The media *could* be an important engine of democracy, if it so chose.

>+◆>+O+◆+<

Reading list

Aristotle, *The Art of Rhetoric* (Penguin 1991).

Aristotle, *The Athenian Constitution* (Penguin 1984).

C. Carey, *Lysias: Selected Speeches* (Cambridge 1989).

Kenneth Dover, *Greek Popular Morality in the Time of Plato and Aristotle* (Blackwell 1974).

L. Foxhall and A.D.E. Lewis (eds.), *Greek Law in its Political Setting* (Oxford 1996).

Homer, *The Iliad* (Rieu-Jones, Penguin 2003).

Joint Association of Classical Teachers, *The World of Athens* (second edition, Cambridge 2008).

W. Lamb, *Lysias* (Loeb Classical Library 1930).

Stephen Newmyer, *Animals, Rights and Reason in Plutarch and Modern Ethics* (Routledge 2006).

[7]

Crime, punishment and education

More law

When election times come round, our politicians are always promising to 'reduce the size of government' and 'simplify bureaucracy'. Why they bother remains a mystery. We and they know they are saying it simply for effect, because in the same breath they are always saying that they will change everything. But change, by definition, means more government, bureaucracy, etc. – otherwise, how can anything be changed?

One obvious example of government failure to 'cut red tape' is in the number of laws that find their way relentlessly onto the statute books year in year out, most of them (as we know) from Brussels. Since 1997, for example, 3,000 new criminal offences have been placed on the UK's statutes! According to *official* figures, 11 million crimes a year are currently committed. The number rises to 14 million when it includes 'repeat' crimes committed against the same target, but is, in fact, nearer 60 million.

The ancients thought far too many laws were being made and did not hide their concerns about it. The Roman historian Livy, for example, devotes a section of his *History* to a discussion of the origin of Roman law in the XII tables (c. 450 BC, see p. 118). But even these, he tells us, were originally only X, made coincidentally by X men, the Decemviri: 'as heaps of statutes are [today] piled one on top of another, [the original X] are the fountainhead of all public and private law.' When, however, it came to finalising them (a job the *people* did, by the way), they found they still needed II more – a 20 per cent increase.

Indeed, so serious had the expansion of laws become by Livy's time that one of the things Julius Caesar tried was to:

'reduce civil law to fixed limits, and out of the huge, straggling mass of statutes include only the best and most essential in the fewest number of volumes'.

Poor law

Like all such projects, it was doomed to failure, and not only because Caesar was assassinated shortly after. At a later date, the great historian Tacitus took it upon himself to discuss

'the origin of legislation and the processes which have resulted in the countless and complex statutes of today.'

He compares the simplicity of the XII Tables – 'the last example of equal law' – with what he thought of as the modern disease: laws made in the heat of civil conflict and the desire for power, so that

'when the state was at its most degenerate, laws were most abundant'.

Tacitus (as usual) put his finger on an exquisite paradox. Laws were made to be obeyed. If there were so many of them, why was society so corrupt? Or was it the other way round: that the more corrupt the society, the more laws that were needed to try to control it? The paradox applies with equal force today: dog laws, gun laws, sporran laws (certain types have to be registered, if you can believe it), smoking laws, mobile-phone laws – where does one begin, let alone end? – all raise precisely the same question.

But the crucial point is this: if laws are to work, either people must respect them, or the laws must be enforced. Passing *more* laws is entirely irrelevant to bringing about either one or the other. But that is all Parliament is good for.

Hanging law

The Greeks of Locris (in Southern Italy) reckoned their ancestors had done such a splendid job of organising the state that they passed only one new law in two hundred years. This was to accept the proposal of a man with one eye, who had been threatened with having that eye put out by a man with two eyes. His proposal was that such a man should lose both eyes so that their sufferings would be similar.

In so doing, the one-eyed man was putting himself in mortal danger. This was because the Locrians decreed that anyone who proposed a new law did so with a rope round their neck. If the proposal was rejected, the rope was pulled tight and he was dead. Hence the lack of new laws.

It sounds a scheme well worth adopting in Parliament. Imagine the excitement when it comes to the vote for a bill, its proposer gazing down into the black hole of eternity as the MPs troop through the lobbies! Sky would surely bid for the rights, and interest in Parliamentary proceedings would rocket.

Education, not law

This was a problem the Greek philosopher Plato (c. 380 BC) had long foreseen. In his *Republic*, Plato argues that people who are always legislating are like the sick. All they can do is stuff themselves with different varieties of medicine in the hope of getting better, when what they should be doing is changing their way of life.

What is required to break this miserable cycle, Plato argues, is a sound education for the young that depends not on rules but on principles. Then, he goes on, proper behaviour like 'being silent in the presence of elders, giving up your seat to them, standing when they enter the room, and looking after your parents' is automatic, and issues of 'hairstyle, clothing, footwear and the general way one presents oneself' solve themselves. Significantly, he continues:

'In my opinion only an idiot would legislate on such matters. These rules do not come into being, nor would they remain in force, through being formulated and written down'.

In expressing these hopelessly liberal views, Plato was clearly under the influence of Socrates, a man who would never have made it as a teacher today, in school or university. The reason is that the one thing ministers endlessly bang on about is the amount of our money they have spent on 'resources' for education. But Socrates did not use them.

Resourceless teaching

What Socrates wanted to do was discover, with the help of his pupils, what goodness was. Having done that, he could then teach it. As a result, everyone would be good, and therefore happy. He made no use of hand-outs, computers, visual aids or eye-catching noticeboards (he did occasionally draw in the sand), but relied on labour-intensive small-group discussion. Admitting to ignorance of what 'goodness' was, he spent most of the time trying to find out from students. Attendance records, schemes of work, modules, lesson plans, bullying initiatives, assessment procedures and health and safety issues relating to projection equipment played no part. His only stated aims and objectives were to leave students more baffled at the end of the lesson than they were at the start. He had no respect for authority and abused visiting lecturers and politicians regardless of status.

His research record was poor. Though he made one break-through in discipline theory – that no one does wrong willingly – he never found out what 'goodness' was and published nothing. He even refused to take payment from his pupils.

He was, of course, one of the world's most influential teachers. And the terrible truth is this: that is the only thing that *really* counts in education. Ask anyone what (if anything) they valued about being at school, and interactive whiteboards will not come high on the list; old Duchy, Parky and Hobbo will.

Platos or Aristotles?

The reason is that the great teacher knows what to teach, why he is teaching it and how to put it across. This is thoroughly Platonic: he believed that one could have confidence in a system of education only when one knew what its end in view was, and why it was the right end. So he would have thoroughly disapproved of the 'Platos', the prizes awarded by the *Guardian* every year to the 'best teachers'. This is because the criteria for the selection of winners depend overwhelming on their personality, communication skills, enthusiasm, imagination and so on, i.e. the 'how' of teaching – how you persuade your charges to learn – and not the 'what' or 'why'. For Plato, there was a critical difference between persuasion and truth, and it was the responsibility of anyone in a public position, from politician to teacher to artist, to know the difference. The 'Platos', in his view, would be putting rhetoric before substance. (Not that they are called 'Platos' any more, but the 'Teaching Awards'. Presumably the teachers who received them had no idea who this Platos chap was, which rather proves the point.)

Plato gives a striking example of what he means in his dialogue *Phaedrus* by pointing out what the consequences would be if you were persuaded that a horse was an animal with the longest ears. Hearing how essential horses were for success on military campaigns, you would proceed to buy a herd of donkeys to accompany your troops into battle. Plato goes on: 'What sort of harvest do you suppose rhetoric would then reap from the seed it had sown'?

Time, therefore, for a new competition for teachers, the 'Aristotles'. Like Plato, Aristotle was interested first and foremost in the purpose, the 'end' of things, and 'Aristotles' would be awarded purely on the quality of knowledge being presented to pupils. It would be fascinating to see if the winners of the 'Platos' also picked up the 'Aristotles'. Naturally, the only resources allowed to an 'Aristotle' contestant would be a squeaky blackboard, a badly focused epidiascope and perhaps a little sand.

So what *is* being taught?

Plato and Aristotle would be in despair of modern schooling generally, for any number of reasons but especially because 'education' does not feature anywhere. The Department for Education has been replaced with the moronic and mealy-mouthed Department for 'Children, Schools and Families'. According to its website, its top priority is now 'Health and Safety'. It has actually made it illegal, i.e. a *criminal* offence, for primary schools to interview pupils and parents in case some children turn out to be cleverer or more advantaged than others. How one expects to develop skills and abilities without identifying, and then catering for, them escapes me.

In his *Dialogue* on the decline of oratory, the Roman historian Tacitus thought the problem was getting boys to concentrate on education in the first place. They were lazy, and their parents neglectful. Only races, gladiator shows and the theatre interested them – today's football and TV:

> 'What boy talks about anything else? What else do you hear when you go into their classrooms? And that is the sole topic of conversation their teachers engage in with them too. It is not by strict discipline or capacity to teach that they get their pupils [education was all private] but by sucking up to them.'

In fact the government has completely given up on the idea of education or the young actually learning anything. Schools are little but an extension of the social services and job-creation schemes. For example, ministers now feel it their duty to issue instructions about playing conkers, the contents of lunchboxes and issues 'around' equality, smoking, bullying, parenthood, etc. The Department for Kidz'n'Stuff has decreed that cookery classes will be compulsory from eleven to fourteen, 'to tackle the problem of obesity'. So – you do not want them to eat so much, so, you teach them how to cook. Brilliant! Meanwhile, the government plans to replace specific 'subjects' at A-level with a generalised 'work-based diploma', and has dealt a killer blow to adult education by proposing to withdraw all grant-funding support for adults who register for a qualification equal to or lower than what they already have – *unless job related*. Farewell, then, the Open University and Lifelong Learning. At this point both Plato and Aristotle would have committed suicide.

Children will respond to the demands made on them. Make no demands and there will be no response. One day someone will wake up and discover that it is 'education' they are missing out on. For the argument, ancient and modern, is really about means to ends. Plato was not hostile to jobs and getting things done, but reckoned that getting them done *right* was really quite important, and that could not be divorced from *living* and *thinking* right. Gordon Brown bleats on about 'va-a-a-arlues' from his windswept highland sheep-steading. It seems he has only business ones in mind.

Grown-ups know best

The result is an education system with an interest largely in what government needs from children, not what children need for *themselves*. So, for example, government loads schools with national curriculums and league tables, all quite irrelevant to the educational development of any individual child. It keeps them all in school, by law, when many children would be far better off out of it. Is that what it means by 'liberating' children? Equally pointless are the endless 'qualifications' that government demands children get, most utterly worthless (as many businesses know all too well). Most paradoxically of all, it claims to be meritocratic, while condemning anything that is 'divisive'. But is not the whole purpose of meritocracy to divide people – by merit? At the same time it appears to want to stamp out schools dedicated to helping their pupils become meritorious. Plato took a quite different view of the child's needs in his *Republic*, reflecting a time when the connection between education, intellectual excellence and moral virtue was taken for granted.

Plato sees the young person's mind as a citadel which can, in the wrong circumstances, be stormed by any fleeting desire that takes its fancy. If the mind is drugged on the concept of 'liberation' and consequently sceptical of the value of inhibition, self-control and moderation, it loses the capacity to differentiate between right and wrong desires, and develops no natural defences against what is evil. As a result, it is easily stormed and taken by whatever passing pleasure attracts the attention.

Such a liberated person

> 'one day gets drunk at a party; the next is sipping water and trying to lose weight; sometimes takes exercise, sometimes slobs out without a care in the world, and then takes up philosophy'.

In other words, they 'submit to every passing pleasure in turn until it is satisfied, and then submit to the next.' Taken to extremes, the demand for freedom means that

> 'fathers are afraid of their sons and sons neither respect nor stand in awe of their parents; the teacher fears and panders to his pupils and the pupils despise their teachers ... the old then adapt themselves to the young, aping them and mixing frivolously with them, because they do not wish to be thought strict and disagreeable.'

This was shocking to the ancients because (unlike today's parents) they firmly believed that adults knew better than their young. They did not regard children as fashion accessories or extensions of their own personalities (as we tend to), but as small adults, needing training to turn into proper adults and bring credit to their parents and community (cf. p. 244). So 'innocence' was not a quality they associated with children, rather 'no sense'. That meant inculcating principles and teaching them virtues like, for example, reason, self-control and respect. Indeed, the modern complaint that children 'grow up too quickly' would have been greeted with amazement: for the ancients, they could not grow up quickly enough.

Since the job of helping children to internalise virtue, once the main purpose of education, is no longer on the table, the new theory is that children who go wrong need 'role models' to help them become human. These, naturally, are to be drawn from celebrities on the television, the universal purveyor of values before which all must grovel. Apparently the first list of role models will feature WAGS, 'wives and girlfriends' of footballers. It should be 'wives or girlfriends', of course. No wonder children these days just wish to be famous.

On the other hand, it is just conceivable that the young go wrong not for lack of role models but because they see no purpose to their lives, and therefore no use, and therefore no value and therefore have no sense of self-worth. So they look around for someone or something that will value them or give them a sense of worth, and find it in gang culture, or doing whatever they feel like, such as asserting their own importance (i.e. nuisance value) before the world. That would be well in keeping with the prevailing ethos that the world is populated by autonomous individuals, beholden to no one (let alone 'authority'), doing their own thing as of right, without reference to any other norms than their own feelings and desires (see box, p. 227). The ancients, by contrast, had a very strong sense of what their children were *for*, in the context of state and family (see pp. 107, 244). Adults, in other words, though they complained about the behaviour of their young as much as we do, were not as disoriented or as lacking in confidence in their authority as we are.

Meanwhile modern social workers bang on about every child needing 'a quality attachment to a caring adult . . . services should be structured round this.' I think they mean 'love'. It is heartening to know that 'services' can now provide that.

Legal lunacy

Plato does not confine his views about the inculcation of principles to education. He is happy to apply it equally to the commercial world as well,

> 'otherwise they'll spend their whole lives making rule after rule, and then trying to improve them, in the hope that they'll hit upon a successful formula'.

He concludes that it is the mark of a badly governed society to need rafts of legislation about everything. Such law-makers, he goes on in a brilliant image, 'are unaware of the fact that they are slashing away at a kind of Hydra' — the many-headed monster which grew two heads for every one chopped off.

University education, Plato-style

Talk to students in school and many will say 'I want to go to university'; and indeed, 80 per cent of those who apply achieve their lifetime's ambition. What they should be saying is 'I have a passionate desire to know more about Homer's *Iliad*, or the coefficient of expansion of copper, or the mountain ranges of Peru'. Exams do not necessarily tell you anything about a pupil's desire to know and to learn – and that is what should be the test of going to university: not what you know now, but (like Socrates) what you know you do not know and desperately long to know. And this was a principle enunciated by Plato, who saw interaction between teacher and pupil as the very heart of education: he talks of 'truth flashing on the learner's soul like a flame kindled by a leaping spark'.

His university interview technique consisted of describing to potential students the nature of the whole subject, the various stages it went through, the time it would take and the effort it entailed. Those who were captivated and believed that life could be lived in no other way passed the test; the others did not. This test, he argued, 'has the advantage that a student has only himself to blame if he cannot meet the demands of the subject, and his teacher is absolved from responsibility'. The onus is therefore on the student to keep up with the pace. Nothing could be more alien to today's educational culture, where some universities have moved lectures to the afternoons because students complain they cannot get up in the morning, and repeat them in the evenings for students who cannot even do *that*.

Plato is describing the absolutely crucial difference between active and passive education. He came up with a telling image to describe those who were turned off by the prospect of real engagement with the subject: they were the sort of people who were satisfied with 'a superficial veneer of learning, like the tan men get from exposing themselves to the sun'. What a wonderful image of passive education: shoals of obese, be-trainered students at SunTan U, clutching their mobile phones, iPods and bottles of water, lying in a lecture hall like beached seals, using their skill and judgement to roll over now and again until lightly educated on both sides.

So we need to ask Plato's question: who will benefit from university education, and how will we find out? The answer has an awful simplicity to it. All students with minimum qualifications, who wish to, pay to go to university for one year. At the end of the first year, the universities decide whom to keep and whom to reject, without government interference. Those who are kept on get the rest of their education absolutely free – and should be the pick of the bunch, whether from state or private schools.

Most responsible universities would, I guess, reject up to 50 per cent of their students at the end of the first year, ensuring that the highest standards are maintained and that only those with a real commitment and passion for learning make the cut. That would, I guess, make free university

> education affordable by the state to all those who merit
> it. And that is the point: there are lots of excellent
> students around – curious, hard-working, enthusiastic,
> questioning – and they deeply resent the presence of the
> suntan set.

Amen to that in the modern world where, if you are a brass band and want to play *Jingle Bells* at a Christmas charity event you will have to get a licence for it on pain of punishment (it is 'not religious content'), as you will if you want to hold a poetry reading, backed up with a didgeridoo, in an Oxfam bookshop before a maximum of 25 people. Meanwhile, you are breaking the law if you attempt to sell wine in quantities that are not 125 ml, 175 ml or multiples thereof. Plato would have thought this stark, staring bonkers, certifiable lunacy. And he would be right. It would be difficult to think of a more efficient way of bringing the law into contempt.

Justifying punishment

Before one can draw up a system of punishments, it is vital to be able to demonstrate that people can be held responsible for their actions and, at the same time, to *blame* for them (the two are not the same. Roman lawyers argued endlessly over the problem, and politicians still do: Peter Hain was responsible for the cash donations he received but did not declare, as he admits, but was he to blame?). Only then can one argue about what actions should be punishable, and what not. The philosopher Aristotle did just that, arguing as follows.

A man wishes for an end. He decides on the means to reach that end. He chooses those means and acts on them. Now, a mere *wish* is neither here nor there: goodness is all about what we *do*. So goodness will find its expression in the way we deal with the *means* to the wished-for end, i.e. the decisions we take about our choice of means and how we put them into effect. If that is the case, he goes on:

'virtue and vice depend on ourselves, since where it is in our power to act, it is also in our power not to act, and where we can say "yes", we can also say "no".'

What, however, if we are careless or thoughtless? That surely renders us incapable of controlling our behaviour. Aristotle will have none of that. Our ability to act well or badly depends on our character, the sort of person we are; and our character is controlled by the actions we *choose* to engage in – how we spend our time, whom we mix with, and so on – all of which is entirely up to us. Choose to act like *this*, and *this* will be the result (Aristotle draws an analogy with people who keep on practising to win at games). Moreover, he says, it is unreasonable to maintain that a man who acts unjustly or self-indulgently does not *wish* to be unjust or self-indulgent. Mere wishing cannot make him become *just*, for example, any more than it can make a sick man healthy. The person who throws a stone decides to let go, he says; once you have done that you cannot call the stone back. But you had the power to decide whether to throw it in the first place.

Aristotle leaves the crunch argument until the end. If it is the case that we have control over the decision whether to be good or bad, it follows that both virtue and vice spring from the same source: ourselves. So any argument:

'that absolves bad men of responsibility for wickedness would also deprive good men of responsibility for virtue.'

Aristotle is, of course, right: it would make no sense to reward some and punish others if men had no ability to make a choice about behaving well or badly. We, however, do not take such a black-and-white view of matters. The argument about 'responsibility' and 'blame' has been muddied for ever by the invention of Freudian psychology, which argues that there are deep-seated, unconscious reasons why men act as they do, and to punish them for that would be unjust. The ancients were well aware of cases where considerations of that sort would come into effect (a Roman lawyer says you would not punish a lunatic or a child – at least not a child under the age of seven – for causing damage). But they would tend, I suspect, to regard the Freudian argument not as an excuse for acquitting people, but rather as another reason for stringing them up: not only has X committed murder, but he has also done so for unconscious reasons, which means he is very likely to do so again.

Punishing schedules

The 6th-century-BC Greek thinker, poet and politician Solon said that society was glued together by rewards and penalties. The Roman Cicero (1st century BC) thought that *vindicātiō*, 'desire for revenge', was implanted in man for the same purpose. All agreed, however, that society would be far better served if crime was not committed at all. An ancient and modern 'solution' has been to demand that penalties be far more severe, on the assumption that the more afraid people are of the consequences of crime, the less likely they are to offend. We do indeed hear of a range of the most ghastly punishments in the ancient world: crucifixion; burning alive; burial alive; throwing off a rock; throwing to wild animals; and pouring molten lead down the throat, to name but a few.

The sophist Critias, however, took a different line. In a fragment from a play he wrote, he makes the evil Sisyphus suggest (for the first time that we know of) that the gods were invented to keep men afraid of divine vengeance and therefore more likely to obey the law:

'Then, when the laws prevented men from open violence, but they continued to act violently in secret, I believe that a shrewd and subtle man invented for men the fear of the gods. His aim was that there might be something to frighten the wicked even if they acted, spoke or thought in secret. For this reason he introduced the conception of divinity. There is, he said, a spirit enjoying endless life, hearing and seeing with his mind, exceedingly wise and all-observing, bearer of a divine nature.

He will hear everything spoken among men and can see everything that is done. If you are silently plotting evil, it will not be hidden from the gods, so clever are they. With this story he presented the most seductive of teachings, concealing the truth with lying words . . . So, I think, first of all, did someone persuade men to believe that there exists a race of gods.'

And Critias was right to this extent, that unless we have (somehow) internalised beliefs about civilised behaviour, no amount of law is going to make us 'good'. Nor, in fact, is any amount of punishment: it is not its severity that counts, but the certainty of detection. Inculcating a fear that the gods will see you, even if humans do not – however unjustified that fear, as Sisyphus says – may indeed be one effective way in which society can encourage that internalisation. As the worldly Roman poet Ovid put it much later 'It's useful that gods should exist, so let's suppose they do.'

Crimes and punishments

In the absence of judges, ancients usually linked specific crimes to specific punishments. There was no room for doubt on the matter: be found guilty of *this*, and the law said *this* would be the consequence, with no remission for good conduct. You have killed your father? Right: you will be tied up in a leather sack with a dog, a monkey, a snake and a cockerel and thrown into a river.

But that leaves the question: capital punishment apart, what did ancients hope the punishment would achieve? It is a question to which we still have no agreed response. For example, there is currently a plan to release 25,000 prisoners eighteen days early, every year. There is always outrage when such proposals are made, and dire warnings are uttered about them 'offending again' when they should still have been in prison. But what grounds are there for believing that another two and half weeks in prison will *prevent* them offending again?

Plato's purposeful punishment

In 5th-century Athens, as we have seen, the concept of 'the law' was well understood, but democracy encourages debate and argument, and thinkers of the classical period reflected hard on what punishment was for. In fact, we have still not got much further on the five broad purposes of punishment deduced by Greeks, the first three of which were by far the most common:

- retribution
- compensation
- protection of society
- deterrence
- reform.

Perhaps the most interesting of the thinkers who tackled the problem of punishment was Plato. Believing in the importance of experts (primarily himself), he had little time for democracy or the 'people' – many Greeks were intense critics of Greek culture – and when he thought about how his ideal state would work in practical terms, he drew up a law code in which the people had no active role to play at all.

Plato uncontroversially argued that the criminal should be restrained and made to pay compensation, but went on to claim that any means were justified in ensuring he never committed a crime again. He even suggested that rewarding him for staying straight was not to be dismissed, a move which often seems to be touted in the modern world ('Don't murder that old lady, and win a pair of trainers!').

The reason was that Plato regarded criminality as a disease that could be cured, and the ultimate purpose of punishment was to cure it. If that turned out to be impossible, the death penalty was the only option, he thought (so here deterrence came into play). It is interesting that Plato had no time for the concept of retribution. For Plato, the criminal was ill/diseased/ignorant/disordered/not thinking straight, and therefore to be pitied.

Education would sort him out. For Plato, punishment was essentially humanitarian:

> 'When anyone commits an act of injustice, serious or trivial, the law will combine instruction and constraint. The result will be that, in the future, either the criminal will never again dare to commit such a crime voluntarily, or he will do it a very great deal less often; and in addition, he will pay compensation for the damage he has done. This is something we can achieve only by laws of the highest quality. We may take action, or simply talk to the criminal; we may grant him pleasures, or make him suffer; we may honour him, we may disgrace him; we can fine him, or give him gifts. We may use absolutely *any* means to make him hate injustice and embrace true justice – or at any rate not hate it.
>
> 'But suppose the lawgiver finds a man who's beyond cure – what legal penalty will he provide for this case? He will recognise that the best thing for all such people is to cease to live – best even for themselves. By passing on they will help others, too: first, they will constitute a warning against injustice, and second, they will leave the state free of scoundrels. That is why the lawgiver should prescribe the death penalty in such cases, by way of punishment for their crimes – but in no other case whatever.'

There is indeed something extraordinarily irritating about having to see our taxes spent on looking after criminals in prison anyway, let alone without any guarantee about their conduct when they are released. About 76 per cent of teenagers who leave prison go straight back to crime.

Democratic sentences

For the most part, as we have seen, crime and punishment were statutorily linked: be found guilty of X, and Y will be your punishment. But in Athens there was one exception: in a limited number of actions, if a guilty verdict was delivered, the punishment was up for debate. Such a case was that involving Socrates on a charge of corrupting the young and introducing new gods (399 BC). He was found guilty, and that triggered the procedure.

It worked as follows. The prosecution and the defence both proposed punishments; and the jurors then voted on their preference. In Socrates' case, the prosecution demanded capital punishment. Socrates, on the other hand, argued that he had been of enormous benefit to the state, and his punishment should therefore be to enjoy free meals and a pension for the rest of his life, though he does say he could afford a fine of 100 drachmas. It was a Socratic irony too far. His appalled friends quickly clubbed together to propose instead a fine of 3,000 drachmas, which Socrates grudgingly accepted, but the jury voted for the death penalty, and Socrates was executed.

The procedure strikes me as a brilliant, democratic compromise. The point is that *both* sides can have a say. If the defendant takes a Socratic view of the matter, he is asking for trouble. But, given the prosecution spoke first, the defence had the chance to adjust its proposal in the light of the other side's recommendation, as well as of their own understanding of the jurors' prejudices. If the prosecution went for the ultimate option, it was up to the defence to come back with an equally irresistible, if less severe, offer. Not something that a man like Socrates would have been interested in complying with, however.

The virtue of such a system in the modern world is that it would immediately do away with the 'out of touch' judge. It leaves the punishment to representatives of the society against which the crime was committed, whether to go for the defendant's (presumably more lenient) or the prosecution's (presumably more severe) proposal. It sends a public signal to law makers about what, in today's world, is and is not acceptable.

Nevertheless it does not solve the problem: what guarantee is there that the offender who serves his term will *not* reoffend when he is released? And, as Plato would have it, what is the purpose of punishment if it does not cure the offender? Should we release people only when we can be certain they will go straight from then on?

To make the Athenian system even more democratic, there was even a proposal (never enacted) that the jury itself rather than the opposing sides should decide the punishment. Aristotle reports the idea, and does not seem to have been against it in principle. He merely points out that, if every juror had the chance of a say, it would be very difficult indeed to get them to agree.

Cui bonō? The death penalty

Whatever the law said, Greeks (as we have seen) tended to ask themselves in any situation: 'Where do my interests lie?' The Romans were precisely the same. The orator Cicero argued:

'Our ancestors wrote laws whose sole aim was the stability and interests of the state. The state is best off when governed according to laws, but all laws should be interpreted in the light of that goal. Epaminondas of Thebes rightly passed over the *letter* of the law, thinking it sheer madness not to interpret in terms of the stability of the state a law that had been enacted for that stability. By assuring the stability of the state and looking to the common interest, he could not possibly fail to obey the laws.'

Take, for example, the final solution: the death penalty. Ancient Greeks had no compunction about imposing it. It was quite common even for *stratēgoi* (the top ten political and military figures in the state, see p. 94) to be condemned to death for failure or fraud at the end of their year of office (though any *stratēgos* who had a whiff of that outcome made certain he either never returned or immediately disappeared into exile, cf. p. 96).

But the decision was not necessarily automatic. There was an occasion in 427 BC when the Athenian Assembly debated how to punish the town of Mytilene, which had revolted from them. Should all the males be executed, or just the ringleaders? 'Execute the lot' was the Assembly's decision. But next day, the people had second thoughts, and the Assembly was recalled to debate the issue again (the Assembly could, and did, change its mind: the contrast with Parliament is striking). Thucydides reports the two main speeches that informed the subsequent debate: Cleon (see p. 78) for keeping to the original decision, Diodotus for executing only the guilty.

Cleon argues that Athens' power depends on its strength. To show weakness at a time like this would be disastrous. Fancy arguments are no substitute for firm action ('the man in the street knows best', he says). Mytilene's revolt was deliberate, calculated and unprovoked. Athens had done them no harm, and they took advantage of Athens' good treatment of them. Other states will follow their example if Athens does not crack down.

Diodotus' reply has two main threads. First, he objects that the prospect of the death penalty has never deterred anyone if they thought they could get away with it: it will not stop others revolting. Second, he argues that failure to distinguish the guilty from the innocent within Mytilene will drive the innocent to the extremes of despair and therefore to extremes of resistance, because they will realise that innocence will never protect them from the ultimate penalty. This will cause endless trouble for Athens, now and in the future. Diodotus emphasises that the question is not one of 'pity or finer feelings', but only 'how Mytilene can be useful to us'.

Since Diodotus won the day (by a whisker), it is clear that the Assembly of the people was sophisticated enough to see the force of his argument: that, whatever one felt about the Mytileneans, what ultimately counted were Athens' long-term self-interests, and in those terms, it was better not to execute the innocent.

Like the Greeks, the Romans too did not hesitate to use the death penalty, but could be equally circumspect about it if it suited them. When the Roman aristocrat Catiline was – probably unjustly – made out to be fomenting revolution in order to seize the lands of the rich and redistribute them among the poor, there was an intense debate in the Senate about what to do with some of the captured ringleaders of the 'conspiracy'. The consul-elect

Silanus made the case for execution. Then Julius Caesar inter-vened, pointing out (among much else) that these conspirators were citizens, and citizens faced with the death penalty had the option of going into exile. He quotes examples from history where emotion had got in the way of intelligent judgement, and when kings and peoples 'allowed anger or pity [!] to lead them into error'. He goes on, as the historian Sallust reports:

'These men deserve their fate, but you must consider the precedent it will set. Bad precedents all emerge from measures good in themselves. When power passes from you into the hands of unworthy and ignorant men, the precedent you will have established by imposing an extraordinary punishment on men who deserve it will be used against the innocent, who do not deserve it.'

Cato, however, had the last word, the Senate was persuaded and the Catilinarians strangled.

The point is not that Caesar was against the death penalty in principle. He was against its use in this instance because he thought it would, in the long term, break with tradition and lay innocent Romans open to slaughter at the hands of the ignorant and ruthless.

Modern capital punishment

The contrast with today could not be starker. European law forbids Parliament even to *discuss* the issue of capital punishment, let alone restore it. Yet up to the early 20th century, it had been standard practice throughout history across the world, and still is in many countries. It raises the question – why in our age is it such anathema, at any rate in much of the West? It is no use arguing that 'we' might be responsible for the death of an innocent person. That argument has always been available (see Julius Caesar above), but only in the last century has it been assumed to be unanswerable (and at a time when the law has never been more sympathetic to criminals, and scientific evidence better able to help us deliver a secure verdict).

Perhaps the reason is that, when Christian observance was common in the West, it could be argued that God would make it all up to the victim in heaven. If that is the case, it may explain why America, which is a much more 'Christian' land than Europe, still retains capital punishment in some states. But what is wrong about executing a person who is, actually, *guilty*? We have no problem about confidently assigning guilt in other cases. Why not for murder, for example, too?

It may be because we live in predominantly secular times, when we feel (perhaps) that there is only one life for all of us, with no hope of another, and life is therefore infinitely precious. In that case, it is ironical that the argument is based on the 'sanctity' of life – a thoroughly religious concept (Latin *sānctus*, 'sacred') and one that no Greek or Roman would have given a second thought to. Then again, we live in a welfare state, whose aim sometimes seems to be to look after every one of us every minute of our lives, even those determined to do away with that life. We live at a time when medical advances often seem on the point of offering us immortality, unless murderers get us first. Perhaps the slaughter of the two world wars has also left an ineradicable mark on Western consciences (but that has nothing to do with murder).

There is, in my view, a strong case for saying that we should ask the Greek question in instances where transparent enemies of the public, effectively at war with us and bent on taking life for the sake of it (train bombers and so on), are found guilty: what is it in the best interests of our society to do with these people? The ancients, at any rate, would have been amazed that we think it is in our best interests to lock them up for life in high-security prisons where costs on average are nearly £50,000 per prisoner per year, and much more for category A prisoners. But they would also understand Diodotus' and Caesar's argument that capital punishment could, in certain circumstances, have dangerous consequences. What they would not understand was the blanket ban on it, let alone on even any mention of it.

Humane treatment or public interest?

When Caesar made his point about exile as an alternative to execution, he was referring to the law of *aquae et ignis interdictiō*, 'refusal of water and fire', i.e. food and shelter (we might say 'hearth and home'). Originally, this made an 'outlaw' liable to be killed by anyone with impunity. But under quite recent criminal legislation, the law had been changed, and citizens now had a *right* to go into exile. They could not be prevented or killed *en route*.

This was an interesting development. As Cicero indicated (above), the *ūtilitās pūblica* was for Romans the crucial factor in determining the law and its attendant punishments. This may be one reason why an option for a criminal was to be drafted into a gladiatorial troupe. At least he would give the public some (by Roman standards) innocent entertainment, and even (perhaps) set them a fine example of how to die heroically – a common ancient justification for the games. And Cicero remained, at heart, a committed *ūtilitās* man.

But at the same time, Romans were proud of their *hūmānitās*. Given the way they could treat slaves and criminals and foreigners (when it suited them), this may seem utterly bizarre to us, but Romans would have said they were talking about Roman civilisation for civilised people – a categorisation which, by definition, excluded non-citizens like slaves or those not worthy of it like criminals (cf. Caesar's argument, above). Pliny the Elder was admiral of the fleet and died trying to rescue people from the explosion of Vesuvius in AD 79. His everlasting achievement was to write a simply wonderful 'Natural History', an encyclopedia of all things Roman in thirty-seven books, and in it he described Italy as:

> 'nurse and mother of all lands, chosen by the will of the gods to cast light on heaven itself, to unite scattered empires, to moderate lifestyles, to use a common language that

harmonised the discordant and savage tongues of so many peoples, to give mankind *hūmānitās . . .'*

Later, he rejoices over the Romans' destruction of Druidic rites in Britain:

'It cannot be estimated how much is owed to the Romans, who did away with monstrous rites in which killing a man was the highest duty of the pious and eating him the key to good health.'

That was what the Romans meant by *hūmānitās* – bringing civilisation to mankind. Though this was what we said we were intending to bring to our Empire, it is not something that the West, at any rate, is allowed to bring to people these days. Nevertheless, few people outside the West seem to have furious objections to some of our medical, technological, sporting and educational products, like liver transplants, football, university education, surface-to-air missiles, trainers, computers, mobile phones, the internet and baseball hats. Where would Osama bin Laden be without them?

A degree of *hūmānitās* spilled over into Rome's legal thinking. For example, Romans established courts so that provincials who thought they had been badly treated could bring Roman officials to trial. Robert Harris' novel *Imperium* deals with one such case, when Verres, the corrupt governor of Sicily, was brought to trial by Cicero, on the urgings of members of the Sicilian community. If you were a Roman citizen sentenced to death, the emperor Claudius permitted you to choose your own method of dying, to keep your property, be buried and not undergo a humiliating public execution. The crime of treason, because it was directed at one man (the emperor) and not at the whole people, came to be treated with a degree of moderation. When Christians were burned alive as state enemies, there were strong protests at the savagery of the punishment.

But there was never any consistency. There remained a tension in the Roman world between *ūtilitās pūblica* and *hūmānitās*. It was always possible to argue that the death penalty served the latter as well as the former because it would ensure the good conduct of future generations. Meanwhile, one cannot but muse on the concept of 'exile' and feel it would have its uses today. There was any number of desolate islands dotted round the Mediterranean that Rome used for the purpose. It sounds a perfect project for the EU, which would bring much-needed 'jobs' to such areas, while ensuring criminals had the best of everything, including their rights. The islands would prove excellent training grounds for future EU administrators, lawyers, judges and human rights supremos. One could hold the Olympic Games on them.

On the other hand, we could outsource exiles to countries with spare prison capacity. What state are the Gulags in these days? They were officially closed in 1960, but restoring them would make a good training in 'skills' and do wonders for the Russian heritage business. Many were in areas of rich climatological and geological interest, like North-east Siberia and the steppes. For the Roman poet Ovid, exiled by Augustus to Constantsa on the Black Sea coast of Rumania, the experience produced some wonderful poetic outpourings.

One law for the toffs …

In one major respect, however, Roman law was radically different from ours. St Paul was a Greek-speaking Jew from South-east Turkey. The area had been granted Roman citizenship, which Paul duly inherited from his father. In AD 58, Paul was arrested by the Roman authorities in Jerusalem for causing a riot. The commander of the garrison, Claudius Lysias, ordered him to be flogged. While they were tying him up, Paul asked the centurion if it was legal to flog a Roman citizen without trial. The centurion dropped everything and told Claudius.

Claudius too dropped everything and confronted Paul. 'Are you a Roman citizen?' he asked. 'Yes' said Paul. That was that, and Paul was shipped off to Rome for trial – after a fascinating conversation in which Paul said that he was born a citizen, and

Claudius admitted that he had bought his citizenship 'at great price' (he may originally have been a slave in the service of the emperor Claudius).

That was what it meant to be a Roman citizen, and that is the difference between our and Roman law. The sentence someone received under Roman law depended crucially on whether you were free or slave, rich or poor, male or female, citizen or non-citizen. This eventually became crystallised into two broad categories – *honestiōrēs*, 'the better sort' and *humiliōrēs*, 'the lower orders' – though it is impossible to be accurate about who precisely fitted into which category (slaves formed a third grouping).

Here are some legal opinions of the 3rd-century AD jurist Paul:

'Anyone who knowingly and with wrongful intent forges a will ... *honestiōrēs* are deported to an island, *humiliōrēs* are either sent to the mines or crucified.

The Cornelian law imposes a penalty of deportation on anyone who kills someone or walks about with a weapon, etc. It is laid down that in the case of *honestiōrēs* such acts are punished by a capital penalty, but *humiliōrēs* are either crucified or thrown to the beasts.

Under the Julian treason law, anyone at whose instigation arms were taken up against the emperor or the state ... used to be exiled. But now *humiliōrēs* are thrown to the beasts or burnt alive, *honestiōrēs* are punished capitally.'

The issue here is status, and the Romans' fear of humiliating, shameful public degradation. The *honestior* did not evade punishment, but expulsion, deportation and/or confiscation of goods did not propel him into the popular limelight, let alone humiliate him there. Even if he was sentenced to capital punishment, an execution was a comparatively quick and clean death, in the face of which he could win credit by exhibiting proper stoic fortitude. The *humilior*, on the other hand, was sent to the mines, crucified, thrown to the beasts or burnt at the stake; the first a slow death sentence, the last three carried out in public, before mocking crowds in the arena.

The humiliation was increased when such punishments were presented as entertainment. The gladiator, as we shall see, at least had a chance to die nobly, or even win his freedom by performing brilliantly and becoming a popular icon. But Romans developed a taste for executing criminals by staging shows in which they met their death, for example, where a criminal would play the part of Icarus. He was the son of the inventor Daedalus who flew too close to the sun so that when the wax holding his wings together melted he fell into the sea. So the criminal would plunge to his death on the arena from a great height and to the cheers of a delighted crowd.

Romans would therefore have sympathised with the predicament of the *honestior* Lord Archer when he was banged up for four years for perjury and was shocked to find himself living with *criminals* behind bars and steel doors. This is not the way for a Lord to be treated! So he wrote to the Home Secretary to inform him of this appalling state of affairs. Apparently the Home Secretary was already aware of the situation. Still, the brilliant prison-reforming novelist was one up on his great personal friend Charles Dickens, who also wrote novels and was a passionate prison-reformer but never went to prison.

Law enforcement

In the ancient world, where no one was a policeman, everyone was a policeman. This cut both ways. On the one hand, the thought that everyone could be watching and might be prepared to 'have a go' could have been a deterrent; on the other, if the criminals looked numerous and/or nasty enough, there must have been a strong case for turning a blind eye. For all that, community outrage, appeal to local 'bosses' and a culture of revenge may have guaranteed at least some form of victims' 'justice', however summary.

In that situation, making more laws made very little difference. But we are in the same boat, not because the weak are in principle defenceless but because there are so many laws and so few police that it is impossible for the laws to be properly effective (and those police that are around always seem to be doing something else). Two million crimes a year are reported but not followed up. So decent people living helplessly in estates infested with drug- and gang-culture are in a different situation from Romans. Romans had no policemen ordering them not to 'have a go'. So they could always phone up friends and try their luck. In such situations today, where the only deterrence seems to be the cast-iron certainty of detection, the establishment of rewards for bringing and winning a case might play more of a part (cf. p. 106).

There is a rough calculation that 100,000 persistent offenders cause half of all crime. But only 20,000 of these are locked up at any time. Would it not be wonderful if we could take the Platonic view of punishment, i.e. the criminal is ill, and therefore no release until cured? Recently, however, there has been a small step in that direction: the introduction of 'imprisonment for public protection', as a result of which the criminal is freed only when he is no longer considered a significant risk to the public.

>─┼─◆>──O──<◆─┼─<

Reading list

Aristotle, *The Nicomachean Ethics* (Wordsworth Classics 1996).

Richard Baumann, *Crime and Punishment in Ancient Rome* (Routledge 1996).

Livy, *The Early History of Rome* (Penguin 1960).

M.M. Mackenzie, *Plato on Punishment* (California 1981).

Plato, *The Laws* (Penguin 1970).

Plato, *Phaedrus and Letters VII and VIII* (Penguin 1975).

Plato, *The Republic* (World's Classics 1993).

Sallust, *Jugurthine War; Conspiracy of Catiline* (Penguin 1963).

[8]

Celebrity games

Crowd-pullers

The word 'celebrity' comes from the Latin *celeber*, whose basic meaning is 'busy, populous, well attended', i.e. someone or something that attracts the crowds. In the ancient world that meant physical crowds: bums on seats or feet on ground. But in the modern world, with its extensive aural and visual media, which can bring names and faces into every home, virtual bums are good enough. For example, in 2006, calculations based on hits on Google produced the following top ten 'celebrities': 1. Bill Gates 2. Bill Clinton 3. Jesus Christ 4. The Beatles 5. Albert Einstein 6. Jennifer Lopez 7. Paul McCartney 8. Tiger Woods 9. John Lennon 10. Anna Kournikova.

It does not matter that this faintly disgusting collation was put together off the internet, and that it consists of a collection of living and dead sportsmen and women and pop singers, a scientist, a politician, a computer guru and the (by many reckonings) Son of God. (How the ancients would have loved that! 'And now, a big hand for Jupiter, or is it Zeus? Ha ha! Great to see you, by Jove, arf arf. Yes, just take a seat on the sofa beside Elton there, sorry SIR Elton ha ha! He's a big fan of yours, Elton is – oh, and you like Elton too? Great!' 'Thanks, Wossie, and can I say what a great privilege it is to be here? I've always wanted to meet you and, er . . .').

It does not matter either that celebrity-gathering by any other focus group, for example, members of the Joint Association of Classical Teachers, would produce a different list. The conclusion would still be the same, i.e. people are 'celebrities' for no other reason than that sufficiently large numbers of people have turned them into celebrities. The 'celebrities' cannot necessarily be blamed for that. Further, crowds being notoriously fickle, there is no point in trying to draw conclusions about the nature of the celebrity that attracts the crowds. Albert Einstein and Jennifer Lopez? Quite apart from the fact that it must be rather cheapening to be mentioned in the same breath as one who never even had a number 1 record, let alone bottom.

Never, in other words, has a word been more accurately derived. But we can be a little more discriminatory than that. Crowds can generate celebrities who:

1 do not *set out* to be celebrities – for example, Einstein – but have it thrust upon them. These are people with serious achievements under their belts, for whom celebrity status is an unintended, irrelevant and possibly unwelcome by-product of their achievements.
2 desire to be celebrities because it is good for the business they are in, such as pop stars and film stars. These people have trivial achievements under their belt, but they are at least achievements.
3 have no worth, merit or achievement of any sort whatsoever: for example, Tony Benn and participants on the TV show *Big Brother*. For such people, recognition is a fulfilling end in itself.

Ancient celebs

The ancient world can boast plenty of celebrities under the first two categories. Socrates would be a good example of no. 1. He did not seek followers, but when young men in particular (we are told) saw him making fools of the great and good in Athens with his relentlessly sharp and probing questions, they flocked to him.

In the second, most populous, category would come the 'sophists', freelance professional educators, who charged hefty fees both for teaching the young and giving seminars and displays of public eloquence. These were Athens' TV academics, the David Attenboroughs, Patrick Moores, Simon Schamas and David Starkeys of their day.

Take Prodicus, from the island of Ceos, born about 460 BC. He had a reputation for love of money, an expensive lifestyle and generally exhibitionist behaviour, and knew the big bucks were in Athens, where he came regularly to declaim and teach. His lectures on the correct use of words were especially famous. Socrates went along to them, and (ironically) wished he had been able to afford the full fifty-drachma course as opposed to the one-drachma show he managed to attend. Aristotle, discussing how to hold an audience's attention, recommended Prodicus' tactic of 'slipping in a fifty-drachma touch when the audience begins to nod off'.

Actors too had virtual pop-singer status (and, incidentally, freedom of travel and immunity from military service, so important a part of communal life were they felt to be). Like Bianca Jagger, film star and one-time wife of the lead singer of the Rolling Stones who is a goodwill ambassador for the Council of Europe and heavily involved in Amnesty International, and 'Spice Girl' Geri Halliwell, who became a goodwill ambassador for the UN, well known ancient Greek actors were used to promote causes on embassies. Neoptolemus and other famous thespians were used as ambassadors by Philip II of Macedon (father of Alexander the Great) in his clash with Athens, and attracted the scorn of the great Athenian patriot, orator and statesman Demosthenes. But the biggest stars in the ancient world were the sportsmen, winners of the Olympic Games, the most hotly contested and prestigious Games of them all.

Olympic heroes

The ancient Greek for 'contest, competition' is *agōn* (root of our 'agony'). It was used of games, battles, dramatic festivals (where plays were in competition with each other) actions at law and speeches, and originally seems to have meant 'a crowd gathered to watch a contest'. That, in Greek eyes, was the point: competition meant nothing unless it was engaged in public, because it was only when people witnessed your victory that you could gain the glory that you longed for.

Modern-day sportsmen, for whom games played behind closed doors are a peculiarly exquisite kind of torture, are celebrated by appearing in advertisements and having things named after them ('Shearer's' is a bar in Newcastle United's stadium). Ancient Games' winners and their sponsors paid sculptors to put up statues of them for public display (that is why the ancient site of Olympia was full of them) and commissioned poets like Pindar to celebrate their achievements in song and dance in their hometowns. In his poems, Pindar pointed out that winners came as close to divinity as any man could hope – we know the 'worship' bestowed by fans on modern sportsmen – while the losers kept quiet about the fact: Pindar described them as having no glad homecoming, but creeping along the back alleys, keeping well out of the way of their enemies.

No Greek liked to be laughed at in public, and losers knew that was the fate that could await them. Satirical stories abound of hopeless athletes like Charmos, who came seventh in a field of six (a friend who ran on to encourage him beat him) and Marcus, so slow that the groundsman locked him in the stadium for the night, thinking he was a statue. It is said that the prospect of public humiliation drove the England rugby team to greater heights than anyone could have hoped after being thrashed 36–0 by South Africa in the first game of the World Cup in 2007. Athenians must also have been encouraged by their city's habit of honouring victors with cash rewards, a lifetime's meals at public expense, the best seats at the theatre and tax exemptions. MBEs are routinely doled out to our sportsmen who win something important.

All must (not) have prizes

It says something for our contrasting attitude towards sport that Eddie the Eagle was a public hero. Greeks would not have put up with him – an insult to Zeus (p. 184). The ancient Olympic Games Committee demanded that all contestants turn up at Olympia a month in advance to train and to show that they were up to scratch. Obvious failures were sent home. Likewise, a contestant who, seeing what the competition was like, knew that he had no chance, could find some excuse to abandon his entry. This was very common in the contact sports like boxing and all-in wrestling. Inscriptions survive announcing that so-and-so had won first prize *akonīti*, 'without dust' – i.e. without actually competing: all his rivals had taken one look and slipped away.

Hence no Greek said 'It's the taking part that counts', or 'Everyone's a winner'. The Greek *āthlētēs* means 'one who competes for a prize', not 'one who partakes'. Winning was the whole point; everyone but the actual winner was a loser. There were no prizes for second or third in the Games. Were this system and culture adopted, small countries would be saved vast sums of money and much pointless effort. It would also save the spectators the endless tedium of 'heats'. The Olympics are not like school, where anyone who does not win a prize will obviously be scarred for life.

Picking the winner

Ancient Greeks got it right in another respect: the relationship between driver and management in the really expensive sports, like Formula 1. We tend to become outraged when management tells racing drivers what to do. At the Austrian Grand Prix in 2002, for example, the Ferrari driver Rubens Barrichello was ordered by management to pull over and let his world champion team-mate Michael Schumacher win. In the 2007 championship, there were tales of conflict between the management of the McLaren team and their two star drivers, the experienced Fernando Alonso (who thought he should be given priority) and the rookie (British) pretender Lewis Hamilton (who did quite well too).

The parallel here with the equine events in the Olympic Games is striking. They required phenomenal outlay – horses, stables, chariots, etc. – and were therefore the prerogative only of the rich. As a result, chariot victories carried by far the greatest prestige of all. But the crucial point is that when it came to celebrating the winner, the poet Pindar sang the glory not of the jockey or chariot-driver, but of the *owner*. Winning was down to the horses. The jockey/driver was merely a technician. He did what he was told – or was out of a job. (We even hear of a horse, Breeze, that threw its rider at the start but still won in superb style and was duly given the prize.) As a result, Pindar's odes for equestrian victors concentrated not on the jockey/rider's skill but on the glory the owner had gained, his great wealth and his willingness to spend it on a good cause.

It was the owner who made horse racing possible. It was the owner, therefore, who ran the show and took the credit. The same is true of Formula 1. The drivers, sitting behind their funny little steering wheels going brrm brrm, may be brave and brilliant technicians, but that is all they are. Only their lives and reputation are at stake. But the owners' money is at stake. That is far more important. So in relation to the owners, the drivers know their place. Nowhere.

But at least Greeks were spared one ghastly feature of modern sport: athletes were not plastered all over with logos and advertisements. How could they be? They competed stark naked. Well, one *hopes* they could not have been, but no doubt a modern advertising guru would leap at the chance to advertise – well, one shudders to think what, let alone where.

Stop it at once!

Sex also raises its weary head. Apparently lorry-loads of contraceptives have to be shovelled daily into great bunkers in the Olympic villages where the athletes stay; and discussions in the papers are intense about the effect of their WAGS on footballers before a big game.

Greeks would have thoroughly disapproved. This was because semen was identified as the vital constituent of male strength. The doctor Aretaeus (1st century AD) says:

'If any man is in possession of semen, he is fierce, courageous and physically mighty, like beasts. Evidence for this is to be found in athletes who practise abstinence.'

Even involuntary nocturnal emissions were thought to be enfeebling, threatening one's endurance and breathing. The thinker Philostratus (3rd century AD) says in his *Gymnastikos* that those who have had one

'should take exercise carefully and build up their strength more than usual, since they now have a deficit in their system ... their workouts should be easy to do but spread out over a longer period of time, so that their lungs may be exercised.'

Prevention, however, is better than cure, and the doctor Galen (2nd century AD) recommends that athletes take precautions against them:

'a flattened lead plate is an object to be placed under the muscles of the loins of an athlete in training, chilling them whenever they might have nocturnal emissions of semen.'

Some athletes refused to tolerate even the mention of sex in their presence, walking out of the room when the conversation turned that way (if that were common practice today, not a single match of any sort at any level would ever take place). The pankratiast Cleitomachus is said to have averted his gaze when he saw two dogs mating. Even so, in the homoerotic atmosphere of the ancient gymnasium, the naked athletes were aware of the temptations. Infibulation, tying up the foreskin, may have been practised in an attempt to avoid the embarrassment of over-excitement in the heat of the moment.

The critics

By Roman times there were hundreds of Games round the Mediterranean out of which top athletes, by now thoroughly professionalised, could take their pick. Indeed, Rome was happy to see look-alike 'Olympic' games franchised out to parts of the

Eastern empire (e.g. Alexandria and Ephesus. The Premier League was hoping to pull off the same sort of trick by staging an extra league soccer fixture every year at a venue outside the UK). There were even guilds of athletes doing the circuit like the Harlem Globetrotters, some demanding appearance money (nothing new there, then).

As today, great sporting heroes were enormously popular, among men and gods. One Theagenes from Thasos was unbeaten in 22 years and apparently won 1,400 titles in all, and on his death the Thasians erected a statue of him. A rival attacked it, and was killed when the statue toppled over onto him. The statue was found guilty of murder and dumped in the sea. When a famine hit the town, however, the oracle at Delphi said it must be recovered. It was, developed healing powers and for eight hundred years had sacrifices made to it. (The base, fitted with metal rings to ensure no one could steal it, can still be seen today.) So any Sunderland supporter who attacks the statue of the Newcastle footballer Jackie Milburn set up in his hometown of Ashington had better watch out.

But athletes also attracted criticism, as sport still does. Today's vast salaries and grovelling adulation of players, generating their enormous self-importance, were even in those days the subject of comment, as was the inability of many of them to think about life beyond sport. The Greek doctor Galen made the point:

'Perhaps it is because they make such huge sums of money, much more than anyone else, that athletes put on airs. And yet you can see for yourself that they are all in debt, not only when they are playing but when they retire.'

Winning was pooh-poohed by the 6th-century BC Greek poet and thinker Xenophanes, who pointed out that, however much the victor at the Games was honoured,

'the city would not thereby be better governed, nor its granaries filled.'

Aristotle thought:

'the athlete's style of bodily fitness does nothing for the general purposes of civic life, nor does it encourage ordinary health or the procreation of children. Some exercise is essential, but it must be neither violent nor specialised, as is the case with athletes.'

So when the minister for schools recommends that frisbees and yoga would be a good exercise for children, Aristotle would be on his side (unless, of course, they became part of the Olympics, another feature of the modern Games that Greeks would have thought deranged: the vast increase in types of sport allowed, from beach volleyball to synchronised swimming). Cicero was even more contemptuous of Games: when Milo, a famous wrestler grown old, saw young men practising and lamented that his own arms were now dead, Cicero said

'No, you fool, *you* are dead, since your nobility came not from yourself but from your arms and legs.'

As for the stadia and the horrendous costs involved (cf. p. 23), the ancient Greeks knew far better. For the 1,200 years of their existence, the Olympic Games were held every four years in exactly the same place, a sanctuary of Olympian Zeus in a backwater of the Western Peloponnese, thus avoiding today's fatuous and corrupt competition between cities to stage the Games. The overall judgement, then, of Greeks critical of the Games rather hits the nail on the head – unproductive, unhealthy, ignoble and pauperising.

Gossip columns

There is another feature of the modern celeb which has its parallel in the ancient world: people's fascination with their private lives (see *Heat* magazine, biographies of Princess Diana and so endlessly on). The essayist Plutarch points out that anyone who becomes a politician must watch it because

'men in public life are responsible for more than their public words and actions: their dinners, beds, marriages, amusements and interests are all objects of curiosity.'

This is never better exemplified than in the public servant and historian Suetonius' *Lives of the Caesars*, which are full of the most splendid tittle-tattle one could imagine about the emperors and their associates.

Did you know that, even in old age, Augustus still had a passion for deflowering young girls, collected for him by his wife? That Caligula committed incest with each of his three sisters in turn? That Claudius planned to legitimise farting at table? That Nero would prowl the streets at night, stabbing people and throwing them into the sewers? That Galba introduced tightrope-walking elephants? That Vitellius never feasted out for less than 4,000 gold pieces? That Domitian was such a good archer that from a distance he could shoot arrows between the splayed fingers of his slaves? Read Suetonius. It is all there.

The reason for all this wonderful stuff is not merely public gullibility and love of a good scandal. The point is that the imperial court (unlike senatorial politics in the republican era) was a closed shop, inhabited by the emperor and his intimate associates, and no one else. That sort of system is bound to generate rumour, because nothing else is available. It is exactly the same with contemporary politics, never better exemplified than by Tony Blair's sofa- and Gordon Brown's throne-style of government. Whatever happens in public, the real business is done in private among a closed circle of friends and advisors. Since the media have nothing else to go on, gossip is the order of the day, wherever it comes from. Hence all the stuff about Cherie Blair, Carol Caplin and so on.

Gladiator chic

The Roman equivalents of the sporting celebrity was the gladiator (chariot-drivers too, but I shall concentrate on the gladiator). Gladiators ('sword-men', Latin *gladius*, 'sword') were outsiders, criminals or slaves trained up to bring amusement to the populace by killing and being killed. As Rome's rather nasty foundation myth suggests – Mars, god of war, fathering Romulus and Remus, who are suckled by a wolf and raised by shepherds in the wild – the Romans had no qualms about the inhuman. But gladiators could be seen as more than bloody entertainment fodder.

In 221 BC, in a funeral speech for his father, a son listed the achievements that made him outstanding, and at the head of the list, above wisdom, glory and high office, stood 'he wanted to be a warrior of the first rank'. In the Roman legion, that meant an expert at single combat. Gladiators exemplified that *virtus* in a particularly uncompromising way. They had no other *virtus* to offer. But Cicero conceded that there could be 'no better schooling against pain and death' than gladiatorial contests. Pliny the Younger argued that that such contests offered the public 'nothing to weaken manly spirits' but inspired them to

'face honourable wounds and look scornfully on death by demonstrating a love of glory and desire for victory even in the persons of criminals and slaves.'

If inferiors could set such an example, how much better would free citizens do it?

This was part of what it meant to be Roman. As the empire spread, so did local enthusiasm to stage games and prove local communities had got what it took. One sees the same thing happening across the British empire. The introduction of a game like cricket was a way of exporting British values and ways of doing things, fair play, umpires, cream teas and all, to the grateful barbarian.

Brutalising games

There were dissenting voices. The philosopher Seneca, who was disgusted by the brutalising effect of the games on the viewer, said:

'in the morning they throw men to the animals, but in the afternoon they throw them to the spectators'

and talks of the crowd *egging on* the stewards when the gladiators were not putting on much of a show with cries of 'Kill him! Lash him! Burn him!' and, when the intermission came, 'Can't we have a little throat-cutting to pass the time?' After watching such a spectacle, Seneca concludes,

'I come home more greedy, ambitious, voluptuous, cruel and inhuman.'

All this reminds us of the arguments surrounding boxing today and other brutal contact sports. At least today such contests are controlled by law between boxers of (apparently) similar weights and abilities. The bottom line, however, is that, then as now, such shows were *public entertainment*. What the public wanted was action and lots of it. Gladiator troupes were run by promoters, and a successful troupe, while it could be highly lucrative, was a very expensive investment. Gladiators had to be bought, trained how to fight for their lives and to fight well, equipped, fed, housed and transported. They could even be transferred from one troupe to another. It was the world of the professional footballer.

And when the public did not get a good show, the gladiators paid for it. We hear of some fighters 'so old and decrepit they would have fallen over if you blew on them'. They were flogged after the show for putting on such a pathetic performance. Modern audiences do not hesitate to show their disapproval if similar performances are put on in the ring.

Making good

By the same token, as first-rate 'entertainers' gladiators could win the favour of the crowds. In replicating the fighting so dear to the heart of all Romans, the outcome of that fighting was also replicated – death or *glory*.

So while gladiators were seen as the lowest of the low, the

successful were hugely admired. As a result, the gladiator who became a crowd favourite could make a fortune in prize-money put up by the show's promoter, win his freedom and retire. Their performances were keenly discussed by fans, and graffiti were common, both eulogising them ('Celadus makes all the girls sigh', 'Crescens holds the hearts of all the girls') and picturing them in action. The satirist Juvenal takes up the theme: 'All women adore the sword', he moans, well aware of the *double entendre*, and anticipating today's heart-throb sportsmen like, we are assured, the French rugby 'caveman' Sébastien Chabal.

Though gladiators could not hold the copyright on their image as today's sportsmen can, entrepreneurs understood their worth and a whole industry grew up around them. Souvenir shops sold knives, lamps and pottery with scenes from the amphitheatre; their images were carried on everything from mirrors to perfume containers and babies' bottles.

The result of all of this was that those who put their money into the business did not want to see lots of dead gladiators. Nor did the crowds. They came to see a terrific fight, and if they got one, they did not want to see the loser killed. They wanted to see him fight again. *Missi*, 'let off, discharged', is frequently found in inscriptions listing what happened to the gladiators in any one set of games. There is good evidence from gladiatorial lists that combat was not the outright bloodbath that Hollywood would have us believe, any more than modern-day wrestling results in the broken limbs that always seem to threaten. This is business: you do not want your star turns injured or, even worse, dead.

Political celebs

At the start of this chapter I defined three categories of celebrity, of which the third was people who had achieved nothing at all but had become famous simply for being recognised, usually through fortuitous media appearances. It is extremely difficult to find any serious parallels for this in the ancient world. You had to have achieved something to become a celebrity in the ancient world:

you had to be famous for something other than merely being famous.

What one does find, however, is important political figures in Rome using their wealth and influence to try to become stars in the popular entertainment world. This, it seems to me, is quite rare in the modern world. Boris Johnson may appear on *Have I Got News for You?* but Gordon Brown is not in training for an appearance on *Strictly Come Dancing,* nor does Her Majesty plan to hold down her own tightly scripted breakfast show. Princess Anne, it is true, is an Olympic rider, but that is because she is very good at it, as is Prince Philip at carriage driving (he has represented Great Britain in World and European championships).

The emperor Nero, however, was convinced he was a supreme instrumental and operatic star and athlete, and set about demonstrating it. And when the emperor laid his credentials, however non-existent, on the table, people tended to find them extremely impressive. Since Greece was the home of culture in the ancient world, it was there that Nero went to display his talents, and as artist, aesthete, showman and PR man, he certainly was a tremendous hit with the locals. Indeed, in AD 66–67 one ancient historian tells us he carried off 1,808 first prizes at the various arts and athletic festivals he attended! Not stupid, the Greeks; and Nero responded in kind, liberating the Greeks from Roman rule and Roman taxation. As we have seen (p. 67), his last words were 'Dead – and what an artist!'. Aristocratic Romans held him in utter contempt for this pandering to the likes of actors and sportsmen.

It is ironic that the one role Nero could not play was that of emperor. It is equally ironic that the modern world has reversed the Roman practice. Then, political figures yearned to become stars (the emperor Commodus, with his passion for gladiatorial combat, is another example). Nowadays, stars yearn to become political figures. Think Ronald Regan, Arnold Schwarzenegger and our own Glenda Jackson.

It is easy to see why. Something else you rarely find in the ancient world is the 'Cool Britannia' phenomenon of the Tony Blair period, when pop stars, films stars, artists and sportsmen were invited to unfold their thoughts on the Great Issues of the day and were listened to with the sort of reverence and humility one might have accorded to the views of a Pericles or Marcus Aurelius (but cf. p. 152, and Mick Jagger, p. 219). One cannot think that artists would listen with similar respect to David Miliband's views on art.

One can conclude only that the world of the arts and sports, film and pop music has become too professional for amateurs these days. Politics is the one arena left in which the amateur can flourish. One notes that the new prime minister of Thailand, Samak Sundaravej, is a TV cook. He does not, apparently, plan to give up his show.

>─┼◆>─O─<◆┼─<

Reading list

Edward Champlin, *Nero* (Harvard 2003).
Mark Golden, *Sport in the Ancient World from A to Z* (Routledge 2004).
Keith Hopkins and Mary Beard, *The Colosseum* (Profile 2005).
E. Köhne and C. Ewigleben (eds.), *Gladiators and Caesars* (British Museum 2000).
Nigel Spivey, *The Ancient Olympics* (Oxford 2004).
Thomas Wiedemann, *Emperors and Gladiators* (Routledge 1992).

[9]

War and peace

The end of the glory days?

In 2003 it was revealed that two British commandos from the Special Boat Service had escaped capture in Iraq by trekking some hundred miles across mountainous terrain, by night, to the Syrian border. Who were they? Nobody knows, nor will know.

The SBS's motto is 'Not by force, but by guile'. This is a truly classical antithesis. In the epics of Homer, we hear of a debate about how Troy will be taken, whether by force or trickery, and in the end we know it is taken by trickery – the trick of the Wooden Horse. The Wooden Horse was the idea of Odysseus, the ultimate tricky hero, who after the war engaged in endless deceptions on his epic journey home to his wife Penelope; the contrast with the ultimate impulsive man of violence Achilles is marked.

But one attitude to war, the opposite of the SBS's, links both Odysseus and Achilles: the determination that men shall *know* of their heroic deeds. The Homeric hero, for example, risked life and limb to remove the armour of the opponents he had killed in battle. He needed the visible evidence that he had done so to reap the full benefit back home. For that is the only route to *kleos*, the reputation for greatness that lives on after death – man's only hope of immortality.

The modesty of so many of today's soldiers is a very striking difference. Obituary writers of those who served with supreme bravery in the Second World War are constantly amazed how frequently a family will know very little indeed about their father's or husband's heroic achievements. Perhaps the experience of the First and Second World Wars – arguably the first in which *everyone* experienced catastrophic loss, winners and losers alike – has in many ways removed the 'glory' from it.

Those wars may explain why we in the West think of war differently now. We are currently living in a longer period of continuous peace than any in the whole of our history, and rather agreeable it is too: each of us does not have to be prepared, quite literally, to fight an enemy hand-to-hand in order to survive. Anti-war movements and media disdain for the military are common-place. If war is declared, we demand not only that it be a just war, but that there be just behaviour *in* war. So for the soldier, warfare must now sometimes seem more like lawfare, such are the legal chains that seem to bind his every move. But at least such re-strictions probably do more to create the conditions in which a war can be said to be 'just' than any amount of theorizing (see box). That said, when fighting successfully was the single pre-condition of *every society's existence* in the ancient world, one can understand why there was little room for niceties. *Inter arma silent lēgēs*, 'In battle, laws fall silent', as Cicero said, broadly (actually, with the words in a different order and an introductory *enim* 'because', i.e. *silent enim lēgēs inter arma*). Only if the enemy is equally nice can one afford to be nice oneself. Soon our soldiers will have to ask for the enemies' signed agreement (in triplicate) to be shot.

Killer beliefs

Ancients, however, would be astonished that we are currently fighting wars over religion: or at least, that religious motives are driving the forces against us. With few exceptions (the Old Testa-ment and Rome's battles with the Jews from AD 66 until their final diaspora in AD 135), such wars were not fought in the ancient world because no humans thought gods would be offended by the exist-ence of other gods. For example, when Romans captured a new place, they immediately sacrificed to the local deities. So in Britain we find an altar to Campestres (the Roman parade-ground gods), Mars, Minerva, Hercules, Victoria and – Epona. Who? A local horse-god. An altar to the 'Spirit of Augustus' has 'Vanauns' attached to it, whoever, or whatever, he may be. This, explains Minucius Felix (3rd century AD), is why Rome was so successful; they brought local gods on side at once. Ancients would wonder why Americans had not done the same in Iraq.

The seeds of religious wars are to be found in the development of the idea of the one true god who insists on no other gods but him. That was fine as long as it was kept local (Yahweh, for example, seemed content as long as the Jews had no other gods). But the Christian church took a different attitude. All nations had to worship Him, with rewards for believers, if not in this life, then in the next, and damnation for non-believers, a cry taken up with renewed fervour by Islam after its beginnings in the 7th century AD. Islamic extremists continue to take the view that those who do not worship their version of god must be murdered, guaranteeing the murderers a glorious afterlife.

Greeks and Romans would have thought all this madness beyond belief: what sort of god was it who wanted to prevent fellow gods being worshipped? And why (as Cicero said) did a god need humans to protect him or her? Gods were perfectly capable of avenging themselves (grounds on which Cicero might have defended the blasphemy laws – who knows what punishment an irate deity might impose?).

Most important, the ancients were very keen on aligning their own gods with those in other cultures. Here is an eastern goddess Astarte. She is a sex goddess. She must be the same as Aphrodite. So it would have been self-evident to them that the Christian God and Allah were exactly the same god (as, indeed, they are). This would have made attacks by believers in the one on believers in the other quite incomprehensible, and (even worse) infuriating to God too, who was thereby losing worshippers.

The just war

Popular wisdom has it that St Augustine first outlined the case for the 'just war'. But the Roman statesman and philosopher Cicero got there before him. In his *dē officiīs* ('On Obligations', 44 BC), Cicero argues as follows:

'There are two ways of settling a dispute, by discussion or by force. However, the former is characteristic of man, the latter of animals. So we must resort to force only when discussion is no longer possible. The only excuse for going to war is that one may live in peace, unharmed.'

He now lays down the various conditions:

- No war will be just unless (i) an official demand for satisfaction has been submitted, or (ii) a warning has been given and (iii) a formal declaration made.
- Cicero distinguishes between wars fought for the sake of survival, and wars fought for the sake of *imperium* ('rule, control'). In the latter, *glōria* is at stake. Both must be justified in accordance with his original principles, but wars of *imperium* must be fought 'with less bitterness'.
- The victors have a duty to treat the vanquished mercifully – as long as the vanquished have themselves acted without cruelty or barbarism.
- Only legally enlisted soldiers can fight.
- All promises must be strictly observed.

It is noticeable that Cicero sees that (i) the interests of Rome are the sole justification for war, and (ii) both self-defence and expansion of empire are sufficient motives for action. Such a vision suited the most powerful state in the ancient world. Cicero's call for mercy for those of the enemy who decide to agree with Rome is equally self-serving. As he goes on to say, Rome's ultimate aim is 'peace without treachery'. Rome needed all the friends it could get.

Virgil talks of Rome's mission as 'pardoning the defeated

and warring down the proud'. Rome, however, decided
who fell into which category. All very von Rumsfeld.

Laconic words

Given the conditions under which war is fought, one can understand why there is a long-established military culture of 'action,
not words' among soldiers. Colonel Tim Collins's brief but
pointed address (c. 500 words, about four minutes' worth) before
leading his troops into battle in Iraq is a case in point. For the
soldier, the fewer and punchier the words, the better. The great
masters here were the Spartans (who lived in Laconia), famous in
the ancient world for their cracking military one-liners – morale-
boosters (so important in battle) to make the spine tingle. When
Panthoidas, visiting Asia, was shown a great defensive wall, he
commented: 'Magnificent women's quarters'. When the three
hundred Spartans defending Thermopylae were told by the
Persians that their arrows would blot out the sky, Dieneces replied
'Excellent. Then we shall fight in the shade'. King Agis used to
remark that he never knew how *many* the enemy were – just *where*
they were. Even the Spartan women joined in – most famously
ordering their sons to return either with their shield or on it.
When one young man complained to his mother that his sword
was too short, she replied 'Then lengthen it by a stride'. The
shortest soundbite in history occurred when an enemy embassy
announced that they were about to invade Laconia and if they
succeeded, Sparta would be razed. The Spartans replied 'If'.

But the ancients were not automatically gung-ho for battle.
When in the *Iliad* a duel between Paris (who stole Menelaus' wife
Helen and started the Trojan War) and Menelaus is set up to
decide the conflict one way or another, Greeks and Trojans alike
cheer with relief. In Homer, Ares, the god of war, (Latin Mars) is
the most hated god of all, and war is constantly described with
the epithet 'with its many tears' as well as 'where men win glory'.
The 5th-century BC Greek historian Herodotus puts in the mouth

of the defeated king Croesus of Lydia the following terrible words:

> 'No one is so stupid as to prefer war to peace. In peace, sons
> bury their fathers; in war, fathers bury their sons.'

Don't families still know it? Pericles said of the death of young
Athenians in battle:

> 'The spring has gone out of the year.'

War in the ancient world was business – every man's business, as
the Trojan hero Hector put it, especially his. There was no option
if you wanted to survive. Rome's war against Hannibal makes
that point – and the even more important point that, as the British
in Northern Ireland, Iraq and Afghanistan already know, and
America is fast finding out, an enemy must *agree* that it has been
defeated before victory has been gained. When in 2003 President
Bush stood on the deck of *USS Abraham Lincoln* and announced
'major combat operations in Iraq have ended', the Iraqi resistance
did not, unfortunately, agree.

Hannibalic lessons

The first war between Rome and Carthage (264–241 BC) was
fought over Sicily. It is called the first Punic war because Carthage
was originally a colony in North Africa founded from (modern)
Lebanon, the land of peoples whom the Greeks called *Phoinikes*
(Phoenicians). 'Ph' was sounded in Greek as in 'top hat', and that
word was romanised into *Punici* (the –*es* plural ending in Greek
being replaced by the –*i* plural in Latin).

Carthage failed to exploit its superiority at sea and when it sued
for peace, Rome turned Sicily, Sardinia and Corsica into its first
provinces (the Roman Empire starts here). Carthage, hit by a
gigantic indemnity and with inflation rampant, shifted its overseas
power base to the silver-rich south of Spain, and in 218 BC the
second Punic war began when Hannibal marched his army and
elephants from Spain, over the Rhone, across the Alps and down
into northern Italy.

Hannibal was banking on his tough, experienced army; his own brilliantly innovative generalship; and (the great imponderable) his ability to win Italians to his cause. He made a terrifying start, crushing the Roman army at Trebia (218 BC), Trasimene (217 BC) and, most devastatingly of all, further south at Cannae (216 BC). After such victories, he had every reason to expect Rome to surrender.

But the Romans did not *agree* that they had been defeated, and poured money and manpower into proving it. They learned from observing Hannibal's tactics: how he lured the enemy into fighting on terrain advantageous to himself, how he hit the legions (used to fighting front on) from the side. They saw that the way to deal with him was to harry and worry him, not confront him. They needed to prevent Hannibal being reinforced, so they ensured their coastline was secure.

By the same token, they took ruthless reprisals against Italians who defected to him: since Hannibal could not be everywhere at once in Italy, they waited for Hannibal to move on and then took revenge on the defectors. Finally, and most brilliantly and courageously of all, they took the battle to the Carthaginians where Hannibal was not, i.e. Spain and eventually North Africa. Serious military thinkers, the Romans.

None of this could have been done without overwhelming manpower: a citizen army that could be constantly replenished after terrible losses. It was a matter of survival. It was business. In what was now a war of attrition on enemy soil, an unsupported Hannibal could never win. In 203 BC, claiming to have killed 300,000 Romans and sacked 400 towns, Hannibal reluctantly returned to Carthage, where he was defeated by Scipio at Zama in 202 BC. And from then on, Rome had an experienced citizen army at the ready for anything – the ultimate enforcer.

After Cannae, with 50,000 Roman corpses covering a few square miles of open plain, Hannibal's cavalry leader Maharbal said to him *vincere scīs, Hannibal, victōriā ūtī nescīs*, 'You know how to win, Hannibal, but not how to use your victory'. Whatever Hannibal did, he could not persuade the Romans to agree that they had been defeated. Taliban and al-Qaeda are of precisely the same persuasion. Experts at hit-and-run, able to replenish forces at will and moving the enemy around difficult terrain in a war of attrition on (for their opponents) unfamiliar soil, they are fighting a very Romanesque war.

Afghan Alexander

Alexander the Great found out about this style of fighting when, having finally defeated Darius III and his Persian army in 329 BC – the purpose of his expedition – he pushed into Afghanistan (Bactria/Sogdia, as it was then) to pursue the leader of the Persian resistance, Bessus. Bessus was duly turned in by his treacherous Bactrian lieutenant Spitamenes.

But Alexander needed to feed his army and secure his rear, and did so by plundering widely and garrisoning the main villages. Further, he refused to allow the locals to do what they had always done in relation to their war dead, i.e. leave their bodies in the field for vultures to consume. All this raised the locals to revolt, and when Alexander decided to turn to Spitamenes for suggestions about how to deal with it, he found that Spitamenes was the ringleader. The furious Alexander immediately sent 2,000 troops to Samarkand to sort him out. Knowing the terrain, Spitamenes laid an ambush. It was a massacre. Alexander at once mustered 7,000 elite troops and raced 180 miles across the desert in three days (!) to take revenge. He searched up and down for him but found, precisely, nothing.

The guerrilla attacks continued for nearly three years. Spitamenes kept on the move, making alliances where he could in an area which Alexander increasingly dominated, and attacking at speed and without warning – surprise raids on garrisons, ambushes and instant retreats into the desert where he could not be followed. The result was that Alexander effectively gave up, simply ordering the troops in Spitamenes' territory to keep a lookout 'on the chance of laying a trap for him, in case he should be riding round in the neighbourhood.'

It was not often that he was reduced to such a counsel of despair. Spitamenes was finally nailed only when his troops felt his luck had run out, beheaded him and sent his head to Alexander as a gesture of friendship.

A fiercely independent tribal world, with its own way of doing things which we have to learn, where guerrilla warfare is incessant, executed at speed in very difficult terrain, fought by a people whose capacity for endurance is matched only by their hatred of foreigners and where no alliance can be guaranteed – there are situations in which the 'lessons of history' for our troops there are more than wishful thinking.

One lesson in particular is being taken on board fast: that local tribes can be turned against each other. This makes the recent decision to send home two western officials because they have been having discussions with tribes that 'are perhaps undecided whether they are supportive of the government of Afghanistan' look like complete madness. In his conquest of Gaul, Julius Caesar was constantly in touch with local tribal leaders, willing in principle to strike deals with them, even though he thereby deprived himself of the possibility of the plunder and slaves on which he was so keen.

Keeping onside

Another lesson should be taken on board faster, though it does ultimately depend on willing cooperation. The Roman Empire to the West had a secure boundary – the Atlantic Ocean. To the North there was the Rhine-Danube, to the South the Sahara desert. To the East – Iraq, Persia – there was no such natural barrier, and Romans played it by ear in deciding where, precisely, the cut-off point should be.

The bottom line was to ensure that everything within the limits of the empire was safe and secure (the main purpose of, for example, Hadrian's Wall, which announced 'Civilisation this side, Scotsmen that side'). Clearly the military had an important part to play in the earliest stages of provincialisation, and bringing locals into the Roman army was a central element in Roman tactics. Effective civilian administration came next, and here the key was bringing onboard those local elites who had always run it, with orders to carry on the good work under the generally light touch of overall Roman supervision. This was crucial. No state likes to be invaded anyway – that is humiliation enough – let alone run by someone else. So, for example, it was disastrous for the Americans to have destroyed the existing institutional structures when they first moved into Iraq. The result is that the West has been perceived as working not with but against people's interests. Rome would never have done that.

Most important of all, however, was Roman investment in infrastructure, especially roads, i.e. reliable and fast means of communication. The reason is straightforward: this was the way to plant on the doorstep of those inside and *outside* the limits of empire all the economic, political and military resources of the Mediterranean world. The point is that areas at the limits of empire did not suddenly stop trading with those outside. What the Romans wanted to do was to show those outside what enormous benefits there were for them in having the Romans on their doorstep. For Romans simply did not have enough legions to be able to impose rule by force from Britain to Syria. So the only way the empire could succeed was if it was able to persuade those it provincialised or dealt with that, on balance, the benefits outweighed the disadvantages.

When the West too can prove its interventions have had this effect in Iraq, its problems will begin to end. True, it will take a huge effort to bring their economies into the fold of the global economy, and that will not be achieved until law and order are restored. That is the key; and that – on the self-governing principle – must be done by Iraqis, not Americans. So it can start to happen securely only when the West has left. When Western businessmen start flooding into Iraq, the job will be done.

Eventually, after all the bloodshed, economics will win.

No less important for Romans were deals with local monarchs, the *socii et amici*, 'friends and allies', as they were called, of the Roman emperor. They too were lured by the prospect of having the Roman Empire on their side, and were not unaware of the advantages of having ties, even distant ones, with the emperor himself. Elite Romans made their way in Rome by their ability to establish good 'client' relationships with a wide range of people (the Mafia comes to mind here). They transferred this skill to working up 'client' relationships with often resource-rich foreigners too. So, for all the difficulties it can generate, Americans are doing precisely the right thing in trying to bring into alliance those territories bordering the areas of conflict in which they are currently engaged (e.g. President Musharraf of Pakistan).

Cooperation and trust are central. The Americans are doing something else right in going into battle together with the new Iraqi army. It is no coincidence that the Greek for 'treaty' was *summachiā*, 'fighting together'. The cast-iron agreement to wage war *together* against anyone who attacked any of the treaty's signatories – in some treaties the clause 'having the same friends and enemies' is added – was absolutely critical to the establishment of trust between former enemies. (When will the British Army open a recruiting centre in South Armagh?)

Of course the Romans would have thought it madness to train up a local army beside their own, but that was because they were usually taking over states, and not intervening in sovereign territories with an intention of eventually withdrawing. As we have seen (above), what Romans did was to bring locals in large numbers into the *Roman* army. Indeed, the only way they maintained their vast empire was by recruiting locally for the simple reason that there were not enough Romans or Italians to go round. All the same, since the British army in particular urgently needs to recruit, why not recruit Afghanis and Iraqis? The Roman army was a powerful means of teaching locals the Roman way and acting as a stepping stone for them into Roman society (see box, p. 73). On the other hand, some of the disgraceful treatment meted out by the Home Office to our great allies, the Nepalese Gurkhas ('never had country more faithful friends than you' says a memorial) – now at last being righted – was precisely the wrong message to send out. When you joined the Roman army, you were all in it together.

Which all raises the question of NATO allies who are not committing troops to these difficult areas and therefore not fulfilling their side of the alliance. The Athenians knew the answer to that one. When they controlled a maritime empire, they demanded allied contributions either in warships (triremes) *or money*. So come on, allies: prove you are our allies, 'fighting together' with us, by at least opening up your chequebooks.

Mercenary tactics

One aspect of the deployment of our military forces would have struck both Greeks and Romans as dangerous: making commitments in places thousands of miles from home where self-interest is in doubt and the endgame unclear. Indeed, a recent Strategic Defence Review suggested that the job of the armed forces is no longer to defend Britain but to 'react rapidly' to crises anywhere in the world and to 'build Britain's reputation in the international community'. Are we talking of Her Majesty's Armed Forces – or mercenaries?

Ancient mercenaries served anyone, anywhere. In the course of conquering the known world from 334 BC onwards, Alexander the Great enhanced his international reputation with some 50,000 of them. It was their expertise that was so much admired. The general Xenophon observed that the Spartan cavalry had been pretty much of a muchness until Dionysius I of Syracuse sent them a troop of his own fully trained mercenary cavalrymen. Aristotle backs up Xenophon's analysis:

'War seems filled with empty alarms that mercenaries particularly have become knowledgeable about. They are effective and able to avoid suffering because of their experience. They know how to use their equipment and how best of all to use it to attack and defend themselves.'

Indeed, so organised did the system of employing such forces become that many states concluded agreements among themselves, giving them exclusive rights or first choice on available troops. Soon the Greek words for 'mercenary', 'foreigner' and 'soldier' became virtually interchangeable.

The British Army is one of the best in the world. But the idea that it should be deployed to provide 'services' for 'customers' elsewhere would have struck the ancients as grotesque. However, there is no reason why it should not train mercenaries to do so. After all, it is training the Iraqi army at the moment, so it has plenty of experience, and plans are afoot to privatise the actual training of the army anyway. The mercenaries could be hired out to friendly powers from the UK and relieve the strain on our serving forces – potentially, a very nice little earner too. There are plenty of businesses in Iraq looking for security guards, and at the moment they simply take people away from the army.

Paying the price

But the poet Virgil would add something else – the human cost. In his epic *Aeneid* (19 BC), the story of and justification for Rome's rise to worldwide dominion, his hero, Trojan Aeneas, insists that Rome is on a mission of peace. He laments the slaughter that he foresees must ensue when he lands in Italy to find locals determined to resist him and his men. He talks of 'the shields, helmets and bodies that the Tiber will roll under its waves' and the poet asks himself at one stage:

'Was it your pleasure, Jupiter, that nations who were to live in unending peace should clash with such violence?'

Aeneas himself pledges that, if he is victorious,

'I shall not order Italians to obey Trojans; I do not seek royal power myself. Both nations shall move forward in an ever-lasting treaty, undefeated, equal before the law.'

Of course the *Aeneid* is a panegyric of Rome and its emperor Augustus, but not at the price of *hūmānitās* and *pietās*, equality before the law and the blessings of Roman peace (cf. box, p. 72).

Festivals of peace

When he was Chancellor, Gordon Brown identified our national genius with a series of grinding abstract nouns: 'enterprise and inventiveness, tolerance and belief in liberty, fairness and public service, and internationalism' (don't ask what that last abstract noun means). When Pericles gave his famous 'Funeral Speech' after the first year of the Peloponnesian War in 430 BC, he too identified Athens' genius, and he did so far more intelligently, by contrast with its enemy at the time, Sparta.

First, Pericles emphasises the extent to which citizens past and present have been prepared to sacrifice themselves for the common good:

'by their courage and virtues they have handed our state on to us, a free country . . . so that it is perfectly able to look after itself in peace and war.'

Next, he stresses how different Athens is from regimented Sparta. Athens is a democracy, where all policy decisions are taken together and everyone is equal before the law, 'free and tolerant in our private lives but law abiding in public'. Athens is

'accessible to all, not needing to expel foreigners to preserve our secrets, and relying not on preparations and deceptions to protect ourselves but on the courage and readiness for action inherent in all'.

Athens is a festival society, where people enjoy public as well as private relaxations and do not gripe about their neighbours' habits. As a result, he argues, citizens can fulfil themselves through the leisurely and gracious lifestyle which Athens encourages. All in all, Athens was 'an education for Greece'.

For Pericles, Athens was a self-sufficient society that flourished because it strove to sustain an individual's freedom and self-fulfilment – a remarkable vision entirely free of Brown's plodding attempt to attribute to the British qualities that he would *like* them to have. One cannot really see the English sitting down for afternoon tea and passing the time by reflecting to each other on their enterprise and belief in public service and internationalism.

Most striking for us, perhaps, is Pericles' insistence that Athens is a festival society. Athens was renowned for the vast number of festivals it put on – state and local – and they were occasions dedicated to the worship of the gods. They were characterised by high spirits: good food, good company, plenty of drink and opportunity for sexual high jinks. This is not quite our idea of what religion is all about, but it was the ancients'; and festivals could be properly enjoyed only when their world was at peace.

>—I—‹›—O—‹›—I—‹

Reading list

Adrian Goldsworthy, *The Punic Wars* (Cassell 2000).
Homer, *The Iliad* (Rieu-Jones, Penguin 2003).
Homer, *The Odyssey* (Penguin 2003).
Robin Lane Fox, *Alexander the Great* (Penguin 1986).
Thucydides, *The Peloponnesian War* (Penguin 1972).
Virgil, *The Aeneid* (Penguin 1990).

[10]

The pleasures of paganism

'Everything is full of gods'

Ancient religion is fundamentally different from Christianity or Islam. In the absence of authoritative scriptures, pagans looked about them and took the view that there were many gods and goddesses ('obvious' when you look around at the many different forces at work in the world), that they were not primarily moral beings (because if they were they would enforce morality in humans), but that they must be interested in regularities like the heavens and the seasons (because they would not be regular if the gods did not want them so). Since farming (and fighting) were the main preoccupations of most Greeks, and successful farming depended crucially on seasonal regularity, the importance for Greeks of keeping the gods sweet at the vital times of the year cannot be overemphasised. Our church harvest festivals reflect the same concern.

Greeks also believed that the earth (Gaia) existed from the very beginning (see p. 192), and that it was she who actually gave birth to the gods and goddesses and all the world's natural features, like mountains, rivers, seas, night and day, and was ultimately responsible for the world's abstractions too, like Fear and Pain and Grief, equally conceived of as divinities. So the gods were not external to the world, nor did they make it; they were internal to it, just like us. Further, being all-powerful, immortal and able to do whatever they liked, gods looked to their own interests, not to anyone else's, let alone humans'. Humanity was there to be tolerated, not cosseted, by divinities who saw themselves as an aristocratic elite.

The Christian idea, however, was of a single God of love,

external to the universe; He revealed Himself through scriptures and denied all other gods; He was concerned about humans, though He also made heavy moral and spiritual demands on them, and expected them to strike up a close 'personal' relationship with Him. This is not a model the ancients would have found especially compelling – let alone a God who also came to earth as a baby, was humiliated and executed.

Nor would ancients have recognised the religionist Karen Armstrong's claim that 'All religions are designed to teach us how to live joyfully, serenely and kindly, in the midst of suffering'. Indeed, Greek myths – no Bible but simply traditional, communal stories of gods and humans – go out of their way to emphasise how precarious life is, how fraught with danger and difficulty, how unjust. In such a world religion offered little or no comfort. Only humans could do that.

In AD 178 Celsus composed his *True Doctrine* to reveal all this Christianity as nonsense. What mighty god would want to be transformed into a human, especially one born into a poverty-struck, powerless family, and eating ordinary food and not nectar and ambrosia? How could the dead join company with the gods, when in ancient religion gods and the dead were kept strictly apart? Why did Christians attack the worship of idols when they worshipped a corpse? Why did they rely on faith and not proof? Pagans did not need to have 'faith': they reckoned their own experience provided cast-iron *guarantees* of the existence of the gods, however fickle.

But none of this was a problem for the ancients (except intellectually), as long as Christians reciprocated by tolerating pagan deities.

The religious threat

But when Christians made it clear that their God was the one true God and all other gods were false idols and to be done away with, the Romans constructed that as a possible threat to their world – a world which their own pagan gods had clearly allowed to grow and flourish for hundreds of years (a matter of solid fact for them, not faith). It was the equivalent of terrorism, and had to be headed off before it could get a grip. Their response was exactly the same as ours to extreme Islam: get in first. But unlike us, no law constrained them. They therefore got in hard too. It was, however, not a matter of *policy* to destroy Christianity. Only when it seemed 'expedient for public order' did the authorities take action: and that was up to the authorities to decide. So if they felt the need for a whipping boy on any occasion, Christians (like Jews) were as good as any.

The Romans had acted less temperately in 186 BC when a cult was introduced which they did decide was a serious threat to their way of life – the cult of Bacchus. Stories spread of secret midnight rituals, drinking and sex, murder and other crimes. The cult does not seem to have had any political agenda at all, but it did have a strong organisation, complete with officials and private funds, and was spun as a conspiracy against the state. Its adherents were savagely repressed before it could spread any further.

We do not do ruthless extirpation today, even when some adherents of Islam express the desire to extirpate us. Indeed, our authorities for some reason feel compelled to 'celebrate' Islam as a wonderful thing. Romans would have been baffled by this. New religious cults regularly arrived in Rome but no authority felt it necessary to wax ecstatic about them or their worshippers. Religion was no one else's business but the adherents' – unless it was the state religion, or the adherents turned nasty.

Getting it rite

Ancients took the view that gods were best worshipped through actions – in this case, rituals like sacrifice and festivals. It was obviously crucial that they were properly carried out, otherwise they would not 'work', and the state could be threatened by withdrawal of divine favour. This is a feature of contemporary religious life that is wholly familiar, most obviously in the Eucharist and Islam's feelings about the Arabic Koran. The use of Latin in the Catholic Church offers an irresistible case study. Until relatively recent times, the Catholic Church insisted that sacred acts required sacred language, and that Latin, and Latin alone, was to be used in the mass and the sacraments. So when Jesuit missionaries opened up China in the 17th century, Chinese priests had to learn Latin.

The problem was that they could not pronounce it. When a priest tried to say *ego tē baptizō in nōmine Patris et Fīliī et Spīritūs Sānctī* 'I baptise you in the name of the Father and the Son and the Holy Spirit', it came out *nghe ngho te bapetiso in nomine patelisu nghe te filli te sepilitusu sanketi*. It was not simply that this was gibberish; there was the grave theological danger that the rite was being rendered invalid. But when the Jesuits urged Rome to permit a Chinese liturgy, all their requests were rejected.

That is the nature of sacred ritual: it requires time-honoured routine, couched in time-honoured language. Only that guarantees its effectiveness. To that extent the ancients would have wondered how on earth Christianity today could possibly 'work' when there seems to be no end to the changes in its language, creed and ritual to make it 'relevant to today's world'. It needed to be relevant to the *gods'* world, evidence for which could be drawn only from successful past practice.

The thinker Isocrates reflected on the reasons for Athens' rise to power in the following terms:

'In religious matters (for it is right to begin with them), our forefathers were neither inconsistent nor irregular in their worship or celebrations. They did not make a sacrifice of three hundred oxen merely when it seemed a good idea, while neglecting (at whim) the sacrifices instituted by their fathers. ... Their only concern was not to weaken the religion of their fathers, nor to introduce unwanted innovations; for in their eyes, piety consisted not in lavish expenditure, but in leaving untouched what their forefathers had bequeathed to them. So the blessings of heaven were visited on them with unbroken regularity and in due season for ploughing and for harvest.'

In other words, since success in this life was clear proof of divine favour, it was in your interest to continue playing the same game. Empirical self-interest therefore governed your relationship with the gods. Even critics of aspects of paganism (of whom more later) were not so foolish as to miss out on what it had to offer by way of relaxation.

The good things of life

All the great festivals that we hear of in the ancient world were religious occasions in the sense that they were carried out to honour a god. The Olympic Games were held in honour of Zeus, god of Olympus, and the theatrical festivals in Athens in honour of Dionysus. They were celebrations, and the ancients duly celebrated. Disastrously, such agreeable rituals could be interrupted or curtailed by war. Their full communal celebration was a mark of the peace, leisure and pleasure to which Pericles (p. 178) was referring.

In this sense, religion in the pagan world was central to the good things of life for everyone, particularly when it came to taking it easy and forgetting the cares of the world. Since 95 per cent of the ancient world dedicated almost every day of their lives to ensuring they would have enough to eat, because that was the only way they could stay alive (bad harvests spelled death for thousands), leisure was a very precious commodity. Hence the importance of religious festivals: the gods actually *sanctioned* free time for fun in the course of the daily grind. It is not clear that fun is a major component of religion in today's Western world, except perhaps on Christmas day.

Taking yourself on holiday

Leisure for us is connected with religion at Christmas and Easter. But it has nothing to do with what we call our 'holidays' (despite the derivation from 'holy days'), those precious few weeks of the year when we are not tyrannised by jobs, can do exactly as we like and indulge in the annual ritual of going away to enjoy ourselves as tourists. This is not quite the message the Pope put out for World Tourism Day, when he argued that the purpose of tourism should be to help people 'discover themselves and others' by experiencing 'other ways of life, religions and ways of looking at the world'. He seemed, in fact, to be groping towards the view of tourism espoused by the younger Seneca, millionaire philosopher and briefly adviser to Nero. For Seneca thought that travel was largely pointless.

In *Letter CIV* to his friend Lucilius, Seneca begins by discussing the effects of his retreat to his villa at Nomentum (ten miles north-east of Rome). Seneca's health was not good, and while he agrees that he is feeling physically all the better for it, he goes on to point out that a mere location is not enough by itself to deliver benefits: only mastery of the mind will do that. He tells the story of someone complaining to Socrates that travelling abroad had never done him any good, to which Socrates replied 'Not very surprising, really, since you took yourself along with you'.

Seneca's conclusion is that, if a man really wants to change and escape the things that trouble him, he needs not to be in a different place, but to be a different person.

> 'Suppose you have arrived in Athens or Rhodes' [the height of sophistication for Romans]; 'suppose you have arrived anywhere you like – what difference does the character of the place make? You will be bringing to it your own.'

If one is wracked by fears of poverty, lust for honours, or terror of death, tourism will not help. Travel, he argues, has never helped anyone check his impulses, control his temper or develop sound judgement. It merely makes an already unstable mind yet more unstable, and therefore dissatisfied. All it does is

> 'distract us for a while through the novelty of our surroundings, like children fascinated by something they have not come across before'.

Not that there is anything wrong with seeing new sights, Seneca goes on: the Nile and the Tigris are very interesting.

> 'But this information will not make us better or saner. To do that, we ought rather to spend our time in study and in the writings of wise men; we should try to make sense of the truths they have discovered, while searching for truths as yet undiscovered ourselves. This is the way to free the mind from its miserable slavery and win it into freedom.'

A mere change of scenery cannot cure a disordered mind any more than it can heal a broken leg, says Seneca. All this suggests that the Pope should start offering holidays in the Vatican Library.

Thought for leisure

The Greek for 'leisure' is *skholē*, origin of our 'school' and 'scholar'. One of the consequences of leisure time in the ancient world was the rich, subtle and influential vein of ideas that emerged from those who used that time to grapple with big problems like the nature of the universe and the best way to leads one's life. But the long periods of leisure required for this activity were available only to the wealthy or those determined enough to generate the time to indulge in the luxury. We do not realise how lucky we are today to be members of a society so leisured that virtually anyone who wants to can be educated, producing nothing, for nearly *twenty years*. Then add on retirement. In the ancient world, you retired only when you died. As an ironic Latin grave inscription says:

> 'All a person needs. Bones sweetly reposing, I am not worried about suddenly being short of food. I do not suffer from arthritis. I am not in debt because I am behind with my rent. In fact, my lodgings are permanent – and free!'

Slavery

Slavery was commonplace across the ancient world. Most slaves were bought at slave markets – men, women and children captured in war, or taken by pirates and sold on. They were just like you or me, with our different interests and abilities, except that they had been taken captive. It was not a matter of racial destiny: just the worst of bad luck.

In poorer homes, slaves were workhorses, doing what servants would have done a hundreds years ago. In wealthier houses, they could include highly educated people. War and pirates were no respecters of persons; there might be a Stephen Hawking among their number. The point is that slaves were all highly valuable: they could be your childminder, your children's tutor, your cook, your washing machine, your shopper, your cleaner, your secretary, your caretaker, your builder, your financial assistant, your research assistant. You looked after them, if you wanted to get the best out of them. Some of them felt part of the family. Ultimately, however, they counted for nothing unless you actively decided to make them count for something.

To point up the extremes: Greeks used slaves to work the silver mines: dreadful work; Roman emperors selected intelligent slaves to use in often quite sensitive advisory or financial positions because they knew slaves would be loyal: their position in society depended on the emperor alone. Slave revolts were non-existent except where slaves were gathered together in very large numbers, for example, working large estates in the Roman world. Even so, revolts were rare. Some poor families even sold their own children or themselves into slavery because that at least would guarantee a roof over their head and regular meals, not something that the poor could ever rely on.

At this point it is obligatory to put on a grave face,

etched with concern, and say how awful slavery was (its nearest modern counterpart in the West is probably human trafficking). Phew! Done it! Virtually no Greek or Roman would agree, but there it is. It is interesting today, however, how many people get used to it. Mobile phones can be programmed with electronic calendars run by a central authority telling you what to do, and when. No one apparently objects. The ancients, for whom independence was of the highest importance, would think that approached a form of slavery – as, indeed, was any kind of working under someone else's orders.

The harvest of Greek and Roman thought was amazingly rich. The invention of democracy, atomic theory, philosophy, biology, logic, rational medicine, history, geometry, tragedy, comedy, the idea of worldwide citizenship, many architectural and sculptural forms, and major contributions to our ideas of politics, empire, law, education, urban civilisation and so on bear eloquent witness to the extraordinary fertility of the Graeco-Roman mind. Their language has also had a deep influence on the world (1.2 billion people speak a language derived from Latin) and our Anglo-Saxon. It has been calculated that about 80 per cent of our language of education, science and intellectual discourse is Graeco-Roman, imported into Anglo-Saxon English by the church, the Norman conquest of 1066 and during the Renaissance, for precisely that purpose. Had not Greeks and Romans been there, done that?

And the wealthy took full advantage of the leisure they enjoyed, whatever else they were doing (they knew that it was what you *do* that makes you happy, not what you have). Take some Roman examples:

- Julius Caesar, a brilliant soldier and general and a ruthlessly far-sighted politician, wrote an important book on one of the hottest topics of the day: linguistic theory. He was between battles, crossing the Alps at the time.

- Cicero, politician and lawyer, effectively invented Roman philosophy.
- Pliny the Elder, as we have seen, as well as being admiral of the fleet, wrote an encyclopedia of the Roman world. Drawn from (literally) thousands of books, it embraces all things animal, vegetable and mineral. It deals with everything from the lives of artists to wine production, from the properties of cabbage to shoemaker's black and the dimensions of continents. He also wrote a twenty-book history of German wars, and a thirty-one-book history of the early Roman Empire (neither survives).
- Tacitus was a career politician, consul and provincial governor, and one of the world's very greatest historians.
- The emperor and Stoic philosopher Marcus Aurelius' *Meditations* have brought comfort to millions.

One casts one's eyes over today's highly educated politicians and – no. Don't go there. Probably the reason is the rise of the 'professional' politician, who has never done anything else, unlike, for example, Gladstone, Disraeli and Churchill (even Heath). But it is simply astonishing that those who ruled the ancient world had – or rather *made* – so much time for serious intellectual pursuits as well.

On the other hand – is it? We live in a world where we are instructed to pick a specialism and stick to it, to focus on our 'number one priority', our 'personal brand'. A jack of all trades is master of none, a dilettante, a dabbler. Greeks and Romans would have found this bizarre. Hippias from Elis, near Olympia, a well known academic and lecturer, had a gigantic range of intellectual interests – maths, astronomy, music, linguistics, literature, painting, sculpture and mnemonics (he could remember, he said, fifty names at a single glance). And he made his own clothes, ornaments and pots. He was always being asked by the people of Elis to represent them abroad. Plato mocked him, but there is no hint of this in other sources.

That is an extreme example, but one does find rather a lot of them. Aristotle wrote on logic, metaphysics, biology, sleep, dreams, divination, age, ethics, history, rhetoric and literature. Besides his copious law-court and political work, Cicero wrote (bad) poetry, and major works on rhetoric and philosophy as well as brilliant letters to friends. A real man was *expected* to develop a range of talents and interests, and not forget physical fitness either. Renaissance man had his origins in the classical world.

Critics of paganism

Which brings us back to paganism, because many ancient Greek thinkers took advantage of their leisure to put their mind to religion, and became highly sceptical about various aspects of it. The philosopher Xenophanes (c. 540 BC) said:

> 'Homer and Hesiod have attributed to the gods everything that men find shameful and reprehensible – stealing, adultery and deceiving each other.'

He saw good reason for believing the gods were simply modelled on humans:

> 'If cattle, horses and lions had hands, or could draw and do what men do, horses would draw gods looking like horses, and cattle gods like cattle.'

Plato would have banished Homer from his ideal state because of the immorality of the gods he depicted. The philosopher Protagoras said:

> 'Concerning the gods, I am unable to discover whether they exist or not, or what they are like in form; for there are many hindrances to knowledge – the difficulty of the subject and the shortness of life.'

It is indeed tempting, Richard Dawkins-like (and he also has the leisure), simply to regard any religion as a fiction, out of contact with objective, scientific reality, and therefore to dismiss it out of hand. But despite intellectuals' objections, it was not fiction to Greeks. Religions are designed to take criticism of this sort, happy to admit that the god is knowable by mere mortals only within specific limits, and the rest is a 'mystery' – an entirely logical position.

Further, it is not the purpose of religion to be in contact with objective, scientific reality. Like all religions, paganism was a system that enabled people both to interpret and respond to the external world, to make 'sense' of that experience and to help them think about their place within it – their relationships, behaviour and feelings. A useful comparison has been drawn between a religion and a language. Both are quite incomprehensible to those who do not use them, until you have learned their 'rules' and the inexplicable (to an outsider) inconsistencies and absurdities that always break those 'rules'.

So Richard Dawkins can pontificate away (from the Latin *pontifex*, 'a priest in control of public religion in Rome'), but he will make little difference. If 'faith' is declining, it is not because of rational, let alone scientific, doubts, but more something to do with people's religious experience or, rather, lack of it. Since religious feeling is primarily a matter of habituation, but churchgoing is increasingly a minority commitment, it is difficult to see how the situation can be changed.

Justifying belief

That said, as human experience time and time again makes clear, no religion offers any *guarantees* that gods will do what humans want. In this respect Greek religion is no different from any other. How, then, did pagans explain the efficacy, let alone the purpose, of the man–god relationship? In precisely the same way that the devout do now: where things seemed to go wrong, it was man's fault. 'The gods must be angry with us' was a typical Greek explanation. It is a modern explanation too: the Bishop of Carlisle blamed the June 2007 floods on God's anger at our degeneracy, while emphasising that the people affected were (*of course*) innocent. Discuss. But none of this need have the slightest effect on the religion's adherents (it has been well said that only atheists demand statistics).

Bridging the gap between gods and the world

Two thousand years of thinking about the nature of the gods can still make a contribution today. For example, one of the big current debates is about the relationship between the universe and any divinity that might be behind it. It usually emerges in the form of (God-driven) 'intelligent design' as against (godless) 'natural selection'. Ancient Greeks knew nothing of this debate, of course, but nevertheless came up with an interesting take on it.

Greek thinkers worked on the hypothesis that the world was rationally ordered, and everything in it (including man) had a function for which it was fitted, i.e. the best way to live must be as part of the natural order of the cosmos.

At the same time, they also thought of the world as inherently 'divine'. After all, Mother Earth was Gaia, who existed long before the gods ever did: indeed, by copulating with Ouranos (Uranus, the sky god) and then Cronus, she actually produced those gods and goddesses (so the epic farmer–poet Hesiod tells us). So there must also be a critical link between divinity and the rational world we inhabit. The ancients therefore did not think of 'science' on the one hand and 'gods' on the other as being at eternal loggerheads, as so many scientists today seem to. While ancient philosopher–physicists insisted that their explanations of the way the world worked must rest on human reason alone (see p. 211), that did not prevent them finding a place for divinities in the great scheme of things.

Cause and meaning

According to his 2nd-century AD biographer Plutarch, Pericles was once sent from his country estates the head of a one-horned ram. The prophet Lampon, seeing how strongly and solidly the horn grew out of the middle of its forehead, interpreted it to mean that, of the two people currently fighting for the ear of the people in Athens (Pericles and Thucydides – not the historian), one would emerge victorious – Pericles.

Pericles' mentor, however, was the natural scientist Anaxagoras (on whom Socrates was once keen, cf. p. 216), and he would have nothing to do with this tosh. He had the skull dissected and showed that the single horn had grown, quite naturally, as the result of a skull deformity. That settled Lampon's hash! But not for long. Shortly after, Thucydides was ostracised (see p. 85) and Pericles was left as the most influential man in Athens. So Lampon was right after all.

Plutarch goes on to say that both men were right. Anaxagoras was right, because he had shown how the single horn had come to grow in place of the usual two. But Lampon had understood what it *meant*. Plutarch points out that merely explaining the cause of a phenomenon does not automatically do away with the phenomenon's potential significance, and draws a parallel with sundials. You can, he says, explain the cause of the shadows they cast; but if you do not understand their significance, you have missed the whole purpose of the sundial.

So, he concludes, if you do not know how the world functions, you will be terrified and confused about the role of the gods; but if you do, you will put your superstitious fears about the natural world behind you and replace it with an 'unshaken piety, with good hopes'. The gods, therefore, were revealed *within* nature, not beyond it.

Observe the way in which for Plutarch 'nature' and 'the gods' work in indissoluble harmony, different sides of precisely the same coin. The sense that the gods, for all their ultimate unknowability, were critically tied up with this material and human world, and if you wanted to think intelligently about the gods you could not do so unless you thought about man and nature too, was a crucial feature of ancient thought.

The upshot of all this is: if you asked ancients if the world was purely mechanistic or if there was a Grand Design, many would have answered: 'Both'.

>─┤─◆>─◦─<◆─┤─◄

Reading list

Guy de la Bedoyère, *Gods with Thunderbolts: Religion in Roman Britain* (Tempus, 2002).

James Davidson, *Courtesans and Fishcakes* (HarperCollins 1997).

Hesiod, *Theogony; Works and Days* (World's Classics 1988).

Homer, *The Iliad* (Rieu-Jones, Penguin 2003).

Mary Lefkowitz, *Greek Gods, Human Lives* (Yale 2003).

Daniel Ogden (ed.), *A Companion to Greek Religion* (Blackwell 2007).

Robert Parker, *Polytheism and Society at Athens* (Oxford 2005).

Françoise Waquet, *Latin or the Empire of a Sign* (Verso 2001).

[11]
Peering into the future

Horror scopes

One particular aspect of the ancient world inevitably causes those who live in a post-scientific world to wonder why the ancients have been credited with such a reputation for intelligence, namely, their belief in oracles, divination, soothsaying and such like. How on earth could they have been taken in by such transparent nonsense?

But before we mock, many ancients questioned these as intensely as they did almost everything else. In his two-book *dē dīvīnātiōne* (published 44 BC, just after the assassination of Julius Caesar) the orator, politician and philosopher Cicero destroys horoscopes for ever. Defining divination as 'the foreknowledge and foretelling of events that happen by chance', Cicero lays about it in fine style:

- First, there is no area of life which the diviner can deal with more efficiently than the expert: for questions of illness one goes to a doctor, for nature to the natural scientist, for right and wrong to the philosopher, for statecraft to the politician, etc. The diviner has no role anywhere.
- Second, the definition makes no logical sense. If something happens 'by chance' it cannot, by definition, be predicted: otherwise it could not be said to have happened 'by chance'. If an event were truly to happen 'by chance', Cicero goes on, even the god would not be able to predict it. So how could a diviner? *Dīvīnātiō* is therefore impossible if everything is controlled by chance.

Let us then assume, Cicero argues, that everything is controlled by Fate. In that case:

- It is hard to see what advantages *dīvīnātiō* can bring, for, if something is fated, it will happen, come what may. No amount of divination can help a person avoid it – and how ghastly to know everything that is going to happen to you, Cicero goes on, quoting the example of the recently assassinated Julius Caesar.

If, on the other hand, Fate can be turned aside, then nothing is certain. In that case:

- *Dīvīnātiō* is pointless too, since it is supposed to deal with what *is* certain, and nothing can be said to be 'certain' which can be prevented.

Cicero now takes each type of divination in turn – interpretation of natural phenomena like entrails and lightning, the taking of auspices, casting of lots, horoscopes, oracles and dreams – and shows what nonsense they are. He ends by making the point which Plutarch makes (see p. 193), that superstition has disastrous consequences for its adherents:

'for it is at your heels all the time, pursuing you at every twist and turn – when you listen to a prophet or an omen, offer sacrifice, watch the birds, consult an astrologer, see lightning. Since these signs are given all the time, no one who believes them can ever be at peace.'

But 'the knowledge of nature', which Cicero associates with religion, offers true understanding and peace of mind.

Astrology

Ancient astronomers knew enough about the heavens to be able to contrast the unchanging regularity of their movement with the chaos of life on earth. From there it was a short step to argue that the heavens were divine. If so, they must exert some influence upon the earth.

But how? First, Greeks observed the palpable effects of the sun on the seasons and the moon on the tides; the moon was also thought to produce dew and control menstruation, i.e. fertility. So the heavens did have some obvious physical effects. Second, Greeks had a belief in a general, holistic 'cosmic sympathy', i.e. that everything was ultimately connected with and had influence upon everything else. So the famous 'four elements' (see p. 220) out of which the cosmos is constructed – earth, air, fire and water – represent cold, dryness, heat and moisture. And look! The heavens consist of fire and air; life depends on earth and water; moisture is 'feminine', dryness is 'masculine', etc. etc. Expand these beliefs to extremes and it is possible to see how the heavens could also be thought to affect human lives. Since, therefore, the movement of the heavens was predictable, so must life be too.

Mystic mugs

In the light of Cicero's assault, then, we might do better to enquire why, in our world, the modern equivalent of divination, i.e. astrology (see box), continues to hold such a grip on humanity – or at least seems to, judging by the number of papers (even broadsheets) that publish horoscopes every day. That said, though, modern astrology is certainly not what it was. It has, in fact, been considerably dumbed down. Astrologers are now very well aware that horoscopes are not 'scientific' since no connections between an individual's star sign and his life on earth can be demonstrated; horoscopes do not respond to the criteria of repeatable experiment and predictability; and whatever else astrology does for its users, 'foretelling the future' is not among them.

So nowadays horoscopic advice does not deal with the future ('Tomorrow Terry Wogan will call to paint your kitchen green') but with attitudes, hopes, fears and personal relationships, expressed in suitable vague terms susceptible to many interpretations, i.e. they are basically cod psychology ('cods' being testicles, i.e. balls), cast in mystic mode for those who for some reason need life to be wrapped in mystery. But such transparent piffle is probably harmless enough, makes a talking point and can hardly do more mental damage than half an hour of Ant and Dec.

The Delphic oracle

But what about the Delphic oracle? Did that not predict that Oedipus would marry his mother and kill his father, and 'Gone with the Wind' in the tartan noseband would win the 2.30 at Corinth Park? Well, no: or not the last one, at any rate. And that is the point. Be their balls never so crystal, Greeks were not stupid, and the Delphic oracle was a highly respected institution, not a joke like Mystic Meg or some sort of funfair turn by Harry Potter out of Gypsy Rose Lee.

There are, of course, stories credited to the oracle that were designed to display its 'Mystic Meg' side. Herewith a famous example, one of many that established its reputation. Croesus, king of Lydia (in Turkey), who had a genuine respect for all things Greek, had a big decision to make about whether to attack the Persians. So he decided to check the reliability of the best-known oracles (there were over 120 in Greece alone, and nearly 300 all round the Mediterranean). He sent out ambassadors with instructions to ask the oracles, on the hundredth day of their departure from Sardis, what Croesus was doing. On that hundredth day, Croesus decided to boil a lamb and a tortoise in a bronze cauldron with a bronze lid. When the answers came back, only Delphi got it spot on.

The working of the Delphic oracle

The Pythia was the name given to the woman who spoke the oracles. It is now fashionable to believe that she uttered them in a frenzied rant, brought on by ethane, methane and ethylene issuing from the spring which once flowed under the oracle. Since the first stages of ethylene inhalation (widely used as an anaesthetic in the past) do indeed induce in patients a 'frenzy', it is suggested that was how she generated her *aperēus*.

This, I fear, is tosh. Ethylene occurs naturally only in plants (it is a maturing agent). Even if by some remote chance it could occur naturally in streams, it is impossible that enough could be generated at one point to have any effect on humans. It is also historical tosh. No contemporary ancient historian says anything about frenzied rantings at Delphi. The one time there is a record of the Pythia gabbling unintelligibly, it demonstrated her behaviour was *untypical*.

This is not to deny that the ecstatic had (and has) a place in religious experience. Female worshippers of Dionysus, the Bacchae, were known to whoop it up in the woods and mountains from time to time. But it was not the rule in the Greek world. They did not expect the Pythia to rant and rave when she uttered her prophecies, any more than we expect the Archbishop of Canterbury to foam at the mouth when he announces the hymns. The boring probability is that the Pythia produced coherent answers, which were written down by her attendants or interpreters before being given to the consultants. Plutarch is quite clear on the matter: the Pythia speaks with her own voice under the impulse of Apollo, he says, who 'puts visions into her mind for her to express in speech as best she can'.

In other words, the Pythia, working under impulse, did her best to articulate what she 'saw'. No wonder she had problems. But that was to be expected. There is a legitimate role for the mysterious, miraculous and numinous in religion. There was much in the world that seemed to make no sense to Greeks (as to us), and if the purpose of religion is to confront ultimate mysteries, beyond the ken of human

> understanding, it is not surprising if it calls up concepts and
> images that will not bear strictly rational scrutiny.

Croesus was thrilled. He made a gigantic 3,000 animal sacrifice to Delphic Apollo and sent fabulous gifts there to win the favour of the god. He then asked whether he should attack Persia. The oracle said that, if he did, he would destroy a great empire.

We all know what happened next, and we all say 'Arf arf, silly old Croesus, he should have asked "Whose empire?"' But Croesus was not daft. He had sent again to Delphi, asking how long he would reign. The oracle replied he would reign until a mule became king. Since Croesus thought that unlikely, he attacked the Persians and their king Cyrus in full confidence. So when he was defeated, he sent to the oracle a third time, asking what the bleedin' hell was going on. The oracle said not only should he have asked 'Whose empire?' but he should also have checked out Cyrus' lineage: for a mule is the offspring of a he-ass and a mare, and Cyrus was a son of parents of different races – hence, a 'mule'.

Interpreting the oracle

The story perfectly exemplifies the reputation the oracle developed over the years – the ability to know the unknowable (the story of Croesus' lamb / tortoise) and the human capacity for misunderstanding it. The lesson to Greeks was clear: the gods could do what people would call miracles, but man could never be certain to understand their messages properly. Oracles, in other words, were a two-edged sword.

No Greek was therefore surprised if the oracle at Delphi came up with something hard to interpret. This was, after all, a god speaking, and through a fallible human (the priestess, the Pythia: see box). The god could also speak (as he did at other oracles) through the flight of birds, the clashing of the metal bowls and the murmuring of trees. This is 'speech', but of a different kind – one which did not communicate through verbal but through non-verbal means, and was even more in need of interpretation by fallible humans. As the 6th-century BC philosopher Heraclitus said of the god of the oracle at Delphi, 'he neither speaks nor hides: he uses signs'.

The democratic response

All this explains why, for example, the democratic Assembly in Athens tended to rely on its own judgement in political matters. Religious matters were one thing; but politics was another. So when there was a major crisis which they felt was beyond their ken, humanly inexplicable or very threatening, like plague, famine or war (e.g. the impending Persian attack on Athens in 481 BC, which produced the famous 'Take to your Wooden Walls' utterance, interpreted to mean 'fleet'), they did consult oracles. But if the Assembly felt an issue was in their power to decide, they decided it. That was what democracy was for.

But by the same token, keeping divinities sweet was of the highest importance for them, and the democracy took enormous care to ensure that traditional religious rituals (of which there were very many) were properly carried out – festivals in honour of the gods, sacrifices, prayers on public occasions (e.g. before going into battle), and temples maintained (temple maintenance was a regular item on the Assembly's agenda, unlike church maintenance today). You could never be too careful where gods were concerned.

In this respect, public religion today would seem to be failing us. True, like the Greeks, we do not consult our religious authority (the Bible) over Parliamentary matters. But Athens got its name because it was the city of Athena. It was her personal fiefdom. It was to Athena, therefore, that Athenians looked in times of crisis. Indeed, the main reason for worshipping the gods and putting on great state festivals in their honour was to ensure they protected you. Athenians would therefore have wondered about a religion like Christianity that did not seem to make the security of the whole nation its main priority. But what emerges from this is that the oracle was not really about *prediction*.

Looking to the present

Prediction of the future is a hot topic these days, most urgently concerning the physical state of the world: global warming, flood, volcano, earthquake, disease, weather. Given the current state of science, it is possible to make some pretty fair short-term guesses on such topics, as long as the data is available and we interpret it right. Long term is more difficult. Human behaviour, too, is subject to recurrent patterns: crowd control at football matches, for example, is now quite a fine art, though the consequences of, for example, introducing a new law are far more difficult to predict.

But these sorts of predictions are the product of a scientific world very remote from that of the ancients, and equally remote from our everyday lives. Whatever the fluctuations in the stock market, whatever the weather, fundamental changes in the way each of us *is* are few and far between. What we as individuals actually want is assurance about the future – the sense that we can handle it. To that extent, it is not so much predictions about what will happen in the future that are important to us as preparing ourselves for the possibilities and creating in ourselves a mindset that can handle them. In other words, we want sound advice, derived from an authority we can trust: we want our present thinking reordered to be ready for anything in the future and be able to make sense of it – good or bad – when or if it happens. Further, in instances where we do actually want a prediction – for example, betting on horses or shares – we want to feel in control, even though our horse trails in last or our shares bomb. That control usually manifests itself in our overall confidence in our *capacity* to make the right decisions, even if they turn out hopelessly wrong.

If that is right, the Delphic oracle fits into a pattern we should be able to understand. The point is that the historical veracity of the stories about Croesus and Oedipus are in severe doubt, since they are tales preserved from the deep past, a combination of folklore and myth. They served their purpose, however, in establishing the oracle's reputation. But the real world was very different. Some 500 genuine consultations and answers survive – they were recorded on public inscriptions to commemorate the event – and they show clearly that the oracle was not a predicting machine so much as a sort of religious advice bureau.

You went to it when, for example, you wanted to know to which god you ought to sacrifice in order that a journey would turn out well; what you should do when you find you have accidentally transported a sacred snake in your wagon back to your hometown; whether you should declare your country inviolable; and so on. It is very revealing that the most common formula in which to pose your question to the oracle was 'Is it better and more advantageous to do X or Y?' The god just chose one or the other. Nothing more was required. And it could also wield political influence if a state chose to consult it on a matter of policy, which some did.

That, of course, did not mean the questioner was guaranteed success. Gods are gods: if you asked the wrong question, or did not interpret the answer correctly, the god had the perfect get-out. But that did not affect your view of the gods' fallibility, only of your own. It certainly did not mean that you regarded the whole thing as hokum.

Handling what life throws at you

So what individuals wanted from oracles, soothsayers and such like was what we (if we are sensible) want when we face the prospect of the future: the confidence that we shall be able to handle whatever the future will throw, or the past has thrown, at us. For the ancient, living in tough times, the basic requirement boiled down to surviving under the circumstances in which you found yourself and, with luck, doing well.

When the Roman satirist Juvenal (writing c. AD 120) put the

question of what that good life might be, it came out in the practical question – what should men pray for? One answer he famously gave was *mēns sāna in corpore sānō*, 'a healthy mind in a healthy body'. One wonders what he would have made of today's men and women in search of the *corpus sānum*, lurching along the fume-filled roadsides in their huge Day-glo trainers, swigging out of their mobile phones while chatting earnestly into the bottles of water clenched to their ears. As he looked at all these perfectly healthy imbeciles pointlessly pounding the pavements, he would surely conclude that the greater the desire for a healthy body, the less healthy the mind. *Mēns īnsāna in corpore sānō*?

Good health, being in many ways a matter of pot luck in the ancient world, was very highly valued. If you survived birth, childhood and disease and could enjoy a respectable diet, you could count yourself pretty fortunate. In such a world anything that could do you good was to be recommended, so exercise was indeed high on doctors' priorities.

In today's world, health is dependent on government intervention. As two professors wrote in the *Guardian*:

'the improvement of health ... will require investment in services and facilities ... that engender sociability and inclusion, life skills, self-esteem and mutual respect.' [Note: this is not a spoof.]

So no chance anyone could actually take a decision off his/her own bat to do a little exercise and eat and drink sensibly. Only the welfare state can do it for you.

Victim culture

The immediate reaction to even the slightest inconvenience these days is to brand it a 'tragedy' and scream for compensation. Every year, for example, there is usually a hitch in A-level marking that means some of Britain's brightest and best 'young people' are 'forced' to undergo the disaster of taking a year out. 'What of the effect on our future careers, income, quality of life and happiness?' they moan, accompanied by a disgusting chorus of sympathy from adults, stoked up by the media. Note too the use of the passive voice to emphasise man's helplessness. 'Millions *forced* to flee hurricane', we are told. *Forced* – to flee a *hurricane*? By whom? No one would need to force me. But 'Millions sensibly choose to flee hurricane' does not encourage the outrage necessary to stoke up demands for the government to do something about it.

Around AD 60, Seneca wrote to his friend Lucilius about their mutual acquaintance Liberalis, who had been much downcast at the news of a great fire that had completely wiped out the proud Roman colony of Lugdunum (Lyons) in two days. Seneca starts by observing that fires, like earthquakes, do damage but rarely destroy a whole town in one go, as had happened on this occasion. So this event has been, he goes on, a serious test of Liberalis' usually steadfast will, especially as it was so unexpected – 'for the unexpected exacts the heaviest toll on us'.

Therefore, Seneca concludes, 'we must ensure that nothing is unexpected by us. Our minds must look ahead at all times and think about, not what usually happens, but what can possibly happen'. He points out that *Fortuna* is able to strike in any number of ways; she can turn our own hands against us or produce disasters out of top hats; one is never safe from her, especially at times of greatest hopes and happiness, and when she strikes, it is with terrifying rapidity. Cities, like mountains, *casurae stant*, 'stand but to fall'.

The consolation in all this is that reverses often lead to a more prosperous outcome. Seneca quotes a friend of Augustus with a grudge against Rome saying that the only reason he felt aggrieved when buildings there burned down was because he knew far better ones would replace them. But at all events, the mind must be disciplined to understand

and endure a human's lot: 'into such a world have we entered, under such laws do we live'.

There was, in other words, a dignity attached to enduring suffering. Ancients would have had little but contempt for our victims screaming 'X wrecked my life and done me 'ead in for ever' at the drop of a hat.

The lamentable idea that you might actually have to do something yourself to improve your lot was typical of all ancient thought. The Roman doctor Celsus, for example, divided the population into the weak ('the large portion of townspeople and almost all who are fond of literature') and those who were healthy, vigorous and their own master. The former group should take care not to overexert themselves, but should take some light exercise, 'enough to make them sweat'. The latter need be under no rules, but should aim to lead a varied life in town, country and farm with a little sailing and hunting thrown in.

The philosopher–millionaire Seneca (AD 1–65), one time adviser to Nero, even extended the daring concept into the intellectual sphere. He did not deny the value of exercise, but argued that without mental health the body 'though very powerful, is strong only as that of a madman or lunatic is strong'. Fitness fanatics unfitted themselves for real study, dulled the edge of their sensibilities, and (worst of all) had to take orders from ghastly fitness trainers, whose high ambition in life was sweating and drinking. No change there, then.

But the mind required training day and night, though a change now and again – a little walking or riding – was beneficial. We should limit the flesh and give free rein to the spirit, Seneca says. Our aim should be a self-contained, self-confident mind, which disdains everything that the mob prays for or Fortune can bestow, and seeks true, lasting happiness. This, unlike physical health which is always liable to relapse, will not fail: 'the mind, once healthy, is healthy for good and all'. What? No sociability, inclusion and life skills? These ancients didn't have a clue, did they?

To return to Juvenal. The *mēns sāna* sentiment is only one of a number of recommendations he makes, all as relevant today as they were then. He begins by pointing up the folly of a number of typical prayers. The most popular one, he suggests, is 'Increase my bank balance'. But when your champagne flames with gold, he warns, that's the time to worry. Others hanker after power, only to find the monuments they erected to themselves dragged down and thrown on the heap (the fate of many an emperor), followed by the insults of the craven mob who yearn only for bread and circuses (*pānem et circēnsēs*) and see everything simply as potential for entertainment. Schoolboys pray for the eloquence of a Cicero or a Demosthenes (persuasion being the key to power in the ancient world, cf. p. 87), but that eloquence destroyed them both. What about success in battle – the victories, the triumphs, the glory? Juvenal witheringly mocks the achievements of Alexander the Great and Hannibal ('On, on, you madman, cross the savage Alps! Thrill schoolboys! Supply essay titles!').

Long life is another ardent plea – but there is no pleasure, says Juvenal, in trembling limbs and voices, bald heads, deafness, disease, and worst of all, mental decay and the death of loved ones (anyone listening out there?). Parents pray for good looks for their children, but he points out that good looks can corrupt those who possess them as well as exposing them to assaults from the lecherous.

So is there nothing worth praying for? Juvenal ends the Satire with his own modest recommendations. In general, he suggests, let the gods get on with it: they will give us what we need, not what we want. But if we must pray for something, make it *mēns sāna in corpore sānō*; a brave, enduring heart, for which death holds no terrors, and length of life is irrelevant; freedom from anger; craving for nothing; a preference for the labours of Hercules over Eastern luxuries; and most of all, *virtūs* (manly goodness). Lady Luck has no power, he concludes: it is we who make her a goddess and place her in the heavens.

Lord Byron was so impressed by this that he thought it should be read at funerals. Which brings us to the underworld.

Pagan underworld

In the absence of inspired scriptures, pagans had as many views on the afterlife as there were pagans. Here is Homer's. When Odysseus goes down to the Underworld to consult the prophet Teiresias with a view to discovering how to get back home, he meets the soul of the dead Achilles. When Achilles had learned at Troy that his beloved companion Patroclus had been slain in battle by Trojan Hector, he vowed revenge. His divine mother Thetis told him this would result in his early death. Achilles retorts:

'Then I die here and now, since I let my companion be killed when I could have saved him.'

Odysseus greets Achilles, calling him most blessed of the Greeks, honoured like the gods in life, and now king over all the dead. Achilles replies:

'Don't try to gloss over death for me, shining Odysseus. I'd rather be a serf working in the fields for a man who owned nothing, scraping a living, than lording it over all the lifeless corpses. Enough! Tell me of my son . . .'

Odysseus reports that Neoptolemus performed heroics in the capture of Troy. Odysseus continues:

'That is what I said, and the soul of swift-footed Achilles departed, huge-striding, across the asphodel fields, rejoicing at my account of his son's great glory.'

For Homer, Hades was not yet a place of judgement, rewards and punishment, but where existence was dull, grey and meaningless because *living* was everything, and in Hades none could strive to be best and reach for the stars. But the dead could still feel stirred by the deeds of the living, and Achilles, reacting with a flash of his old anger to being told how rewarding it must be to rule the dead, turns immediately to news of his son – the only thing that can now count for him. His reaction to the news – his soul 'huge-striding' (!), *makra bibāsa* – sends a shiver down my spine every time.

This is the life! This is the only life!

⊳–◆–○–◆–◁

Reading list

Tamsyn Barton, *Ancient Astrology* (Routledge 1994).

Hugh Bowden, *Classical Athens and the Delphic Oracle* (Cambridge 2005).

Guy de la Bedoyère, *Gods with Thunderbolts: Religion in Roman Britain* (Tempus 2002).

Joseph Fontenrose, *The Delphic Oracle* (California 1978).

Homer, *The Odyssey* (Penguin 2003).

Juvenal, *The Satires* (World's Classics 1991).

Seneca, *Letters from a Stoic* (Penguin 1969).

[12]

The science of living

The matter of existence

When Charles Darwin came back from his five-year journey on HMS *Beagle* to publish (after much thought and over twenty years later) his *On the Origin of Species* (1859), when Einstein told us that $E=Mc^2$ and when Stephen Hawking wrote *A Brief History of Time*, none of them said: 'And as a result of this, you will leap out of bed every day with a smile on your lips and a spring in your step, and all your problems will be solved'. Indeed, Hawking said of his 'vibrating string' theory of matter: 'It won't have much effect on how we live'. But this is precisely what ancient thinkers reckoned their explanations of the natural world *would* have. The great Roman poet Lucretius, in particular, was almost evangelical about the connection between happiness and the way the world was made.

Greeks, as we saw in the last chapter, took the view that there was a critical connection between the activity of divine powers and the natural world; and to understand the natural world was to get as close as was humanly possible to understanding these powers. But that had an obvious corollary. Man too was part of the natural world. The connection was therefore an inseparable three-way one: divine powers – nature – man.

Godless thinking

When Greeks started thinking about the nature of the world, they did not allow themselves *carte blanche* to answer in any way they felt like. There was one rule, a rule invented by Greeks, which was to have a world-changing effect on all subsequent scientific thought: your answer was not allowed to assign any involvement to the gods. That does not mean you did not acknowledge the gods. You almost certainly did (all that drink and sex, see p. 179). But when it came to your speculative work, gods must play no part in your account.

In that respect, your situation is much the same as any modern scientist. (S)He too is in the same boat. (S)He may be Christian, but is not allowed to say 'Sorry, squire, can't answer that legitimate scientific question because that's God's territory'. A legitimate scientific question by definition does not tread on that territory. If it does, it is not scientific. You can blame the Greeks for that.

Logical accounting

There is a consequence of this rule that is equally earth-shattering. Since you cannot appeal to divine authority for your conclusions – a move much loved by religious authorities because, of course, it closes down all debate – you have to win the *argument* on purely human terms. That means, by producing an *account* appealing to *reason* and *logic*, based on evidence – the most powerful analytical tool to which the brain has access.

The Greeks had a word for it: *logos*, covering the range 'word, statement, *reason*, *logic*, *argument*, *account*'. It is, perhaps, the most significant and influential word in the whole ancient Greek language, source of all those '-logies' ('bio-logy' – a reasoned account about *bios*, 'life'). It was even cunningly deployed by St John to bring Christian teaching about the divine (aaargh!) into line with Greek rational thought: 'In the beginning was the *Logos*'.

So if our ancient Greek philosopher-physicist, mulling over the problem of what the cosmos was made of, decided on the basis of a reasoned account that 'water' was the answer, he would be taken seriously, though he could expect heavy assault from the 'fire' brigade in the next city-state, already locked in mortal intellectual combat with the 'air' lot on the island opposite. But if he quoted Hesiod and said 'The universe is the product of divine intercourse, you fools', he would be laughed out of court. A scientist today would say much the same were a fellow scientist to explain the origins of the cosmos by pointing him to the opening chapters of *Genesis*. You can blame the Greeks for that too.

Public understanding of science

Here we get to the nub of the matter. If you live in a free society where there are *no* higher authorities imposing beliefs upon you on pain of punishment in the name of tyranny, religion or tradition, the world is your oyster. You can make of it whatever you like. The only hindrance to your view is the ability of other humans to argue against you and show that you are talking drivel.

In such a society – especially in a democratic one – everything is up for debate. The point about the ancient Greek world is that it is the first of which we know where issues that were (normally) the monopoly of religious authorities or already settled by traditional beliefs – what the world is made of, where it comes from, how we should behave and so on – were debated in *public*, in *humanly intelligible* terms, through arguments based on reason, and not mysticism, magic or the supernatural.

Eclipses

Eclipses of the sun and moon are of high historical importance because they are the only sure way of dating past events absolutely. Since we now know precisely how the sun, moon and earth interact, we can say with absolute certainty when eclipses occurred in the past.

- From the 3rd millennium BC, Babylonians (inhabitants of modern Iraq) were recording the movement of the heavens and kept records, for some 2,000 years, stored in two libraries. In 747 BC, their astronomers systematised the information and used it to date eclipses of sun and moon, to see if any patterns were at work. The first Greek philosopher, Thales (c. 580 BC), presumably knew of this Babylonian work and exploited it to predict the eclipse of 28 May 585 BC.

- Both Greeks and Romans had sequential dating systems; all we require is for one of them to be linked to an eclipse and we can establish some form of accurate dating. Since there are about 250 mentions of eclipses in Greek and Roman literature, we can be fairly certain of the chronology of the ancient world. For example, the Greek poet Archilochus mentions one that we can date to 6 April 647 BC.

- But calendars are difficult to integrate. For example, the solar eclipse of 14 March 190 BC is recorded as 11 July by Romans; the lunar eclipse of 21 June 168 BC recorded as 4 September.

- Since the ancients popularly regarded eclipses as mystical, portents of things to come, they tended to scatter them about at significant historical moments. For example, Herodotus says that when Xerxes set out to invade Greece in spring 480 BC – that date is certain – there was a complete eclipse of the sun. Xerxes asked what it meant, and his obedient Magi replied that the Greek cities would be totally eclipsed. But the only eclipse visible in Persia that year was a *partial* one in October 480. However, there was a total one visible in Persia in April 481, i.e. the total eclipse of 481 was moved forward to make Xerxes' departure portentous.

- Intellectuals rejected these mystical explanations. The philosopher Anaxagoras (5th century BC), who realised that the moon shone by reflected light, produced the correct explanation: 'eclipses of the moon occur when it is screened by the earth [from the sun] . . . and of the sun when it is screened by the new moon [from the earth]'.

That does not mean to say that other cultures could not make important 'scientific' breakthroughs: Babylonians and Egyptians certainly did in mathematics, medicine and astronomy, for example. But it is Greeks who challenged authority and tradition in this world, and threw everything open for anyone to partake in, if they wished, without fear of interference on any other than intellectual grounds. 'I have got it right: everyone else has been talking bollocks' is the constant refrain of Greek thinkers. Big-headed? Of course. Groundbreaking? Without a doubt – one of the Greeks' most important contributions to the whole idea of what we mean by 'the Western tradition': the tradition that tradition (like authority) must be fought.

But one of the problems was this. Greeks had nothing else *but* their grey matter and their senses with which to solve problems. It would not be until the 17th century that technology would start to be added to the battery of means by which the physical world could be understood (and therefore properly experimented on). Only when man could get *below* the level of perception and manufacture reliable measuring implements would it become possible to inject some experimental reality into discussions on the nature of the world. Since the 18th century, of course, man's ingenuity at developing and then using the technology has led to a world of almost daily miracles.

Tyranny by numbers

For all its benefits, however, science has also had a stultifying effect on man's ability to deal with any problems that are not scientific. The reason is that science offers such a phenomenally powerful *model* for solving problems that it is assumed its techniques can be automatically applied to any problem, scientific or not. But the key to good science is (to put it extremely simply) accurate quantification – and that means getting the *numbers* right. Pythagoras, we are told, foresaw this development, arguing that 'number' held the key to the world. In an important sense, it does. But the tendency to see all problems in numerical and statistical terms is to lose sight of the basic truth that, while the physical world may work like that, humans do not. This is infuriating to administrators, who wish they did. It would make their life so much simpler.

So they produce, for example, computer-markable exams and claim this is what is meant by education. The computer is another favourite 'model' for human life, and an equally deficient one too, it having – for example – no sex life, no taste for good wine, no appreciation of a cover drive. One of society's most pressing problems is anti-social behaviour. What will solve it? 'A *system* . . . where the problems are addressed', a chief constable tells us. Good word, 'system'. It sounds logical, organised, scientific. But don't police already have 'systems' in place to deal with crime, usually called 'arresting and charging people'?

Another problem is family breakdown. It is clear from the statistics (ah! More nice, round numbers!) that marriage is the best generator of civilised children. Therefore it is concluded that all you need are mechanisms – that scientific image, as if people are inanimate objects driven by levers – to encourage marriage, and the problem is solved. What is the best mechanism? Why, we are told, money – something else that is a number. But money buys goods and services. That is fine if you need goods and services, but how (precisely) does it ensure a secure marriage?

The simple fact is that no such human problems are susceptible to 'scientific' (let alone 'political') solutions. That does not mean that humans cannot work away at them to learn by experience and reach privately workable solutions. To do that we need all the help we can get. The past is not a bad place to start since, first, the ancients' astonishing literary legacy gives us a powerful sense of what it meant for them to be human and how humans best function, and second, they built their own experience on close contacts with people they knew, not people they met vicariously through magazines, newspapers and TV. Finally, they were not blinded by the promises of science or the vacuous 'things can only get better' culture to hard, everyday realities. Indeed, they looked back to the past as a golden age and assumed things could only get worse. Theirs was an unforgiving world in which fantasy was not easy to sustain (cf. pp. 227, 257).

The study of Mankind

All these human problems bear on the questions that Greeks themselves raised: how far there might be a tangible, purposive connection between Nature (meaning 'the way the world was made and how it functioned') and man. Because, if there was, they argued, the sooner man found out, the better, since it would clearly result in man being able to lead a better-functioning existence. Thus was born the idea of being 'true to nature', of there being a 'natural' (and therefore 'right') as opposed to 'unnatural' (and therefore 'wrong') way of existence.

In this respect, however, Socrates rather bucked the trend. He admits that there was a time when he was fascinated by natural science, and found himself wondering about things like 'whether it was blood that makes us conscious beings, or air, or fire; or is it the brain that supplies us with our sense of sight and hearing or smell? Is it from here that memory and opinion, and then knowledge, come?'

But, he says, he eventually grew tired of it all because the study did not seem to have anything to do with 'the one thing it is in a man's interests to consider, with regard both to himself and anything else – the best and highest good'. It was therefore Socrates who (most of all) directed thinkers' attention away from the workings of the cosmos to what man was doing here on earth; in particular, what man was *for* and therefore how best he could be *good* at it. As Cicero claims, Socrates 'called philosophy down from the sky, set it in cities and even introduced it into homes and compelled it to consider life and morals, good and evil'.

Socrates drew a parallel with the crafts. We know what a shoe is *for*; so we know what a *good* shoe is; and we can find someone who can *make* a good shoe. So what is a man *for*? What goes into a *good* man? And who *makes* him a good man? Well, argued Socrates, we'd first better try to decide what we mean by 'good' –

and another gigantic branch of the Western philosophical tradition began to sprout.

Expertease

Socrates' question also raised acutely the question of the expert. On the craft analogy, it was possible to say who the experts were when it came to shoe-making or ship-building. But who were the experts when it came to making political decisions and exercising judgement about right and wrong, let alone making a good man?

Aristotle took a fascinatingly contrary view here, which would be applauded by all those TV shows dedicated to finding budding 'talent' and inviting the audience to humiliate it. He argued that one of the things that could be said for real democracy was that the more people who had a say, the more likely one was to get a reasonable result, since many brains were better than one; and he applied the same argument to the judging of poetry and plays.

Man, says Aristotle in his *Politics*, is by nature a *politikon zōon* – literally, 'an animal that lives in a *polis*', the Greek city-state. We might translate it 'social animal'. The unique characteristic of *politika zōa* (plural), he claims, is that 'they alone can distinguish between good and bad, justice and injustice and all the rest – and it is sharing a common view in these matters that makes a household and a state'.

As a result, he reasons, democracy is (give or take one or two problems) the best form of constitution:

'It is possible that the many, of whom no one taken singly is a sound man, may yet, taken all together, be better than the few, rather as a feast to which all contribute is better than one supplied at one man's expense. For even where there are many people, each has some share of virtue and practical wisdom; and when they are brought together . . . they become one in regard to character and intelligence. That is why the many are better judges of works of music and poetry: some judge some parts, some others, but their collective pronouncement is a verdict upon all the parts.'

It will not be true in all cases he says, because 'some men are hardly better than wild animals'. But, in general, it is.

This 'Ask the Audience' theory is one to which politicians are unwillingly forced to submit every five years or so. Otherwise they resist it to the death. So too do poets, artists or musicians. They much prefer the views of the 'experts' because these are the people who sit on grant-giving panels and also could not care less what the general public think. All the more reason to try it. After all, if it works for pop music, why not Art? One longs to see Brian Sewell asking the audience to press their buttons in favour of Rolf Harris or Tracy Emin.

The ancient view: artists as technicians

The nearest Greeks got to a word for 'art' was *tekhnē* (cf. 'technical'), which Aristotle defined as 'the trained ability to produce something under the guidance of rational thought'. In the ancient world, the artist was on the same level as our doctor or car-mechanic – one whose purpose it was to serve the public to the best of his technical capacity. So the idea that the artist was someone before whom one grovelled in drooling adulation would have struck the ancients as absurd. The Greek man of letters Plutarch (c. AD 50–120) hit the nail on the head:

'No one of good breeding or high ideals feels that they must be an artist after seeing the work of Pheidias, or a poet because they get so much pleasure out of poetry. It does not follow that because a particular work of art succeeds in charming us, its creator also deserves our admiration.'

That did not mean that people did not admire an artist's products. They certainly did, but rather in the way that we admire the work of an efficient dentist.

Like the dentist too, the ancient artist made his reputation by his public efforts. Art was not for art's sake, but to show off the wealth and taste of the patron, and the most effective patron of all was the public. So the artist devoted his career to a tradition of art that had been approved by public response down the ages. Buildings like the Parthenon were agreed by vote of the democratic Assembly and, for all the expense, hugely popular. The great Pheidias is said to have hidden in his studio and admitted the general public so that he could hear what they said about his latest work in progress.

Novelty and creativity for their own sakes were of no interest to the ancient artist. But this did not mean art stood still. Far from it. Development and innovation were welcomed and admired, but within the context of existing conventions. The result was continuing support from both public and patron. It is a lesson that members of the starving 'Arts' communities, exuding their usual aura of injured self-worth, would do well to learn when they next get their begging bowls out and start ululating about public indifference. In fact, if artists were to think of themselves first and foremost as craftsmen, they might well start to win back the public acclaim some of them once had.

But Socrates' question would not go away, and many subsequent thinkers set themselves up as experts on life problems.

As has already been observed, it is to pop singers, actresses and chat-show hosts that our political figures turn for advice these days, on everything from global warming to Third World poverty. This surely is a fairly new development. I do not remember Harold Macmillan inviting Vera Lynn to head up a think tank on the inner cities. Did it all start in 1967 when the Rolling Stones pop singer Mick Jagger (now, predictably, knighted), accompanied by another renowned social thinker Marianne Faithfull, descended from the heavens by helicopter onto the lawns of the editor of *The Times* to be fawningly interviewed on TV for his views about Yoof and Life and Drugs in company with the Archbishop of Canterbury?

Whether it did or not, Socrates' question continues to make us muse about any expertise our politicians may have that can reassure us we are in safe hands, and wonder what it is about actresses that makes them such Renaissance figures.

Atom theory

Greeks other than Socrates, however, took the idea that man's proper functioning, i.e. the good life, was critically dependent on the physical nature of the world he lived in. One theory was to have enormous significance.

To simplify a complex issue: the first Greek philosophers were really physicists or natural scientists. The big question they asked was: what is the one 'stuff' that lies at the root of the physical world? Various answers were proposed, such as air. But that raised a serious problem: how did that one stuff change into all the other stuffs we see about us? How did air, for example, turn into Neil Kinnock? (Ed. That's too easy. Please think of a trickier example.)

Indeed, the problem of change was felt to be so taxing that the philosopher Parmenides concluded that change was in fact impossible; but because the world we lived in made it look as if it *was* possible, we lived in a world of complete make-believe, where nothing was real!

One compromise solution was to conclude that there were four stuffs (earth, air, fire and water – the famous and very influential 'four element' theory), and the world was made up of mixtures of them. Another solution was to lead eventually to a development that, admittedly some 2,200 years later, would utterly transform our world – the very first atomic theory. 'Atomic' derives from the Greek *atomos* 'uncuttable, indivisible' ('-tomy' words in English are to do with cutting things out, like hysterectomy, and 'a(n)-' is mostly a negative prefix, cf. anaesthetic, literally 'no feeling/sensation'). It was developed by two Athenians, Leucippus and Democritus. To put it at its simplest, they argued that, since Parmenides was right and change was impossible, the basic substance must be something that never changes. It must therefore be something we cannot see. It must therefore be minutely small, below the level of sense perception, and the world must be formed out of the various, myriad ways in which the indivisible *atomoi* (pl.) endlessly grouped and regrouped.

And they were, stunningly, right. Not that they knew it, let alone could demonstrate it. But reason and logic had enabled them, all unknowing, to stumble over a basic truth. And it does not stop there. Since they thought that there were infinite numbers of atoms, existing in infinite space, they speculated that there must be an infinite number of other worlds. One ancient source describes their belief as follows:

'There are innumerable cosmoses differing in size. In some there is no sun or moon, in others they are larger than with us, in others more numerous. The intervals between the cosmoses are unequal; in some places there are more, in others fewer; some are growing, others are fully grown, others again are dying; somewhere worlds are coming to be, elsewhere fading. And they are destroyed when they collide with each other. Some cosmoses have no living creatures or plants, and no water at all.'

Incredibly, this is now one of the latest theories of the cosmos. While many believe that the universe started with a 'Big Bang' about fifteen billion years ago, two leading cosmologists have recently proposed that the cosmos in fact undergoes cycles of expansion and contraction, so that it endlessly dies and rises from the ashes! It is good to know that modern science has finally caught up with the ancient atomists.

Francis Bacon (1561–1626) was an early enthusiast for the atomic theory; but it was the French Jesuit Pierre Gassendi (1592–1655) who wrote commentaries on the issue, duly modified and accommodated to Christian teaching, as the best way of investigating nature. This work came to the attention of scientists including Robert Boyle (like Newton, a keen alchemist), whose work on gases had already convinced him that Aristotle's theory of matter was nonsense. Soon the theory that matter consisted of 'minute particles' became received wisdom, and in 1803 John Dalton founded modern atomic theory with a series of statements about chemical combination (e.g. that elements consist of individual small particles – atoms – which can be neither created nor destroyed).

Aristotle, however, was a four-element man. If the man whose word was law in Western thought for over 1,500 years had chosen the atomic option, the technological revolution might have happened much earlier than it did. So it is, obviously, all Aristotle's fault, and he owes every one of us an apology. I am sure the Greek government, backed up by a tearful Ken Livingstone, will be happy to oblige.

Hypothetical deductions

Since we know the atomic theory of matter is correct, it is very hard indeed to get our heads round the idea that someone like Aristotle – a towering intellectual genius in any terms – opted for the four-element theory. The point is that there was a basic weakness at the heart of Greek thought, a weakness not unique to the Greeks and not resolved, in fact, until the 16th century.

Greek philosophers could proceed only by observing the world about them and establishing a hypothesis about how it worked. That done, they then made deductions from that hypothesis, and that was that: problems solved. The exercise was a rational one, of course: Greeks used reason to establish the hypothesis and reason to make deductions from it. What they never did, however, was *to test the hypothesis to see if it was true*. So if the hypothesis was rubbish – for example, that the cosmos was made up of earth-air-fire-water – the deductions would be rubbish as well. This is the problem with all metaphysical speculation.

There is nothing wrong in principle with the hypothetical method. We still use it. In the realms of higher maths – Stephen Hawking territory, for example – we propose hypotheses about the nature of the universe and make deductions from them. The difference, however, is that these are tested to destruction by what physicists can discover about the nature of the universe (Hubble telescopes and all that) to see if they accord with the evidence. So the Hawking theories may accord with the evidence at the moment, but who knows what disruptive piece of evidence may emerge to blow the whole hypothesis to smithereens? Ancient Greeks would have absolutely adored such debates. They were brilliant mathematicians anyway e.g. Euclid, Archimedes, etc.

And that is the point. Until someone actually thought up the idea of testing hypotheses to destruction, and had the technology so to do (e.g. to see below the level of perception, to measure accurately, and so on) one could not test hypotheses except by looking at the logic of the deductions that flowed from it. Aristotle, of course, knew about the atomic theory but saw logical problems with it that he did not see with the four-element theory (though he was forced to add a fifth, *aithēr*, the ether). Hence his (to us) unhinged conclusions.

One can best see the same hypothetical/deductive way of thinking at work in today's politics. The Tory hypothesises, for example, that (i) the 'market' solves all problems, and (ii) the smaller the state and the lower the tax rate, the happier and more successful we and the economy shall be. The socialist hypothesises the reverse. Well? Which is true? The answer is important because the deductions you make from a false hypothesis, being rubbish, will have very serious consequences. Or is neither true?

Is anyone going to solve the problem for us? Very probably not. As the Greeks knew, once you have established a much-loved hypothesis on which your whole belief system depends, you do not question it. Your world might collapse, and then where would you be? The current assumption that the best thing for all children between five and sixteen is to be educated by the state in schools is another splendid example. Compulsory state education is now 130 years old, and no one ever questions it. Unsurprisingly, it is a failure for the bottom ten per cent. It always has been and always will be. It is called statistics. That ten per cent will fail *by definition*. What is the government response? Pour in more resources.

Why not abandon the hypothesis? Or try a different tack?

Where has our famous English pragmatism gone? When local neighbourhoods ('demes', p. 92) in Attica sent their young men to Athens to be certified as aged eighteen by physical examination, demes were fined for any candidates who failed. Since it is the government that boasts about all the 'resources' it lavishes on education, perhaps it should be fined for every pupil who reaches sixteen or eighteen without the skills even to go to university, let alone get a job. It might make them think again.

The Romans (like the Greeks) would have thought compulsory, state-funded education a nonsense anyway. Had they thought it worth experimenting with, they would have contracted it out and let those who wanted an education get it in the form they preferred.

Epicures for all

One very famous theory to emerge from atomic theory was that of the good life, Epicureanism, named after its founder, the Greek thinker Epicurus (the Latinised form of the Greek Epikouros, c. 300 BC). Its most influential adherent was the great Roman poet Lucretius (1st century BC). He wrote a simply sensational six-book poem *dē rērum nātūrā*, 'Concerning the Nature of Things/ Matter/the World', in which he set out Epicurus' key to how the 'atomic' world worked and therefore to happiness; and it was he, incidentally, who was the crucial influence on Gassendi and the others.

Lucretius' argument went as follows. Man spends his life striving for wealth, celebrity, power, fame, honour, fortune, glory. And a right pain it is. So why do we bother? Because we are terrified of death, against which our only compensation lies in amassing material goods. But if, as Epicurus showed, everything – the universe, our world, men and gods alike – is made up of unchanging and unchangeable atoms, from atoms we come and back to atoms (on death) we must go. Therefore there is no afterlife. Therefore there is nothing to fear about death – atoms to atoms, dust to dust – nor any need to worry about gods, who are simply atoms as well.

But, one may object, how do we *know* that gods, atoms though they may be, do not still keep a beady eye on our doings? Because, Lucretius hypothesised, gods (by definition) are perfect and perfectly happy. The world, obviously, is an imperfect place, full of diseases, wild beasts, death, and so on. Therefore any god worth his salt would need his celestial brain examined if he were to have anything to do with it. So gods have no interest in the universe, but live in a place apart, unconcerned about human affairs. QED.

Which raises the question: with the gods out of the way, and all fear of death removed, what does the good life consist of? Pleasure? Endless lounging on beaches under parasols having one's every desire fulfilled by whomever and whatever takes one's fancy? This indeed was a popular notion of Epicureanism, a word that for us is tinged with ideas of luxury and sensuality. Epicurus disagreed. All these, he averred, may bring temporary pleasure but in the long term they bring nothing but pain – hangovers, brain rot, embarrassment, tedium. No: what we must do is to strive for a life *free from all anxiety*. That meant avoiding desire for everything that was unattainable or had no limits (like wealth and status), because that desire, by definition, could never be satisfied.

A prime example of the sort of thing Epicurus thought was so degrading of, and debilitating for, humans is open in front of me now: it is a handbook describing how to be 'cool'. Apparently there are 'experts' in 'cool' – am I really writing this in the 3rd millennium? – working in association with something called the Coolbrands Council, who tell you that the top twenty 'cool' things are various fast cars and computer-related products. Apparently the 'coolest' international destination is Japan (but what if you are Japanese?). It makes one long to become an Epicurean, whose basic rules were:

- Stick to what is natural and necessary, e.g. food, drink, sex (hmm: perhaps the beach is not such a bad idea).

- Avoid what is natural but unnecessary, e.g. desire for specific varieties of food and drink and sex (the beach *is* a bad idea).
- Avoid even more what is unnatural and unnecessary, like – well, everything connected with the Coolbrands Council.

This line of thinking is all about getting your mind straight in order to deal successfully with the world. Nowadays this exercise is called 'cognitive therapy', and no one doubts its importance. As I write, the government has said it is planning to fund the training of 3,500 cognitive therapists to deal with what it perceives as a growing problem. They could do worse than to turn to Epicurus for the answer.

Stoicism: the alternative to Epicureanism

Stoicism was invented by Zeno (from Cyprus, 335–263 BC), who set up a university in Athens. Stoics believed that god was not a personal god but 'divine reason' – a rational power that guided all things and was everywhere in the universe, like honey permeating a honeycomb. Man, therefore, possessed a rational mind, and this was the 'divine' element in him. They believed the highest product of the rational mind was excellence, or moral virtue – the one thing that really counted and alone led to happiness. By contrast with virtue, everything else – wealth, status, etc. – was a matter of indifference.

This raised all sorts of problems, for example, how the irrational could exist in such a universe, but also had important consequences in encouraging the view (as Cicero said) that 'the world is a common home of gods and men', all sharing in the divine reason. From such a belief, concepts such as world citizenship and the law of nations developed.

The famous Stoic teacher Epictetus was born a slave in Phrygia (the region around Ankara), a Greek-speaking province of the Roman Empire. He was sold to a confidante

---

of Nero, and Nero freed him. He set up a private university in Greece and was visited by the emperors Hadrian and Marcus Aurelius.

Epictetus argued that we have a choice: we can go with the flow (floating down a river is an image that Epictetus uses) and act rationally – because that is the way the universe is – and be happy. Or we can go against the flow, act irrationally and be miserable. It is up to us. The Stoic had therefore to decide what was 'up to him' and what was not, i.e. what he had it in himself to control and what not. The two things they identified as most likely to cause one to *lose* control were the emotions and the desires. So 'endure and restrain yourself', said Epictetus.

Stoics believed in both fate and free will. To explain the paradox, they used the image of a dog on a long leash attached to an ox-drawn cart. The dog has much freedom to roam on his long lead, but ultimately has no option but to go where the cart goes. That is fate. But he can go freely and be happy, or struggle against it and be miserable. It is up to him.

The Romantic Movement that swept across Europe from the 18th century put an end to all that. Set up in opposition to classical rationalism, it was all in favour of creative freedom, spontaneity, sincerity, emotionalism, yearning, dreaming, poking about in the soul with a pole to find 'the truth', a search for something that one felt was there but could never be found: in other words, the priority over all else of 'feelings' (Gottfried von Herder replied to Descartes' 'I think, therefore I am' with 'I am not here to think but to be, to feel, to live!'). This denial of the rational – doing just what we feel like, letting it all hang out – is a regression to behaviour that Greeks would have thought animalistic. It is, of course, very 'inclusive', but ultimately leads to that self-indulgent sentimentality and retreat into dream-like fantasy that are the hallmarks of so much Western life. The 'every child is a genius' theory of

> education is just one example of the absurdities to which
> it leads.

Ancients took it for granted that the 'good life' could not be lived without some reference to the physical nature of the universe. But nature still dealt out some pretty nasty shocks about which one could do nothing – pain, disease, death. So, given that nature could never be transformed, one had to learn to survive these painful blows. The only way one could do that was to develop the inner resources to rise above nature, to transcend it.

Graceful in defeat

It was not just nature that handed out shocks. Humans did too, especially in the highly competitive world of the ancient Greeks, where winning was all and doing down your enemies a particularly enjoyable pastime (cf. p. 95). Greeks therefore, like all cultures, developed ways of dealing with losing. In the modern business world, one way it is handled is to talk of 'spending more time with the family' or 'finding different ways of testing myself' or 'retiring from the rat race to the country'. The famous Greek watchwords 'Nothing in excess' and 'Know yourself', carved on the temple of Apollo at Delphi, were designed to serve Greeks in the same way. The two sayings are different sides of the same coin. They urge a man to know what he can and what he *cannot* do. They therefore prompt a man to minimise the chances of going to extremes and making a fool of himself.

A hysterical example of not knowing oneself was recently provided by Mr Ozzy Osbourne. He is a pop singer who also makes TV 'reality' shows (how Plato would have adored *that* contradiction in terms, cf. p. 257). He was doing a show in North Dakota, and the local police chief, searching for a way to bring in hundreds of petty criminals on outstanding arrest warrants, issued them with invitations to a spoof party to meet this great star. Thirty turned up and were promptly arrested. Mr Osbourne was *outraged*: 'Sheriff Laney should be apologising to me for using my name in connection with these arrests. It is insulting to me and my audience.'

What an exquisite irony. Possibly for the first time in his life, Mr Osbourne performs a genuinely useful service for the community and takes it as an *insult*. The thought that he was good for attracting trash had clearly never crossed his mind. Back to the telly, Mr Osbourne. Best not to know yourself. TV reality is so much more comforting.

Old age

All the books tell you that, thanks to life-prolonging advances in diet and medicine, serious old age is a comparatively modern phenomenon. We can all now make it our ambition to live for ever or die in the attempt. Adam would disagree (he lived to 930) and so would Methuselah, who holds the western world record at 969. These are, however, positive teenagers compared with the Sumerian kings of ancient Babylon (modern Iraq), of whom En Men Lu Anna clocks in at 43,200.

The wrath of God, however, soon sorted out the biblical heroes. Abraham only made it to 175, Isaac to 147 and Joseph to 110, and at *Genesis* 6.3, God fixed the span of human life at a generous 120. Greeks fixed it at a more reasonable three scores years and ten, something resembling contemporary reality though very few of them would have got that far. Interestingly, total possible lifespan appears to have been no different in the ancient world to what it is today. We have a few cases where ancient Greeks clocked in at over 100.

But it is the population figures that count. Around 40 per cent of us Britons are now over 50. Such a figure would have appeared unbelievable to ancients. In the ancient world, for physical, dietary and military reasons, the mortality curve peaked at birth, early childhood and in the early twenties. So you became old earlier in ancient Greece. Some ancient Greek texts suggest you became an 'old man' (*presbeutēs*, cf. presbyterian) at the age of thirty. Those who got that far could well have hoped, I suppose, for another fifteen to twenty years of life.

One consequence of this, however, was to squeeze out middle age: it is an idea you can hardly find anywhere in Greek ancient texts. Pythagoras, for example, fixing human life at eighty years, divides it into 0–20 childhood; 20–40 adolescence; 40–60 youth; 60–80 old age. There is, however, a splendid fable about middle age by Babrius (c. 150 AD):

> 'A man who was middle-aged – he wasn't young any more, nor yet an old man, but his black and white hairs were mixed up together – was still devoting his days to love-making and drinking. But he was sleeping with two women, one young, and the other, old. The young one wanted him to look youthful, so she plucked out all his grey hairs; the old one wanted him to look old, so she did the same to his black hairs. The result was that he went completely bald.'

Well, if one is going to go bald anyway, it would be hard to think of a more agreeable way of doing so. Interestingly, there are ancient beliefs that connect baldness with sexual activity. Some Greek doctors believed that semen was generated in the brain behind the ears, and that during sexual activity it boiled up and scorched the roots of the hair, causing baldness over time. There is still a theory that baldness indicates virility. Can this explain why young men with big, nasty dogs on leads always shave their heads?

Given the angst that middle age causes nowadays, Pythagoras' approach seems very sound: get rid of it. Then, at the age of sixty, one can make the transition from teenage freshness and vitality to toothless senility over the course of a long weekend.

A good death

One way in which the true Roman expressed his mastery over nature was to show that death held no fears for him. Romans regarded dying as an active, not a passive, process, and one which revealed as much about a man's character as his life had done.

Take Cato the Younger. Despite Julius Caesar's offer of clemency, he vowed not to live under what he regarded as a tyranny. So he tried to commit a lonely suicide with his sword, but the wound in his hand made that impossible. The surgeon stitched him up, but he tore open the wound in front of his appalled friends and died in agony. Here was a Stoic bravely enduring a ghastly death in order to proclaim that liberty was more important than life. It offered a lasting model for Romans of what a good death should look like. Death, in other words, regularly presented as a conscious performance, was a privileged moment, an act loaded with moral significance.

Today, as we are endlessly reminded by scientists warning us not to eat bacon sarnies (and demanding money for 'more research' on their transparently lethal qualities) or celebrities pouring out their moving tales of how they bravely 'beat' cancer (they mean their doctors did, but it does not sound quite so heroic), death is not on the menu. The purpose of life is to be kept alive, regardless, i.e. the celebs are all scared stiff. Romans would have regarded them with utter contempt. As the younger Seneca points out, dying is one of life's duties: 'as it is with a play, so it is with life – what matters is not how long the acting lasts, but how good it is . . . make sure you round it off with a good ending.'

Which brings us to medicine.

▷┼◀▸•O•◀▸┼◁

Reading list

Aristotle, *The Politics* (Penguin 1992).

Jonathan Barnes, *Early Greek Philosophy* (Penguin 1987).

Catherine Edwards, *Death in Ancient Rome* (Yale 2007).

Peter Jones, *An Intelligent Person's Guide to Classics* (Duckworth 1999).

G.S. Kirk, J.E. Raven and M. Schofield, *The Presocratic Philosophers* (Cambridge 1983).

G.E.R. Lloyd, *The Revolutions of Wisdom* (California 1987).

Lucretius, *On the Nature of the Universe* (Penguin 1994).

Plato, *The Last Days of Socrates* (Penguin 1993).

Plutarch, *The Rise and Fall of Athens* (Penguin 1960).

T.E. Rihll, *Greek Science* (*Greece and Rome*: New Surveys in the Classics no. 29, Oxford 1999).

R.W. Sharples, *Stoics, Epicureans and Sceptics* (Routledge 1996).

[13]

The doctor could well see you shortly

Natural perverts?

Given that the ancients thought there was a 'natural order' of things, modern medicine in the shape of, for example, quadruple heart-bypass surgery might have looked to them like the grossest of perversions of that natural order, as would atom bombs, aeroplanes and satellite television. Today, indeed, whole branches of alternative medicine have sprung up, hostile to what people see as undue interference with nature.

For all that, Greek and Roman doctors would be green with envy at what modern medicine and technology can achieve. The grounds on which ancient doctors justified their art are clarified by the saying of the 3rd-century BC doctor from Alexandria Herophilus: 'drugs are the hands of the gods'. In other words, doctors did not interfere with nature but used all their skills and available resources to encourage nature to do what it did best – i.e. heal. One doctor did admit that nature sometimes required to be forced into revealing its secrets, but when it did, doctors could see the right way forward. So there was no rupture between medical interference and the 'natural order' because if there was, things went wrong. Modern examples would be rejection of body parts because of tissue mismatch and transfusions of the wrong blood type.

Global warning

Today, the breakdown of the natural order is seen most acutely in the phenomenon of global warming (if, that is, warming is due to environmental misuse). The ancients, who had a dim awareness of the possibility, would applaud today's environmentalists for pointing out the dangers.

Since earth, Gaia, was thought to be a goddess (p. 180), it was commonly concluded that man could exist on it only if he were somehow at one with it and worked closely together with it. But nature was not always friendly. Ancients got round this by crediting it with moral purpose. If, for example, nature at times produced poisons, there must be a lesson there somewhere for man – perhaps 'Do not be greedy'. If man, the elder Pliny argued, had to dig beneath the surface of beneficent earth for gold or iron, he had better beware of the consequences: such products were likely to be corrupting (gold led to luxury, iron to weapons: QED). In other words, there was a moral dimension to the natural world. It was therefore important to work within its limits. Nature would exact a painful price if we went too far in exploiting it.

The Stoic thinker Seneca took the moral argument in a different direction, arguing there was a link between man's corrupt nature and the earth: earth would constantly destroy man and try to produce a better race while man persisted in his decadence. He thought the world would end when it was winter all the year round, sun and the stars failed, and flood and earthquake finally wiped us out. The Roman poet Lucretius, good Epicurean that he was, thought that earth was slowly decaying willy-nilly, and would eventually die, splitting up into its original constituent atoms. Arguably, both are right.

Medical limits

Committed though they were to healing, ancient doctors had only very limited chances of being successful. Nevertheless, medicine is a profession that compels anyone who wants to make a living out of it to resist saying to a patient 'Sorry, squire, haven't the foggiest what's wrong with you, I'll prod around a bit but there are no guarantees'. So doctors oozed a confidence in their abilities far beyond any actual competence.

Their incompetence is hardly surprising. Where physics/

natural science and philosophy had led the way, medicine keenly followed, adopting precisely the same hypothetical principles and practice, but now applied to the body. They had no idea how it worked as a whole any more than anyone else did until almost the 20th century. But doctors did have one great advantage: there were plenty of bodies at hand, including their own.

There was, however, one major proviso to their 'research'. You could observe bodies and examine them, but you could not cut them up. For long stretches of antiquity that was taboo. So doctors had the chance to examine the internal structure of the body only as a result of wounds on the battlefield or injuries incurred in accidents. The results can be seen in Homer's *Iliad*, where the poet occasionally comes up with quite impossible – though unquestionably dramatic – effects. Here Patroclus fells Cebriones with a rock:

> 'He did not throw in vain: the sharp stone caught Hector's charioteer Cebriones, famous Priam's illegitimate son, on the forehead, with the horses' reins still in his hands. It shattered both his eyebrows, crushing the bone; and his eyes fell out and rolled in the dust at his feet.'

Do not try this at home. It will not work. No blow to the forehead could conceivably sever the eyes, attached to their sockets by six strap muscles on each side and to the brain by the optic nerve and blood vessels.

Medical hypotheses

So, here is our ancient Greek doctor, cigar and bottle of Scotch at hand, poised to determine how the body works and what makes for health and ill health. Like other thinkers, he is searching for a hypothesis from which to make deductions. Where does he begin? There are three obvious starting points: first, under what conditions the body seems to function at its best (when a man is fit); second, what the body takes in (food and drink) and what it puts out (faeces, urine, sweat, blood, phlegm, etc.); and third, how philosopher-physicists have decided the world as a whole works.

Lifestyles

One area of medicine was known as 'dietetics', from the Greek *diaita*, 'way of life' (origin of our 'diet'). It is very trendy these days, where people spend inordinate amounts of time and money on gyms, trainers, diet regimes and bottled water ('Best before 2009', we are assured. Amazing how accurately capitalists can predict the date on which a substance millions of years old will go off). In the ancient world, however, this was not exactly rocket salad. Watching what you ate and drank, and ensuring you exercised from time to time, was basic and obvious, a standard recommendation. Especially important was the stomach's ability to digest its food properly. The Greek for 'digestion' is *pepsis* (lit. 'cooking') – the origin of Pepsi.

Going to extremes of *diaita*, however, was not advised. Medical texts are full of observations about the deleterious effects of excess and the absurdity and uselessness of the athlete's body (see p. 158). This is something else our fitness fanatics have got hopelessly wrong. Fitness gyms are not, in fact, about fitness, let alone health, at all: they are about producing a pretty, but otherwise useless, frame.

There is an important point to be made here. Ancients (not just Greeks and Romans) knew very well that, once you fell ill, there was often not a lot they could do about it. They therefore put a great deal of effort into ensuring you did not. Hence the emphasis on healthy lifestyle. We are wise to follow that practice today. This is not because modern medicine is not extremely efficient at making people better. It is. The reason is that getting ill is unpleasant and, more important, *it is in the interests of drug companies that you do so*. That is where they make their money. With a few exceptions, they do not make their money by providing drugs that prevent illness, and they are therefore slow to develop means by which early warnings of illness can be flagged up and prevented before they ever get going.

Four humours

But what if you did fall ill? Here our doctor would bring the latest theories of the cosmos into play, and the hypothesis that won out for the medical profession was the four-element theory (that everything consisted of different combinations of earth, air, fire and water). So, following ancient Greek 'best practice', they then set about determining how the workings of the body could be aligned with that theory. Observation of the body told them that fevers made people hot, like fire; other illnesses made them shiver with cold, like earth; sometimes people broke into moist sweat, like water, etc. Then they observed that the body exuded blood (hot/wet like fire and water), phlegm (cold/wet like earth and water), and other fluids, especially yellow bile (sick) and black bile (doctors began to struggle a bit at this point). Anyway, they proceeded to force these four fluids into a pattern that could be made to match the four-element theory. Doctors then argued that the healthy body kept these various elements 'in balance'. The unhealthy body was therefore excessively hot or cold, moist or dry, and needed to be rebalanced by, for example, taking in suitably cold or hot, dry or moist foods.

As an example of the conclusions doctors drew from the theory, take the following typical health advice from an ancient medical source:

'During the winter, eat a much as possible, drink as little as possible, and this should be wine as undiluted as possible (cf. p. 246). . . . Of cereals, eat bread, roast all meat and fish, eat as few vegetables as possible. *Such a diet will keep the body warm and dry*. When spring comes, drink more, making it more watery; take softer cereals and less of them, and a few vegetables. Cut down on meat, replacing roast with boiled . . . during the summer, live on soft barley-cake, watered wine in large quantities and take all meat boiled. Such a diet is necessary to make the body *cool and soft, because the season is hot and dry* . . . Reverse the process as winter approaches . . . this will keep a man in good health and he will feel less cold, for the season is *cold and wet* . . . '

With some exceptions, this is all rubbish, but rational if you began from the hypothesis that the four-element theory explained the world (the anthroposophical movement, apparently, still believes in its medical validity). So overwhelmingly influential did this theory become that, eventually, it turned into the ultimate theory of everything, encompassing the four ages of man, the four letters in the name of God (YHVH), the four winds, the four corners of the earth, the four grail symbols, the four gospels (and so on and on). Should we extend it even unto the Fab Four? Hush! No joking before the great gods of 'music', as pop nowadays is so reverentially held to be.

Ancient medicine, modern language

The ancient language continues to have its influence on ours. Health, as we have seen, was a matter of keeping/restoring a balance of the four liquids – blood, phlegm, yellow bile and black bile – in the body, and the Latin for 'liquid', 'juice', is *(h)ūmor* (cf. Greek *khūmos*). So:

- If the balance is right, you are 'good humoured'.
- If you behave absurdly, it proves that the balance is *not* right; so you are 'humorous' (we also talk of people being 'unbalanced').

The mixture of these *hūmōrēs* also affected one's 'temperament' – Latin *temperō* 'I mix', giving our 'temper', which originally meant just temperament (the earlier English for bad temper was 'distemper', dis- meaning 'apart, separate'). So:

- If you have lots of blood (Latin *sanguis*), you are 'sanguine, cheerful'.
- If you have lots of phlegm, you are calm and unemotional ('phlegmatic').
- If you have lots of black bile, you are 'melancholic' (Greek *melas*, 'black').

- And all this shows in your 'complexion', Latin *cum* + *plectō*, 'weave together', one's temperament being shown by the blend of colours in one's face.

This nonsense lay at the heart of medical practice for thousands of years. It started to fade away only with the technological and experimental revolutions of the 17th century and (most dramatically) with Pasteur's germ theory of infection in 1878 and the isolation of viruses in 1884. (It is staggering to think that the human race did not know about germs until little over a hundred years ago.)

Medicine good, bad and herbal

So for thousands of years the doctor was almost completely useless. But his medical beliefs and practices were hallowed by tradition; no one had anything better to offer; expectations were limited by what *did* work; and if it didn't work, you were going to die anyway, weren't you? So since no one knew doctors were useless, they were highly respected. It would be quite extra-ordinarily difficult to think of similarly useless people held in high regard for the same bogus reasons in the modern world, would it not?

But one area where ancient medicine often got it right was in its use of herbal remedies (or 'drugs'), another branch of the doctor's art. By 'drugs', doctors meant plants, which anyone could grow.

There were many wonder drugs, beliefs about whose properties were down to folkloric tradition rather than any serious evidence. Take leeks, for example: they were used to stop nose-bleeds, cure coughs and chest infections, pimples, burns and sores; mixed with goat, they cured infections of the ears; mixed with women's milk, they cured singing in the ears and, if poured into the nostrils, headaches. They dealt with poison bites, lumbago, kidney pain; served as a dye for grey hair; and were a pick-me-up after hangovers, an aphrodisiac, and imparted brilliance to the voice. No wonder the Welsh sing so unstoppably.

At the same time, ancients knew about plants that could indeed clean out the system or block it up, prevent pain, heal wounds, act as contraceptives (olive oil), help abortions, deal with local illnesses like pneumonia and eye disease, and so on. They knew that willow bark was good for headaches, pains and fevers (synthesised, it is the source of aspirin). Still in use in Pompeii today for medicinal purposes are local plants that were also used similarly by the Romans, for example, maidenhair fern and parsley (menstruation, abortifacient), common wormwood (colitis), European chestnut (digestion, bowel function), camomile (sleeplessness), chicory (stomach ailments), cyclamen (put in the nostrils, clears the head), oil of larkspur seed (insecticide), figs (laxative, warts), St John's Wort (cleansing the system), lettuce (stomach problems, insomnia), laurel (bowel pains), vervain (internal organs, especially the liver: for Romans, this was the great cure-all plant), and so on.

But credit where credit is due: whatever they got wrong, ancient doctors, Greek and Roman, like natural scientists, had no time for magic or supernatural remedies and made some most stunning physical observations and deductions. They could often *do* little about them, but that does not negate their brilliance. The central, deeply influential point is that their medicine was *evidence-based*, the guiding principle of all modern medicine.

Aristotle on the soul and the abortion question

Aristotle said that a soul (*psūkhē*, Latin *anima*) 'is the fulfilment of a natural body that has organs': in other words, a soul was a prerequisite of a functioning body. No soul, no capacity to function. But what sort of functions? Aristotle homed in on four – nutrition, perception, movement and reason – and established a broad hierarchy of animate existence: nutritional (vegetables), perceptual and locomotional (animals), and rational (man).

So souls were not physical: they were sets of capacities

or faculties. Further, if that was the case, souls could not exist separately from bodies (any more than 'walking' can exist separately from 'feet'). So he disagreed with Plato, who saw the soul as somehow the essence of a man, pre-existing him and surviving him after death: a soul was not the sort of thing that *could* exist outside a body. This led Aristotle to wonder where the human soul came from and how humans began to live. He momentously concluded that each faculty came *in the womb*, at a different stage of pregnancy. The embryo when first formed was purely nutritional, like a carrot. Then it developed movement and sensation, like an animal. Finally, it developed reason and became human – after forty days in the case of a male, ninety in the case of a female.

Thomas Aquinas (13th century AD) adopted Aristotle's view of the development of soul in the womb, but invested it with religious significance. For Aquinas, the soul was not a set of capacities but rather, as it was for Plato, the eternal divine essence of a man, the only feature of mankind that had everlasting value, and whose state was of supreme importance to God.

Hence the argument about abortion. If the *unborn* child has such a soul which enters its body at a specific time, discussions on the foetus are about much more than bald biology.

Two individuals in particular were of prime importance in establishing the basic principles and practice of rational, evidence-based medicine: the Greek Hippocrates from the island of Cos (5th century BC), who was so important that treatises written hundreds of years after his death were ascribed to him, and Galen, a Greek from Pergamum and follower of Hippocrates, who made his name in Rome (2nd century AD). He left us his own frequently dogmatic and pugnacious but deeply influential thoughts on medicine and many other topics, running to nearly three million words. Among many other things, he was a pioneer in understanding the significance of mind–body interaction and the influence of the emotions; stress, such a fashionable problem today, was a particular speciality.

In such works we find, for example, accurate observation of significant symptoms (breath, pulse, fever, discoloration) and careful tracking of the progress of illnesses (Greeks were very good at prognosis); healthy and unhealthy locations and climates were identified (they may not have known about malaria, but they certainly observed its effects); fractures were set, dislocations reduced; nerves were divided into motor and sensory. Cautery was the ancient equivalent of laser treatment, used to seal and clean wounds and haemorrhages and burn off growths, such as warts. A treatise on haemorrhoids describes how to burn them off with red-hot irons and contains the liberal advice to 'allow the patient to shout out during the process because that makes the anus stick out more'. I bet it does.

Womb service

In the ancient world children served two essential purposes: maintaining the family line and serving the military needs of the state. Indeed, anyone in Athens who wanted to serve in an executive position had to pass a test referring to his father, mother, grandparents, cult worship, upkeep of family tombs, treatment of parents and so on. Ancient medical treatises therefore go into massive detail on the subject of producing children, paying close attention to the usual range of beliefs about how the world worked.

The very brief selection of hints here concentrates on three hypotheses about males and females (there were many competing views). First, males are hot and dry, females cold and moist; second, males are right-sided, females left-sided; third, the child was generated from the male seed alone. The woman was merely the receptacle. It was vital therefore that she keep the semen in and not spill it out.

- Age: Aristotle recommended eighteen as the best age for a woman to start having children, and thirty-seven for a man; in this way, they would both reach the end of their reproductive lives at about the same time.
- Womb: Greek doctors thought one cause of infertility was a wandering womb. They believed if it was unused, it dried up and wandered about looking for moister parts of the body. This caused all sort of female problems – headache, palpitations, madness, suicide (cf. 'hysteria', from Greek *husterā*, 'womb'). Foul-smelling substances applied to the nose could repel it into position, sweet substances at the other end lure it. Sexual intercourse and having children also did the business.
- Fertility: the key test was whether a woman's tubes were cleared for take-off. One way of checking was to insert a piece of garlic at the bottom end and smell the woman's breath. If it was garlicky, her tubes were unobstructed.
- Intercourse: soon after menstruation was the best time. To produce a male, a man must consume strong, hot food, lie on his right side and tie up his left testicle (chaps, as usual, have all the fun). The woman must briefly abstain from moist food, bathing and washing her hair. She must cross her legs after intercourse and not take violent exercise. The semen must be hot (Aristotle thought that men with long penises would be infertile because their semen cooled before it reached the woman. So size *does* matter).
- Pregnancy: Aristotle recommended women should moderately exercise their bodies, but not their minds since this would have a deleterious effect on the unborn child.
- Contraception: olive oil was a well known, and effective, contraceptive. Men could drink honeysuckle for thirty-seven days, or the burned testicles of castrated mules, with willow (well, not *all* the fun). *Coitus interruptus* is almost never mentioned (condoms are a 16th-century invention, not widely available until vulcanisation of rubber was invented in 1844).

Children today are demanded as a 'human right' (and by male

and female homosexual couples too, which ancients would have thought grotesque). This produces a strange polarisation of attitudes towards them. On the one hand, children have never been more worshipped and idolised, their early deaths more 'tragic', their every word listened to with such deep reverence and their side taken more ferociously when any figure of authority like a teacher tries to correct them. On the other, they have never seemed less controlled, disciplined and taught how to grow up.

Just conceivably the first phenomenon explains the second. It is as if too many parents have no clear idea of what children are for, or what their responsibility to them is – except the sentimental self-satisfaction of the parents, until they suddenly find they have reared monsters.

Gob-stopper

The government seems to spend much of its time issuing dire warnings about the Great Obesity Battle (GOB), as if no one for the rest of time will ever have the willpower to do anything about it unless the government appoints a Fat Controller with a £50 billion budget. Ancient doctors were aware of some of the problems. The 5th-century BC Greek doctor Hippocrates, for example, knew that sudden death was more common in the fat. Both he and Aristotle thought that fatness in women caused sterility – a sufficient reason for the ancients to condemn female obesity – but we never hear of slim women being praised for their sexual attractiveness or on aesthetic grounds. Anorexia is a good Greek word (*an-orexiā*, lit. 'not-reaching out', 'lack of appetite') but we never hear of that as a medical condition either. Hippocrates suggested that a large physique was pleasing in the young, though not in the old, but recommended moderation in dieting:

'dieting which causes excessive loss of weight, as well as the feeding-up of the emaciated, is beset with difficulties'.

In Greek eyes, obesity was particularly associated with luxury. Ptolemy Alexander, a Greek king of Egypt, needed two people to support him when he left the room to relieve himself. The vast Dionysius, tyrant of Heracleia, in danger of choking if he fell deeply asleep, had to be pricked awake with very fine needles long enough to locate the nerves under the rolls of flesh. Yet he lived to fifty-five, tyrant for thirty-three years, 'excelling all in gentleness and decency'. On their tomb paintings, Etruscans tended to depict aristocrats at dinner as very fat and even more contented.

Spartans took a stern government line: their warriors were inspected naked every ten days for signs of excessive thinness or corpulence. That would make a thrillingly humiliating TV game show for FatConCom to sponsor.

But how to get the weight down? The 'lifestyle' doctor had suggestions:

> 'Fat people who want to reduce should exercise on an empty stomach and eat out of breath ... and take only one meal a day, go without baths, sleep on hard beds and go with as little clothing as possible. The people who want to get fat should do exactly the opposite.'

He also recommends that men should walk quickly in winter, more slowly in summer, and that fleshy people should walk faster, thin people more slowly. Ah – walking. That was the *only way to get around*. No cars, you see. Very good for the weight problem. The Roman doctor Celsus (1st century AD), taking walking for granted, recommended thin men put on weight through rest, constipation and big meals, and the fat take it off through late nights, worry and violent exercise. That sounds as good as anything that will come out of FatConCom, unless government takes the ultimate step and bans all private cars, surely the greatest social and environmental curse humans have ever produced.

Wine-break

When government is not moaning on about the corpulent, it is lecturing the middle classes on the dangers of drinking a glass of wine at home after work. 'Alcohol kills slowly', said a French government-sponsored health warning in the 1950s. Someone added 'So much the better. We're in no hurry.'

Greeks were well aware of the virtues of communal drinking. To judge by the number of occasions on which his heroes eat and drink together, Homer knew that commensality could foster a life-saving sense of fellowship and personal loyalty among soldiers. Military Sparta followed the example in moderation, their soldiers 'drinking only enough to lead the spirits of all towards joyous hope and the tongue to friendliness and moderate mirth'.

Greeks certainly got drunk, of course. They drank alcohol produced not by distillation but by fermentation, probably anything up to 18 per cent proof, though diluted by water in large communal mixing bowls to a ratio of two or three to one. Interestingly, there is no evidence for what we would call alcoholism in ancient Greece.

The going could get tough at the all-male symposium (*sumposion* 'together-drink'). The wise man was recommended to leave after three mixing bowls of wine had been consumed by the symposiasts:

'the fourth leads to violence, the fifth to uproar, the sixth to revel, the seventh to black eyes, the eighth to summonses, the ninth to vomiting and the tenth to madness and throwing things about.'

When it was all over, the party tended to rampage through the streets. The general idea lives on in British cities on most nights of the week.

But Plato was inclined to regard all this as a good thing, under certain tightly (as it were) controlled conditions. He raises the issue in his last work, *Laws*:

'Drunkenness is a science of some importance, and needs no mean law-maker to understand it properly. And I am not speaking about taking or abstaining from wine: I do mean *drunkenness*.'

The crucial condition for Plato is that there is control over the extent of the drunkenness, and that it is guided and directed to fulfil a useful function. If, for example, under guidance from friends you can perform well when drunk, at a party, how much better will you perform with those same friends, sober, when the chips are down. It is good management theory. Plato would probably argue that it should be part of the driving test.

Plato applied the principle to the young. First, since wine releases the inhibitions, it shows people in their true light. This gives the educators invaluable insights into the real character of the young people they are trying to educate. Second, it makes the young more malleable and thus more susceptible to sound advice, and the old (who do the teaching) less grumpy and censorious and so more agreeable. In particular, the young can be rendered mildly plastered under controlled conditions, when their equally plastered elders can educate them in that self-discipline and resistance to pleasure so vital for a happy Platonic existence. The theory is that if they can resist temptation drunk, they can resist it under any circumstances.

Drink, in other words, is a great educational benefactor. Plato's advice would be to get it off the streets, where it really is dangerous, and back where it belongs – in the classroom.

Drugs – or just medicine?

As we have seen, herbal remedies were widely used. Among these were what we would call 'drugs'. Opium – Greek *opion* – was a big favourite here, used as a sedative and painkiller (the source of codeine and morphine today). So were the ancients high as kites most of the time, as has recently been suggested?

The answer is, I fear, 'no'. The reason is that, to give you the 'high' which the Notting Hill set routinely expects after dinner – who can blame them after the company they have had to endure? – ancients would have needed to know about chemical refining and processing; and of that, they knew nothing. So they just crushed poppies, releasing the milky substance which contained the drug, and took it in liquid or edible form. Only small amounts could get into the system this way (though they did know that if you took too much, it would kill you). That is why they knew the poppy as *papāver somniferum* 'sleep-inducing' – it was, basically, a sleeping draft, not an artificial stimulus to make you 'high' and talk drivel and to apologise for when you went into politics.

In other words, drugs were not feared in the ancient world as they are in the modern (see box). What ancients really feared were strange religions that threatened the virtue of their women. Women were thought of as highly vulnerable to the pleasures of sex and drink, and religions for women which dealt in secret, midnight rituals, or hysterical group activity, were highly suspect (see p. 182).

There is, by the way, one reference to what we would think of as drug use in the ancient world, and that is by the historian Herodotus. He describes the Scythians using cannabis. Apparently they threw it onto hot stones inside a tent, where it gave off a vapour, which 'makes them howl with pleasure'. Very barbarian of them. Not the sort of thing a good Greek would do.

Living for ever

At least ancient medicine did not suffer from a syndrome so common today that it is surprising no drug has been developed to counteract it: the feverish announcement, on the one hand, that 'in a few years', thanks to 'gene therapy', we shall be able to cure everything; and the equally feverish announcement, on the other, that 'research shows' that a natural food declared 'good for you' a few months ago has now been demonstrated by a team in Sweden to be, in fact, extremely bad for you (and vice versa). If medical scientists cannot even determine whether a food is healthy or not – today I see a headline questioning whether fruit is good for you – one cannot have much faith in their ability to develop miracle cures from a process currently in its infancy. Coming soon: water – the world's biggest known killer! And: is it not about time mankind found a replacement for oxygen, which has surely outstayed its welcome in the vibrant, modernised 21st century?

Drugs today

It was not until the 19th century that opium could be processed and refined into morphine and codeine (good) and heroin (because it made you feel heroic – 'bad'). It was only then that drugs became thought of as socially dangerous, with addicts who had developed a dependency on them suffering withdrawal symptoms if taken off them, and criminals exploiting their financial potential. In 1930 the Federal Bureau of Narcotics was established in the USA, and the whole business became political, a matter of social control and policing.

Medical ethics

But ancient medicine did not begin and end with the technicalities. Relationships between doctor and patient were widely discussed, and highly professional codes of conduct were drawn up for dealing with patients. Three ancient Greek treatises are devoted to this subject, having much to say about a doctor's appearance, bearing and attitudes. For example:

- He should look healthy and plump, or his patients will think he cannot look after himself.
- He must be serious, but kindly, not given to arrogance (though it can be useful to lay down the law) or vulgar knockabout.
- He must be morally impeccable and in complete self-control, given the intimacy of his relationship with his patient.
- He must know when to talk and when to stay silent; he must not gossip to laymen.
- He must watch out for his patients' misbehaviour, since they often lie about taking medicines that have been prescribed.

And if they do not take medicines they do not like, they can die, and the doctor will get the blame.
- The doctor must treat his patients in a calm and orderly way, diverting attention from what is happening to him.
- The doctor must be careful how he sits, must dress properly, be authoritative, brief, reassuring and sympathetic and meet difficulties with calm confidence. Noise and disturbance must be banned when a patient is being treated.

All who have doctors that follow these prescriptions, two and half thousand years on, will have no complaints. Apart from the disgusting bit about them being *plump*, of course.

Hypocritic oath

Then there is the famous Hippocratic oath (4th century BC) which – much later on – came to be accepted as standard for proper ethical practice. When, however, you look at it in detail, it is almost impossible (as the emeritus professor of medicine Kenneth Saunders has argued) to see why:

- It begins with an oath in the name of the pagan gods Asclepius, Health and Panacea. But gods do not feature in Hippocratic, let alone modern, medicine.
- It continues with the doctor swearing to respect his teacher, teach his sons and his teacher's sons and any indentured pupils – but no one else! We don't do closed shops any more, let alone in medicine.
- The doctor then says he will help and not harm the sick (trite) and will not administer *pharmakon*. This means 'drug' or 'poison', and the difference is largely a matter of dosage. It would be OK if this were a clause against assisting death, but doctors regularly aided suicides in the ancient world.
- The doctor will not cause abortion (commonplace in the ancient world, if controversial now) or use the knife (i.e. will not do any surgery – an absurd clause).

- The doctor will not have sex with patients, slave or free (OK); and never reveal what he hears (OK).

In other words, this is an 'oath' almost as irrelevant to the modern world as it surely was to the ancient, bar a few clauses. Who, then, was it for? The most commonly accepted explanation is that it was an oath taken by doctors who were followers of Pythagoras, who did not condone suicide, abortion or the spilling of blood (see box, p. 103). Somehow, it became accepted as Hippocratic and universal.

For the purposes of comparison, the British Medical Association in 1997 produced the following 'revision' of the oath, notable for its long-windedness, pomposity, repetitiveness, self-righteousness, tyrannical attitudinising and creepy political posturing:

- 'The practice of medicine is a privilege which carries important responsibilities. All doctors should observe the core values of the profession which centre on the duty to help sick people and to avoid harm. I promise that my medical knowledge will be used to benefit people's health. They are my first concern. I will listen to them and provide the best care I can. I will be honest, respectful and compassionate towards patients. In emergencies, I will do my best to help anyone in medical need. I will make every effort to ensure that the rights of all patients are respected, including vulnerable groups who lack means of making their needs known, be it through immaturity, mental incapacity, imprisonment or detention or other circumstance.
- 'My professional judgment will be exercised as independently as possible and not be influenced by political pressures nor by factors such as the social standing of the patient. I will not put personal profit or advancement above my duty to patients.
- 'I recognise the special value of human life but I also know that the prolongation of human life is not the only aim of healthcare. Where abortion is permitted, I agree that it should take place only within an ethical and legal framework. I will not provide

treatments which are pointless or harmful or which an informed and competent patient refuses.

- 'I will ensure patients receive the information and support they want to make decisions about disease prevention and improvement of their health. I will answer as truthfully as I can and respect patients' decisions unless that puts others at risk of harm. If I cannot agree with their requests, I will explain why.
- 'If my patients have limited mental awareness, I will still encourage them to participate in decisions as much as they feel able and willing to do so.
- 'I will do my best to maintain confidentiality about all patients. If there are overriding reasons which prevent my keeping a patient's confidentiality I will explain them.
- 'I will recognise the limits of my knowledge and seek advice from colleagues when necessary. I will acknowledge my mistakes. I will do my best to keep myself and colleagues informed of new developments and ensure that poor standards or bad practices are exposed to those who can improve them.
- 'I will show respect for all those with whom I work and be ready to share my knowledge by teaching others what I know.
- 'I will use my training and professional standing to improve the community in which I work. I will treat patients equitably and support a fair and humane distribution of health resources. I will try to influence positively authorities whose policies harm public health. I will oppose policies which breach internationally accepted standards of human rights. I will strive to change laws which are contrary to patients' interests or to my professional ethics.'

Can it be a parody? It certainly makes the original seem a masterpiece of clarity, compression and good sense.

>-+-<>-0-<>-+-<

Reading list

Aristotle, *De Anima (On the Soul)* (Penguin 1986).
Homer, *The Iliad* (Rieu-Jones, Penguin 2003).

W.F. Jashemski, *A Pompeian Herbal* (Texas 1999).

G.E.R. Lloyd (ed.), *Hippocratic Writings* (Pelican 1978).

Vivian Nutton, *Ancient Medicine* (Routledge 2004).

Roy Porter, *The Greatest Benefit of Mankind* (HarperCollins 1997).

Kenneth Saunders, 'The Hippocratic Oath: A Jaundiced View'
    (*Apothecary* 2003).

Epilogue: dream-world

A Greek or Roman would come into the 21st century West from a world where light and heat could be generated only from fire, and where lighting a fire was such a problem that you kept it going, once lit, for as long as you could. And you walked everywhere. He would come from a world where energy could be generated only by the body (human and animal), and wind- and water-power. One does not move overland even at 5 mph, let alone 70 mph, or indeed through the air at 500 mph, with the ancient world's most powerful living energy source, the ox. Nor use a hairdryer, either. One can do better at sea, but not much.

So it is hard to think of a single aspect of our material world – perhaps the occasional classical façade on a bank here and there – that would not appear to our Greek or Roman pure magic or dreamlike fantasy, from modes of transport, electric light, weapons systems and instant global communications to international cornucopias on every supermarket shelf, from open-heart surgery to films, and men and women freely mingling in streets and bars. So your Greek would be astonished to discover that we still read Homer, your Roman that we still read Virgil. 'Why?' would be his bewildered question, 'When you have all this?'

That would not be the only thing that amazed him. He would find out that the very, very worst thing that can happen to a yoof today is to *lose its mobile* (there's servitude for you). He would see social unrest, yob culture, ignorance, crime and family breakdown everywhere. So he would wonder again,

'Why this discontent – when the world is at your fingertips, when living is so easy, when your every imaginable whim can be so instantly satisfied?'

But when he had recovered from the shock of the transparently impossible, he would know the answer as well as we do. While there is a very great deal to be said for material goods and physical well-being, it is ultimately what goes on in the head that counts: only there are satisfaction, happiness and pleasure generated, and those (as most people eventually come to realise) are more than the sum of the contents of Harrods, though there is no denying that sum can give limited pleasure. And that is the reason why we still read Homer and Virgil.

He might also think another reason was our enslavement to a governmental system that gives us no say over crucial decisions that affect our everyday life. Unengaged with that process – indeed, intentionally kept as far away from it as possible – we say 'What the hell' and go our own sweet way. No wonder the general attitude 'Let the bloody government get on with it. It's their responsibility. There is nothing I can do about it' is so prevalent.

But that is the welfare state for you, which is based on the untested hypothesis that government knows best. But it needs our money to be able to prove it. It therefore compels us, by law, to disgorge into its coffers billions upon billions of pounds for it to spend on its 'vision', i.e. what *it* wants to do for us, not what *we* want *it* to do for us. But only madmen have 'visions', and they often go to doctors to try to get rid of them.

Over time, the result of this is to remove from us the desire to make decisions about our own lives. The government can then say 'Look! We are right! The people *do* need us to do everything for them!' The end result is that, so brainwashed do we become, that no government is able to say 'Sorry, boys and girls, you are going to have to do this yourselves, to exert your own willpower, your own self-discipline, to achieve your ends. *We cannot help you. Get on with it.*'

What a political manifesto that would make! And what a

sure-fire vote-loser – so successful has the welfare state been in depriving us of the will and even desire to demonstrate that we are our own masters, in order to show us that *they* are our own masters – and indeed, that is what government is *for*. It would also mean the government has to give us our money back. Quite recently it suggested that instead of the NHS treating us, we should be given the means to treat ourselves. Excellent idea. But will our taxes therefore drop to take this into account?

So we have been bound into abject dependency on *their* choices on *our* behalf. The broadsheets simply reinforce the message. What is the government going to do about welfare, education, healthcare, transport infrastructure, the *Daily Telegraph* moans today. But government created the problems in the first place. What grounds are there for believing it can solve them? You do not ask back the roofer who, year after year, has failed to stop rainwater cascading into the bathroom. That is what a Greek and Roman would call slavery. And they would be right. Meanwhile politicians beg us not to be so apathetic. The answer is staring them in the face. It's called 'democracy'. It is not an answer to which they will ever respond.

To engage with Greeks and Romans is to enter a world where no government thought its purpose was 'to raise taxes', let alone in order to focus 'not just on the economy but the whole way we live' (Oliver Letwin). Christianity, economics, industrialisation, romanticism, and psychology (forget technology) were quite unknown, as was a banking system which one US president believed is 'more dangerous than standing armies ... the principle of spending money to be paid by posterity, under the name of funding, is but swindling futurity on a grand scale' (Thomas Jefferson, 1816) – a system we now know to be far more dangerous in a 'globalised' world, where a sub-prime problem in the USA can hit every country's economy (see p. 22 on Roman 'banking').

The result is the blissful absence of all the effluent that is indissolubly associated with today's world – literal noise from the mechanical and electronic world around us, and metaphorical noise from politicians, educationists, think tanks, opinion-formers, pressure groups, relationship advisers, and the media and communications industries in all their pestilential manifestations.

The sheer intelligence, articulacy and energy of classical authors – not to mention their influence on nearly all subsequent Western thought – make them especially refreshing and astringent company, in a patronising world like ours where no one is assumed to know anything, let alone to be capable of making their own decisions on any subject and exerting their own willpower without help from 'agencies'. Today the *Guardian* has a 'Fish' supplement. It is entitled 'Fish'. There is a picture of fish as a backdrop. (For those who do not know what a fish is, by the way, it's that slippery thing with fins that swims in water). Open the first page and it is headed 'Where to buy fish'.

Perhaps the greatest pleasure of all is to engage with a world that is free of everything connected with the puerile ad-, celebrity- and TV-driven fantasy of 'living the consumer dream' that seems to be the aspiration of most 21st-century Britons: the dream of eternal youth and eternal novelty and eternal getting ('you are what you own') that seeps insidiously into every aspect of life, destroying anything long term, relationships included, and therefore anything like the prospect of long-term happiness. The point about dreams is that you wake up from them. Plato got this 'culture of unreality' exactly right in a famous allegory.

In his *Republic*, Plato likened man's normal condition to people living in an underground cave. Chained into position from birth, they can see only what is on the wall directly in front of them. Behind them is a puppet show of men and animals, and behind that is the light of a fire (no electric lights). The flickering firelight casts the shadows of the puppets onto the wall in front of chained mankind (so like an old movie!). That is all men can see, while all they can hear is the echo of the words spoken by those working the puppets. Such is the sum total of normal human experience. Reality consists of the shadows of puppets.

Now suppose, Plato says, that one of them should be released. Turning round, he would be dazzled by the fire; and then perplexed by the puppets. Could this be 'reality'? Then suppose he were to be led out of the cave into the open air of the real world above; would his eyes not hurt at the brightness of everything about him, and be unable to see? Of course. It would take him a long time to accustom himself to it.

Then suppose he were to return to the cave. What value would he place on the life of the inmates down there? And when, having with difficulty accustomed himself to the gloom, he told them they were watching shadows of puppets, how would they respond to him? 'They would laugh at him, and say he had gone up only to come back with his sight ruined: if only they could lay hands on the person trying to free them and take them up there, they would kill him.'

Plato had foreseen the PlayStation/television culture. But then calling certain shows 'reality TV' – rich irony – had already given away the true nature of the fantasy medium.

Recently there has been a 'crisis' in this wretched industry, caused by rigged phone-ins and doctored documentaries. It has been greeted with a heaving swell of sanctimonious claptrap from those responsible. Michael Grade (ITV), who has spent his adult life masterminding the flickering puppet show on the cave walls, pompously intoned, 'The contract of trust between broadcasters and their audiences is of paramount importance'. To whom, precisely? The day we 'trust' the media will be a black one.

Incredible as it may sound, he was outdone by Mark Thompson, director general of the BBC, the man who is currently proposing to save money by continuing to pay a sleazy, patronising chat-show figure Jonathan Ross £6 million a year while cutting the budget for the *Today* programme (total cost: £5 million a year). Claiming that 'honesty, fairness, respect' are the 'values' that matter most to people who pay for the BBC (how would *he* know?), he goes on 'But [restoring trust] is not a matter of importing some new culture. It is about reinforcing and celebrating a culture and values which are alive and well across the BBC'.

Too true it is: the 'culture and values', with some exceptions, largely on the radio, of people like Mr Ross, characterised in most cases by fantasy, stupidity, sentimentality, ignorance, bullying, vulgarity and deceit. But what other options do Plato's cave-dwellers have open to them? And with this deadly virus flickering away in almost every child's bedroom in the name of 'entertainment' – no wonder they can't read – government puts health warnings on cigarette packets, tells the middle classes to stop drinking wine and claims that obesity is now as great a threat as global warming. Enter the proposed lunchbox police. But on the intellectual, moral and spiritual degradation visited daily upon children and adults enslaved to that culture – not a peep.

As TV gazes into its mirror on the wall and congratulates itself on the surpassing importance of its 'service to the community', the seven dwarfs of its 'entertainment' culture join in the acclamation: Sleazy, Trashy, Vulgar, Nasty, Shabby, Tawdry and Cheap. Indeed, even some who watch TV know, in their heart of hearts, it is despicable. That is why there is an outcry at repeats. Few people go into the National Gallery and complain that the same old pictures are there. TV knows its winning agenda – never to underestimate the public's taste and intelligence. It is this widespread commitment to and dependency on the tasteless and sordid that would have struck Greeks and Romans as so humiliating, *when so much that is truly excellent is widely and freely available.*

For a Graeco-Roman reaction of amazement to the modern would be entirely justified. We *are* surrounded by miracles, all within the reach of every one of us, from pictures of exploding nebulae 650 light years away – the first stages of the formation of the universe's matter – to electric train sets, replacement heart valves and instant Schubert. Never has information (and misinformation) been more widely and easily accessible.

But what have we made of it all? Thanks to the degrading

'culture' of the world we live in, the real miracles are contemptuously ignored in favour of the trash, encouraging the fantasy that we can (and must) 'live our dream', that anything is possible, preferably effortlessly and at the touch of a button, and that we have a right to it now, at once and immediately, preferably sooner, and the government should pay.

Would I vote for Caesar? You bet I would.

Index